As I remember, Adam

"As I remember, Adam, it was upon this fashion bequeathed me . . ."

As You Like It, Act I, Scene 1

As I remember, Adam

An Autobiography of a Festival

Angus L. Bowmer

The Oregon Shakespearean Festival Association
Ashland, Oregon
1975

ACKNOWLEDGMENTS

If you enjoy this story, you must join with me in thanking those people who made its publication possible. We rejoice in the confidence shown by the 1974 Oregon Shakespearean Festival Board of Directors who decided to publish this book. In good faith they followed the recommendations of Bill Patton and Peggy Rubin. For this much thanks. Happily, Bill Patton also conducted the search which resulted in acquiring the services of Charles Jones as Editor and John Beyer as Designer. Though the story be mine, for the published book we owe much to them. To Peggy Rubin we give thanks not only for her encouragement and many kindnesses, but also for making so many of you warmly aware of the book's existence. Last but not least, we owe thanks to my wife, Gertrude, for her loving care and the hours of typing and rough editing without which the script would never have been viewed by anyone else.

SECOND PRINTING

Composition by Holmes Composition Service, San Jose.
Printed by Graphics Arts Center, Portland.
Book Design by John Beyer, San Francisco.

Contents

DEDICATION

To all those souls both on and off stage whose names do not appear between these covers but whose purchase of tickets, gifts of money, skills, talents and inspiration have made the Festival possible, we gratefully dedicate this story.

Foreword

I first met Angus Bowmer in the summer of 1957. Even then, among theater people I knew, he was a legend. I think my first surprise was that he was not at least a head taller than the people around him. But an even more remarkable facet was his humility. People called him "Gus," or "Angus," and spoke of him as a comrade, friend, or buddy, not usually as a Leader. It is only now, after many years of friendship and collaboration, that I think of him as Mr. Bowmer.

He was, and is, all of a piece. If an actor is one who has a talent for disguise behind a mask so that his true self is obscured, Angus Bowmer is ill equipped to be an actor. In all the roles he has played, including authorship of this book, the true Angus Bowmer was always clear and present. But that never lessened the force of his character nor the delicacy of his art. Theater, to him, was a way of showing things, not disguising them. Hypocrite is not a synonym for actor in Mr. Bowmer's theater.

I came to the Festival as a young Ph.D. expecting to serve Thalia as an acolyte in a Temple dedicated to High Art. My head was full of the Grand Theories of E. Gordon Craig and Robert Edmond Jones, not to mention Harley Granville-Barker, William Butler Yeats, Constantine Stanislavsky, Nemirovich-Danchenko and all those other formidable names. William Shakespeare was a God on Mount Parnassus and we were on the lower slopes of our climb and panting fiercely in the thin air.

But in the Rogue Valley of southern Oregon I met a man with three loves: shakespeare, art, and people; and none of them were capitalized in his mind. The people in Shakespeare's plays were just that: people. And they were no more remote than men and women he met in London hotels or in Lithia Park. His art consisted of introducing them to each other and, like a gracious host, making conversation until both audience and character felt at home together.

Angus Bowmer is a positive man, but a tough one. As I read these pages I realize how much of the toughness is overshadowed by his generosity. Yet that is part of the man, too. He has a North Coast skepticism tempering his Western enthusiasm, but it's the energy one remembers. He knew a failure when he saw it, there was enough in his career to make recognition inevitable. But he was never discouraged by failure. If a director, or text, or actor baffled him, his faith in the essential humanity of each never faltered. Lines of character, of text, of business could be obscure, but never meaningless.

The Festival is Angus and Angus the Festival, but neither are monuments. Both are living testaments to human life in art. Working in Ashland was to come into direct contact with life: life in the plays, on the stage, with the audience. The man who brought all that into being also lives in these pages—not always at the center, not always the *regisseur*, not ever the manipulator of puppets—just there: an actor who instinctively knows the true center of the stage is a little off to the side.

To Mr. Bowmer, Theater is never abstract, no more than his Life is abstract. Both are to be lived as fully as a human being can live them.

And that's what he passes on to those who follow.

——Jerry Turner

"What I have done is yours; what I have to do is yours."

My Grandmother Bowmer

My grandfather, H. L. Bowmer

Our thanks to all the Festival photographers whose work is represented here. Those known to us include: Bob Mallon of Bushnell Studio, Jack Moran, Robert Arbuckle, Anita Fowler, Whitland Locke, Dwaine Smith, Carolyn Mason Jones, and Hank Kranzler, to whom we give special thanks for help in duplicating old prints.

My mother teaching me to "count the house" circa 1905.

*From my father I inherited a more
than generous slice of ham.*

In the back row at the far left I'm in costume for
my role as quarterback at Oak Harbor High School.

Miss Grace Eccles is on the right in this photo of the Oak Harbor faculty. She is the one who advised me to go into theatre.

The role of Adam in Bellingham Normal School's production of As You Like It was my first Shakespearean role in college. I'm sitting second from left; Victor H. Hoppe is standing second from left.

Here I am with my sixth graders at Oak Harbor, where
I taught in 1926. That's where we did a play to earn
money for the Women's Civic Improvement Club and where
I got fired for spending too much time at the theatre.

This production of Love's Labour's Lost at the
University of Washington was directed by B. Iden Payne.
John Conway decorated the stage to resemble an
Elizabethan Theatre. I played Boyet in that enormous
ruff; Virginia Opsvig is at far left.

"And still I seem to tread on classic ground."

July 4, 1893, was opening day for the Chautauqua in Ashland. This frame building, shingled from base to cupola, was 80 feet in diameter, boasted seating for 1000 people and perfect acoustics. It was built in ten days.

The building was enlarged and elongated in 1901.

In 1916 an even larger theatre was covered by an
unsupported wooden dome of 160 feet in diameter. The
Chautauqua ended in the 1920s. The dome was judged
unsafe in the early '30s and pulled down. Our summer
Shakespeare productions now stretch for life within
the ivy covered walls of this old Chautauqua building.

"As I remember, Adam, it was
upon this fashion bequeathed me . . ."

As You Like It, Act I, Scene 1

I

Bequest

MEMORY SOMETIMES CAPTURES a moment in its entirety. Because of some super-stimulation, the senses record and retain for a lifetime the sights, sounds, feelings, even smells of such a time. I can still recapture the scene as the two of us sat in the gloom and moved occasionally to avoid the water that dripped through the stage floor above us. The driving March rain had forced us into the partially excavated dirt basement of the roofless old Chautauqua building which we thought might be made to house a Shakespearean Festival. I was uncomfortably conscious of the sour stench emanating from the piles of dirt on which we perched. Bob Stedman sat beside me as we talked and dreamed.

We were here because we had noted a peculiar resemblance between the circular roofless walls of this old structure and the seventeenth century sketch of Shakespeare's Globe Theatre drawn by Wenceslaus Hollar. It is true that this impression was an illusory one and only possible when the building was viewed from below across the little pond in Lithia Park. But fleeting as it was, this comparison stimulated the germinal idea of a Shakespearean Festival, which in turn became an immediate and exciting challenge for me and my students at Southern Oregon Normal.

We sat there in the basement, Bob and I, unaware of the storm outside, staring at the parallel rows of raindrop craters in the dust at our feet. We had gone over and over all the arguments we could think of to convince ourselves of the appropriateness and practicality of the festival idea, and we tried now to put together all we knew about the building in which we were sitting. It was a large circular structure 180 feet in diameter. The thick, reinforced concrete walls stood 12 to 15 feet above the ground and the earth within these walls slanted in a natural rake toward the stage. The stage, with a 65-foot proscenium arch, had been located in a smaller semi-circular wall two stories high because of the sudden drop of the Lithia Park ground at this point. The auditorium had been covered with the second largest unsupported dome in America. The first W.P.A. project for the City of Ashland involved the removal of this dome and the auxiliary dome over the stage because they had sagged dangerously after years of disuse.

Today, a theatre patron entering this arena in Ashland, Oregon for a Festival play, finds himself in a colorful world apart from the prosaic one he has just left. As he presses through the milling crowd he may patronize one of the colorful booths at the rear of the auditorium, buy sweets or a program from one of the attractive vendors passing through the happy throng. All these attendants and vendors decked out in gay Elizabethanesque costumes, as well as the ticket takers, the usherettes and the numerous red-coated house managers, are some of the 500 community volunteers who are an essential part of this complicated theatre organization. The theatregoer's festive mood is heightened as he moves within the magic circle of the old ivy-covered, banner-topped walls to watch the Green dancers or listen to the sweet sound of the strolling musicians. He may be one of the many people who have seen all 37 of Shakespeare's plays here, or he may be attending for the first time, having read an article by a topflight Eastern drama critic which said that the best Shakespearean productions in the United States were to be seen here in Ashland, Oregon.

As the five-minute trumpet calls, and the Festival flag is raised high over the penthouse of the three-story Elizabethan stage, he finds his way to his seat. Though his is one of nearly 1200, he feels lucky to have a seat, for the chances are much better than even that he will see a long line of "standing room only" patrons waiting patiently at the gate. As he sits in the gathering dusk he can see where the North Star and the Big Dipper hang just over the right side of the stage. In the distance in all directions, the Siskiyou foothills are silhouetted against the brilliant summer night. To his right, just over the walls, he can see the roof of the beautiful, modern Angus Bowmer Theatre where he probably attended a matinee, for the Festival presents 14 performances a week during its long summer season. In addition, there is a "Stage II" season in the early spring.

But back in 1934 all these things were only vague dreams, ideas and longings. There in the basement, the more we dreamed and talked, the more we thought that our venture must be in some way a festival and not merely the production of one play. Had not the Chautauqua been a festival? The decapitated building above us was the third of a series of buildings each one larger than the last to accommodate the enlarging Chautauqua audiences. These audiences were made up of people from all over southern Oregon and northern California. They came with horses and wagons, bringing their families to camp in Lithia Park for two weeks while the Chautauqua series was on. On the boards above our heads Sousa's Band had played, Charlotte Greenwood had starred in *So Long Lettie*, William Jennings Bryan had held them spellbound with his oratory, Billy Sunday had preached to an audience of 5,000. Madame Schumann-Heink was a great sensation. But her appearance was not without its difficulties. That generous-hearted lady, moved by the throngs of school children who lined the streets strewing roses in her path as she entered town, stood up in the automobile in which she was riding, threw them kisses, and invited them all to the concert. The Chautauqua committee, feeling that they had to honor this invitation, nearly went broke that season, handing out passes for school children.

The Chautauqua had died out all over the country many years before I came to the Rogue River Valley in 1931. But Ashland is a very conservative town. Conservatives tend to hang on to the past. Perhaps this conservatism would be an advantage in reviving the festival idea; especially so if the festival were staged within the same walls which housed the old tradition. And Ashland is located ideally for a tourist center. On Highway 99 (now Interstate 5), 17 miles from the California border, this little Oregon town is about halfway between San Francisco and Portland. Nestled in the foothills in an arm of the Rogue River Valley, it is only 12 miles from the larger city of Medford, less than 50 miles from Grants Pass. Over mountain passes lie Klamath Falls, 60 miles, and Yreka, California, 40 miles away. A successful festival lasting several days could be expected to draw from each of these centers.

The tourist industry was already the third largest industry in the state. Ashland was particularly well located to take advantage of the stream of tourists that flowed to and from California. Aside from picturesque surroundings, it is the hub of a perimeter of tourist attractions. Crater Lake National Park, the Oregon Caves, California Redwood groves, ocean beaches and many other spots of beauty and wonder are all within a day's round trip distance from Ashland.

This informal conference under the old stage was followed by many others in more convenient surroundings. Other students like Bob Stedman took up the challenge and contributed ideas. Everyone in the valley who could be enticed into conversation on the subject was consulted or indoctrinated. Dreams were wildly ambitious, and finally we all began to believe that we actually could have a Shakespearean Festival which would eventually draw tourists during a prolonged summer season. For weeks we talked of little else. In groups or in pairs, the people who caught fire boldly projected Festival plans and achievements into a vague and rosy future. Some of that future and those achievements are behind us today and many are still just beyond tomorrow. Eventually it was necessary to get down to the practical aspects of planning the immediate future. How could we get the First Annual Shakespearean Festival on the boards?

Lois Muzzall Bowmer, who had so skillfully (and cheaply) designed and constructed the costumes for my original play, *Andrew Jackson*, would be our Art Director. Robert Stedman would be the Technical Director in charge of scenery and lights. William Cottrell would assist in the directing, I would be the Producing Director. And we all would act.

It was at this stage of the planning that I learned two lessons which were to prove of great importance in the development of the Festival. At this exhilarating period it came as a considerable shock to find that there were people who did not become excited about the prospect of a Shakespearean Festival. At each contact with these individuals, I found my enthusiasm ebbing away. This was alarming indeed, for enthusiasm was about the only ingredient for the Festival that we had in sufficient quantity. If doubt and indifference were discouraging at this point, it could be disastrous when the Festival became a reality. The people who thought it couldn't be done would eventually be won over by success. But what about the ones who just didn't care? Or worse, those who, because of a lack of understanding, or conflicting interests, would actually oppose, if not the whole program, at least some important policy or necessary direction of development? It was easy to see ourselves saying at some crucial time in the future, "These people are stupid and unappreciative. Why should we continue to work so hard when all we get in return is criticism and opposition?" The Festival could very well end like this before all those rosy dreams came true. But if we recognized that these people existed and that indifference and opposition were inevitable, then how could we lay the blame at their feet if we were ever tempted to quit? These people must be out-voted, out-waited or won over, but they could never be used as an honest reason for discontinuing the Festival. This decision has seen us through many a discouraging crisis in more than 40 years of Festival growth.

The second lesson we learned was closely connected with the first because it concerned public relations. In all this general "war dance" period, when we were trying to whip up as much enthusiasm as possible, we did not overlook the newspapers. There were four in the valley at that time and I went to all the news editors to see whether they thought our idea was feasible from a newsman's point of view. I knew that unless we had their enthusiastic support, the Festival would never have a chance. In each case I received encouragement, but not a line of type. At about this time my parents, who had been singing together in public since before I can remember, had a concert engagement at one of the larger churches in Portland. After the concert they met the Church Editor of the *Oregon Journal.* When they learned that he was soon to be in Ashland, they asked him to look me up and mentioned something about the embryonic Festival plans. As a result of his Ashland visit and subsequent interview, there appeared in the *Journal* a quarter-page, illustrated article about the tentative idea. The true lesson came when several of the same valley newspaper men I had talked to called me on the phone and took me to task for letting the *Journal* scoop the local papers! We have always tried to avoid any neglect of the local media people, but I have a firm conviction that public recognition from outside the immediate area tends to encourage more space and time at home.

The Festival owes its very life to the fantastic devotion of the media people: newspapers, radio, magazines and television, both near and far. But I have always felt a special warmth toward the Portland papers which gave us so much initial encouragement in those early days when the Festival was just a gleam in our eyes. Several articles followed that first one, but even more thrilling was an editorial in the *Oregon Journal* giving the whole idea a wonderful boost. It concluded with the hope that the plays given by the

> Ashland-Medford community groups will be so successful that the cities will enter fully into the spirit of the plan and make the festival an annual affair. If the spirit is present, there is no reason why Ashland should not become—as Mr. Bowmer pictures it—the Salzburg of the west.

I have an especial affection for this early evidence that the Festival's present international scope was not the result of an accidental afterthought, but an integral part of those early plans.

As ludicrous as these grandiose schemes might seem in the light of our ignorance of Shakespeare, theatre or even business, the meagreness of our physical equipment and complete lack of funds—they were nonetheless real and inspiring to us. I think that we were dimly aware of the odds against us, but there is excitement in a long shot.

My own thrust of energy stemmed, in part at least, from a vow I had made to myself when I was nine years old. Even at that early age, I had great respect for the talents of the Bowmer family. My cousins, my aunt, my uncles and my parents were all musical. One of my earliest memories is of my father and mother singing in public. And I am proud that my father sang professionally, with his voice still sweet and true, accompanying himself on his big harp guitar, at the age of 85. I could not carry a tune until I was 11 years old!

They were always talking about "forming a company" or "going on the road," but they never did. Later, my father and mother developed a large and enthusiastic radio audience on stations KOMO in Tacoma, Washington, and KWJJ in Portland. But when I was nine, I thought it was a great waste to confine the influence of this wonderful talent to the populace of the several villages in which we lived at different times.

I felt that I should do something "important" one day. My Grandmother Bowmer had taught me that society rewards people for the services they perform for society. Some people contribute only enough to get in return the food they eat and the clothing and shelter they require. For those who contribute something society values over and above what they consume, there are other rewards. But what could I do? I knew that I was the least talented of the Bowmer family, so I decided that I would find some very specialized field, something with very narrow scope, something in which very few or, perhaps, nobody else was specializing. Then I would concentrate fiercely and continually on this (unspecified) activity, and because nobody else was doing it, I would automatically become the best. Little did I suspect that it would be producing Shakespeare on an Elizabethan-type stage.

In order to understand what was back of this peculiar kind of reasoning, you need to know a little bit more about my family. My mother's side of the family was the least spectacular, although I remember my Grandmother Priest telling of hiding under the featherbed in the covered wagon as the horses galloped across the plains in flight from a suspected Indian attack. It was an interesting coincidence that I, having lived so many years in Washington, should move to Ashland in Jackson County, Oregon, to do my life's work just a few miles from the grave of my Grandfather Priest, who was county school superintendent (and candidate for the state superintendency) when he died of a heart attack after climbing Mount Pitt.

My Great-grandfather Bowmer was the most romantic of my forebears. He was a frontier constable, a pioneer judge, an an officer in the United States forces that captured the Emperor Maximilian in Mexico. His second wife, my great-grandmother, was Lorena Hayes, the niece of President Hayes. I wear a ring, inherited from my father, which contains two of the twelve tiny chip diamonds which formed a cluster in her wedding ring.

One of the most frequently retold family stories concerns an incident which occurred in 1856 when my great-grandfather was a judge in Modoc County in northern California. This was a time, so goes the family story, when Judge Bowmer was trying to end the rule of vigilante law and establish orderly, legal trial and punishment of offenders. There had been a murder. The suspected murderer had been captured, and because there was no jail in this frontier community, he was locked up in great-grandfather's log cabin. About dusk, some fifty armed men, all wearing masks, appeared before the cabin. Great-grandfather met them at the door armed with his trusty rifle, and said something to this effect:

"I know that you have come to fetch my prisoner. However, it is my duty as a judge to see him held for trial. Therefore you will have to kill me to get at him. But let me ask you this: which one of you is willing to give up his own life in the exchange? For I will shoot the first man who moves forward from the spot where he now stands."

Then, so goes the family story, two of the vigilantes took off their masks. They were the judge's sons, my grandfather's half brothers!

But the defender of the law was not daunted. He spoke (according to the story) the following words:

"At this moment I am not a father, but an instrument of the law. If either of you two move forward, I will kill you as readily as I would another."

After a pause for consultation, so goes the story, the vigilantes dispersed, the murderer was legally tried and later hanged.

Not long before my father's death, I ran across the story in a volume of early California history by Bancroft. There were certain significant discrepancies in this version of the incident. According to Bancroft, Judge Bowmer made the melodramatic life and death stand before his cabin knowing full well that he would not be harmed. The vigilantes stepped forward, took his rifle away, and carried away the prisoner whom they hanged to the nearest gate post.

I told my father about this less glorious version of the event, expecting him to be indignant or angry. Instead, he looked very thoughtful for a moment or two then he said:

"You know, I don't believe it. I knew your great-grandfather and he was not like that. He was a solid, dignified man standing well over six feet. With his white hair and beard, he was very impressive. Let me tell you another story about him. I can testify to the truth of this one because I was there. I was only a small boy, but I remember it very vividly. At that time, he was constable of Weston, Oregon. Weston might have been the setting for any of the Western movies, with muddy streets and raised wooden sidewalks in front of the stores and saloons. I might add that there were more saloons than stores. The principal, and almost the only, recreation was watching dog fights.

"In those days, there was a gang of young outlaws who lived up in the hills. Every once in awhile they would get drunk, ride into Weston and shoot up the town. On this day they could be heard a long way off, yelling and screeching and shooting off their pistols. Their leader's name was Billy. When your great-grandfather got there, everyone in town was understandably out of sight. Billy had dismounted and came swaggering down the sidewalk, waving a large bowie knife with which he was carving up all the signs along the street.

"Your great-grandfather stepped to the middle of the sidewalk and shouted, 'Billy.' The gangster turned and swayed a bit on his feet. 'Come here.' Billy stood where he was for a moment, and then slowly came toward the constable, still holding the big knife threateningly before him. Your great-grandfather held out his hand. 'Give me that knife!' Billy looked down at the knife as if he hadn't known it was there. He didn't speak. Finally he meekly handed over the knife. 'Now get out of town, Billy. Don't let me see you back here again until you're sober.' Billy turned on his heel, went to where his horse stood, mounted and rode off.

"Now," said father, "I don't see the man who had the nerve to do that behaving as that history book says he did." I don't see him that way, either, after viewing him through my father's eyes. But whether Bancroft had the right of it or not, I suspect that there was a flair for showmanship that may have been passed along through the genes.

My father delighted in telling a story that happened when I must have been no older than four years. Whether or not this incident substantiates historian Bancroft is a matter for conjecture. My parents sang in the church choir and I was seated in the front pew each Sunday. Apparently, in my boredom, I had been something of a disturbing influence during the sermon. I had been warned that, unless I behaved, I would be punished. Mother had always been the wielder of the hair brush, which left the prospect of punishment by my father as a topper. He had always told me that if *he* ever punished me that I would have cause to remember it all my life. One Sunday I sailed a Sunday school card in a frisbee-like orbit around the minister's head. Whether this was by accident or design, I don't remember. But after church, I was assured by my father that the time had come for him to take a hand in my correction. As he was the mildest of men, I did not believe him and managed to laugh, even when he took me by the arm and escorted me into the back yard. It was not until he had cut a switch from a fruit tree and approached me with purpose in his eye that I realized I was for it. I threw myself on my knees at his feet and cried, "For God's sake don't kill me!" At which point he burst out laughing, and I was not punished. In fact, he never again spoke of punishing me himself.

It couldn't have been long after that I had an opportunity to put my penchant toward dramatics to a more legitimate use. I have at hand an old photograph picturing the cast of a variety show with me in the front row. There is a notation on the back in my father's handwriting:

Angus' 1st show—Took part of "Teddy Bear" in camp of Teddy Roosevelt in Africa—just after Teddy's return to U.S. Prop man forgot nursing bottle of milk for "Teddy Bear". Had to borrow real nursing bottle from a mother in audience. Tasted "awful" but even at that early age, Angus had a natural urge that the "show must go on" and drank it down. The program announced this number as

"The Teddy Bear Picnic", and Angus had a ludicrous dance, costumed as a real "Teddy Bear". His father wrote and directed the
show, for the benefit of the Sumas, Washington, Methodist
Church. He was at that time Editor and Publisher of the *Sumas
News*.

I don't remember the dance, but I do remember two things. First, my
father forgot to give me credit for doubling as Kermit Roosevelt;
second, I still remember the "awful" taste of that baby formula. To
this day I can't stand the taste of condensed milk, which I am sure was
the stuff they were foisting off on that poor baby.

I am sure that Dad wrote the above note in later years, after the
Festival was under way. I was always touched by his obvious pride in
the Festival. He never introduced me merely as his son. It was always
"My son, who directs the Oregon Shakespearean Festival." In fact,
these were the last words I ever heard him speak. As he lay dying, he
caught the attention of a pretty nurse and introduced us as we stood by
his bed, with the same old words and the same pride showing through
the signs of death which were already upon him. I hope he knows about
the Angus Bowmer Theatre. If he does, I'm sure he's telling the angels
about it.

When I was in high school, he and I made two important discoveries. We learned about the installment plan which enabled us to
purchase a Buscher alto saxophone. We both learned that we could play
it by following instructions in a book. We later bought him a tenor sax
so that we could both play at the same time. While we did "shows" all
through my young life, I remember this particular period of time most
vividly.

My father's sister, Lorena, her husband, Merle Wiester, and their
three children, "Little" Lorena, Bob and Beverly, all came to Oak
Harbor to live. I can still hear the beautiful "close" harmony of the
mixed quartette rendition of "Sleep Kentucky Babe": Aunt Lorena,
soprano; Mother, alto; Uncle Merle, tenor; and Dad, bass. Our
"WieBow" orchestra consisted of piano, Aunt Lorena; drums, Little
Lorena; tenor sax, Dad; alto sax, me; clarinet, Bev; trombone, Bob.
My! how we worked on the intricacies of "Canadian Capers." Little
Lorena sang character songs like "My Man." I did readings and we all
participated in various "skits." I still remember that there was one
line in one of the skits that Dad thought was so funny he couldn't get
through a rehearsal without breaking up into laughter so violent that
he cried. In performance, I always looked away for I knew that if I

caught his eye we were doomed! Another skit involved Dad and me in a comic rough and tumble fight. I remember that during one performance the audience response was unexpectedly enthusiastic. In fact, they laughed so hard I began to believe we must be very good. When the curtain went down to shouts and cheers, I was considerably chastened to discover the secret of our success. My pants had split from belt line to belt line! I have been highly suspicious of unexpected laughs ever since.

I don't remember how many shows we did during those few years when the "WieBow" organization was functioning. But the mélange of euphoric memories is vivid as I recall the rehearsals, the laughter; the sense of accomplishment when a particularly difficult musical passage came right; the crowds, the laughter, the applause, the smell of grease paint; people telling us we were wonderful, and the laughter, always laughter. It is no wonder that I inherited a flair for public performance.

There was something else, however, which influenced all the doings of the Bowmer family. This was an attitude, a philosophy, if you will, which was not talked about much, and which I did not analyze until many years later. The nearest I can come to giving it a label is to say that it was an unself-conscious dedication to public service.

All the shows we did were, like "The Teddy Bear Picnic" in Sumas, produced for the benefit of the church, the school or some other community cause or organization. They were all amateur in the real sense, for we did them for the love of the doing. But the attitude I speak of went deeper than that. It affected as well the professional activities of the family.

My father and my grandfather were engaged in the country newspaper business during all of my boyhood days. My grandfather started 16 country newspapers in the Pacific Northwest. He learned to set type in Reno, Nevada, and by the time he was 24 he had established and was publishing *The Colfax Vidette* in Colfax, Washington. I remember him best for those ten years after he established *The Oak Harbor News* until about the time I graduated from high school. For 64 years of his life he was engaged in the newspaper business. Most of that time he was editing country newspapers which he had established and operated with the conscious object of building up the little community in which each was located.

The pattern went something like this. He would go into a small rural community where, as his friend, Bill Nye, would say, the principal industry was the crossing of the roads. There would probably be a general store and a blacksmith shop. He would buy a few cases of type (on credit) from the type founders, get an old Washington hand press, and start an immediate political battle for a new road, a much needed bridge or some other project which would bring the community together in support of the common good. In a short time there would be several other business establishments snugged in around the store and blacksmith shop: possibly a feed store, a drug store or even a post office or bank. The citizenry would take on a feeling of pride in the identity of their community. New folk would move in, houses would be built and there would emerge a new town. About that time grandfather would sell out for what he owed the type founders and the paper house, move on to another likely spot and repeat the process. At this point I should say clearly that there never was an issue of any of his papers of which his readers could not be proud. He was a competent craftsman, politically knowledgeable, well read. His editorials were pertinent and couched in the salty, informal style which was appropriate to the Western frontier, a style that lamentably disappeared with the last of the old-style country weeklies.

As a child, it never occurred to me to ask why he moved so often, or to look for any relationship between these frequent moves and the fact that each paper started off as a strong proponent of prohibition, or why my grandmother was always an ardent WCTU worker. My father frequently sold out or quit his job to help his father get squared away before he sold a paper. He frequently ran the paper while his father hunted a new place to land, and he was helpful in getting the new plant established. This meant that my childhood was shot through with moves from place to place on Puget Sound in Washington. But when my parents went off to find a new job, I was always left with my grandmother. She had a profound influence on my life.

After one look at Grandma's face, you wouldn't be surprised that her mother had been born in Dublin, for it was written there in terms of a turned up nose and soft, smiling eyes that could shoot Irish fire. She used to say to me, "I'll snatch you bald-headed," or, "I'll shake your teeth out!" I always somehow understood the hyperbolic nature of these threats, but I had, nevertheless, a very healthy respect for her discipline. She was not for spoiling the child.

I can remember listening to her tell stories as I sat and combed her long, shiny, black hair, which reached well below her waist. She would tell of early days in Virginia City, or recite poetry from memory. But most especially I remember her fanciful tales about an imaginary relative "Sir Goggle-Goggle Cramer" whose castle in Ireland we would all visit "when our ship comes in." "When my ship comes in" was a frequent phrase upon her lips, and was the magic that dispelled despondency over any fancied deprivation.

I suppose, in today's terms, we would have been termed "underprivileged." We lived in tents. Oh, we were quite comfortable. Grandma had lived thus most of her nomadic life. The living room-bedroom tent was composed of two 12 by 14 tents fastened together; floors and three or four foot high walls were of lumber. There was a canvas fly over the top for insulation, carpets on the floor, and portieres between the living room and the bedroom. A wood-burning, "air tight" heater provided warmth, and a Morris chair and a "sanitary" couch (which opened out into a full bed when not serving as a davenport) were the principal furnishings of the living room. In the bedroom were two beds and, for a dresser, two orange crates stacked on top of each other with a cretonne curtain in front.

The kitchen tent was reached by a board walk which had a tarpaulin stretched overhead to keep off the rain. A big wood-burning kitchen range, an oilcloth-covered dining table, kitchen chairs and shelves to hold groceries and utensils were the furnishing there.

None of us ever thought he was unfortunate in these surroundings. I detected a touch of wistfulness in only one thing which Grandma wanted which she did not have. She often expressed her wish for a dresser. I bravely promised that when I got to be a man I would buy her one. This I did, but much too late, for she was long gone by the time I discovered a gloriously ornate piece in an old barn in California. It has a marble top and, with its beautiful mirror, towers all of ten feet high. It stands in our bedroom, but it belongs to Grandma.

She would be the last to complain that she had a hard life. But she reared four children and missed hardly a day working in grandfather's print shop. She literally set type while she rocked the cradle with her foot. At one time she successfully edited and operated the *Milton Eagle* singlehanded! My grandfather, who usually operated a politically independent paper, went to Pendleton to edit the *Tribune* as a Republican paper in the campaign of 1890. Grandma stayed in Milton and operated Grandfather's own paper as a militant Democratic publication.

From the time I could talk plainly, Grandma taught me to "speak pieces" at Sunday School and church programs. I have mentioned the fact that she was an active WCTU member. She drilled young people for declamatory contests, the winners of which won Demerest medals awarded by that organization. All of her children won at least one medal. My father won the silver, the gold and the grand gold medals and my Aunt Lorena won all those plus the highest one: the diamond. I won the silver medal and later a gold medal as the winner of a declamation contest sponsored by the Island County School systems. I still remember the first line of that last declamation:

> The boys of America despise fraud, abominate sham and *hate* political treason!

As a student of Delsarte, who tried to make the performing arts a science, she did not hesitate to use imitation. This was not the stupid mimicry which you see depicted in the pseudo-Delsarte books of the late nineteenth century. Her approach was based on the assumption of certain observable facts about the human mechanism. The forehead and the finger tips are "intellectual," the chin and the palm of the hand are "physical." Thus, to give a simple illustration, if you are depicting a person who is temporarily or habitually engaged in intellectual activity, you might very well place your finger tips to your forehead. I remember that she said the elbows are the index of self-consciousness. Elbows close to the body: weak or vacillating character or movement. Elbows out, hands close to the body: bold or pugnacious character. To make a full gesture with the arm, you lead with the elbow, follow with the wrist and trail with the fingers.

She taught me that, when giving my declamations, I should stand erect, with my chest and chin confidently up, my weight resting on the balls of my feet with a firm stance, so that I might easily move in any direction. The expression of any idea must start with the diaphragm. Thus a step forward or a gesture of the arm or head should first be felt and actually start in the solar plexus.

You can see that all this was a marvelous preparation for the broad movement and open technique so necessary for acting on Ashland's Elizabethan stage.

One more story before I conclude this Bowmer background. There is one more ingredient in the genetic and psychological potpourri that I may have inherited which fueled the start of the Festival in 1935. Let me tell you the story that illustrates the nature of my father's faith. My mother was ill one summer. The doctor recommended that she spend several hours each day outside in their beautiful yard. There was no place for her to lie down, however, so they thought the obvious solution would be one of those porch swings that could hang in its own frame in the shade of the huge cherry tree growing in their back yard. All that would be needed to install it would be some excavation and a solid foundation. At that time they were still paying for the mortgage on the house. Dad had retired, though he was able to take in a little money from a print shop in his garage. But there seemed to be no place they could turn for the money to buy such a swing. After talking it over, they decided to take their troubles to the Lord. For a number of nights they prayed about the matter asking that somehow a way could be found to get Mother a porch swing. One night there was a knock on their door and when Dad answered it, there was a group of young people with a porch swing! They had heard at the church of the folks' dilemma and had pooled their money to buy the swing. There was the answer to their prayers. But that is not the point of the story. They were able to erect the swing immediately, for Dad, while waiting for their prayers to be answered, had confidently built a small brick patio as a foundation for the framework.

Thank God we started the Festival in 1935 without waiting for a government grant.

II

Inspiration

B. IDEN PAYNE was the one who directly inspired the early attempts to recreate productions of Shakespeare's plays on the first of the Ashland Elizabethan-type stages. He was Guest Director at the University of Washington at the invitation of John Conway, acting head of the Theatre Department in the summer of 1930. He produced two plays, and I was able to play a bit part in his *Cymbeline* and also stage-managed and played Boyet for him in *Love's Labour's Lost*. I was so excited about what happened when Shakespeare's plays were placed on the type of stage for which they were written that I asked Mr. Payne why he didn't write a book about it. He smiled a very kindly smile, and said, "This is something to be *done*, and not written about."

Iden Payne had been "doing" things in theatre since 1899, when he joined the F.R. Benson company in Manchester in his native England. I remember I thought of him as elderly, for, in spite of his vitality, he was suffering from an ulcer which kept him on a liquid diet. He carried a thermos of warm milk with him and frequently took a sip during rehearsals. As a matter of fact, he was not yet 50, and later became a member of the Department of Theatre at the University of Texas where he was active into the 1970s. But even back in 1930, he had already done more theatre than most people do in a lifetime. He played a major part in the impetus which the A.E.F. Horniman companies gave to repertory theatre in Great Britain, first as General Manager of the Abbey Players and then as the first stage director of Miss Horniman's famous Manchester Repertory Company. He directed many of the early plays of Shaw, Galsworthy, Masefield, Bennett and Brighouse.

It must have been during this period that he became interested in the work of a man by the name of William Poel. Poel had for many years been an outspoken opponent of the elaborate production methods of Shakespearean revivals made so popular by Sir Henry Irving at the Lyceum Theatre in London. He decried the ignorant "butchering" of Shakespeare's scripts and the resultant mangling of his dramatic structure. The less the public saw of Shakespeare in these productions, the more they seemed to demand the ostentatious spectacle of lavish scenic displays and the interpolation of music and dancing. As a result of the mounting costs, Shakespearean revivals became increasingly rare and the typical nineteenth century spectacular, like the dinosaur, became extinct as a result of its own ponderosity.

His eccentricities kept Poel's work from having an immediate effect upon the public, but his productions and the loyalty and respect created by his zeal and ability influenced profoundly the theatre people with whom he worked. His work also influenced the thinking of several key theatre people outside his own circle of confreres. Among these were George Bernard Shaw and Max Reinhardt. Among the former group were Nugent Monck, Harley Granville-Barker and B. Iden Payne.

Poel used amateur actors in his productions almost exclusively, for he said that professionals could not, or would not, "take the tones." Finally, Iden Payne persuaded Poel to direct one of Payne's companies in some Shakespearean productions. It was at this time that Payne gained a knowledge of and sympathy for Poel's theories, but because he believed them to be impractical for professional theatre, he tucked them away in his memory to be used a number of years later in the United States. He came to the States in 1913, where he organized repertory companies, directed and acted for such organizations as The Chicago Theater Society, The Fine Arts Theatre Company, The Drama League of America, Philadelphia Little Theater, The Schuberts, and The Charles Frohman Company.

He finally left Broadway to become a permanent member of the first Theatre Department of an institution of higher education in the United States, developed under the leadership of Thomas Wood Stevens at Carnegie Institute of Technology. One of the reasons he gave me for leaving commercial theatre was that, on Broadway, an actor no sooner progressed to the point where he could be depended upon to

turn in a good performance than he became a star, at which point he
ceased to act and became a "personality."

Mr. Payne told me that it was several years after he went to
Carnegie Tech that he decided to try Poel's ideas in a production there.
The experiment was an immediate success, and for many years he
directed an annual Elizabethan production at that institution. Moreover, he served as visiting professor and director in colleges and universities all over the United States. There are literally hundreds of
theatre people influenced by their work with Payne in Elizabethan-type
productions who are involved in producing or acting in Shakespeare
productions throughout America.

The respect and affection for this man are universal among those
who have worked with him. And legends about him are numerous. His
age has been a subject for speculation until the last few years. I suspect
his students have always marveled at his vigour "considering his age."
For in the eyes of youth, to be of another generation is to be old.

Whenever two or more of his former students are gathered together, they inevitably get around to telling "Payne stories." They are
countless, but I will limit myself to three.

The first one concerns the fact that Mr. Payne directed John Barrymore in his first starring vehicle on Broadway. Barrymore had acted
a number of times but never in a starring role. With his family name
and with his natural bent, he found acting came easily, although his
great ambition had always been to be a graphic artist. The play was the
American premiere of Galsworthy's *Justice*, and it had been in rehearsal some time when the "angel" of the show came to Mr. Payne in
great agitation. He had just heard some disparaging reports about Barrymore's sense of responsibility and demanded that he be replaced. Mr.
Payne protested, but the man who was backing the production predicted that Barrymore would go on a wild binge with disastrous results
to their enterprise. Mr. Payne insisted that Barrymore stay with the
production, and upon further pressing said, in effect, that if Barrymore
were fired, the management would have to get another director. As a
result, Barrymore stayed in the show which launched him on his career
as one of the great stars of American theatre.

The coda of this story occurred many years later, when a Carnegie
Tech student saw John Barrymore on one of the movie lots in Hollywood. Being something of a Barrymore fan, he knew the story of the
Justice production, and perhaps graveled for lack of matter, he said, "I
bring you greetings from Mr. Payne." The great personage stopped in

his tracks, stared at the young man, and then said softly, "You know, if it weren't for that damn son-of-a-bitch, I'd be a drunken bum in the gutter today."

This next story took place when he was still at Carnegie Tech, and must have happened when he had reached the age at which most of us think about retirement. He was directing a young actor by the name of Howard Miller. (Mr. Miller, when he played Petruchio for us in 1953, was a tall, loose-jointed young man, responding to the nick-name of "Bud.") Bud was alone on stage and Mr. Payne was directing him from the rear of the auditorium. Mr. Payne interrupted the scene and said in his quiet voice, "Control, Mr. Miller, control!" Bud, not knowing quite what to make of the comment, went on with the scene, only to be interrupted again by a louder, more insistent voice. "Control, Mr. Miller, control!" This happened several times. Each time Mr. Payne's voice became louder and more demanding. Now, Mr. Payne has always been known as a gentle person, but it is also known that in the heat of creativity he can build up a head of emotional steam which can cause an explosion. So Bud, wanting to avoid a crisis, stopped and asked, "Just what do you mean by 'control,' sir?' Mr. Payne leapt to the arm of the rear center aisle seat, balanced there on one foot, stepped to the arm of the next aisle seat, and the next, and so to the front of the auditorium, jumped lightly to the floor in front of the footlights, and said, "That, Mr. Miller, is what I mean by control."

The third story took place in 1936-7 when Mr. Payne was producing director at the Shakespeare Memorial Theatre in Stratford, England. In those days all artistic policies and decisions were subject to the approval of the theatre's Board of Directors. Among the plays Mr. Payne submitted for the Board's approval was *Cymbeline.* His suggestion was greeted with indignant protests from a distinguished member of the Board: Mr. George Bernard Shaw.

"Why do you want to produce that play with the ridiculous fifth act?" complained Mr. Shaw.

Mr. Payne turned to the end of the Board table where Shaw was sitting and said very quietly,

"Why don't you write another and more suitable fifth act, Mr. Shaw?"

Nothing more was said on the subject, but several weeks later, Mr. Payne received the manuscript for Shaw's *Cymbeline Refinished.* If you have read it, I hope you agree with me that it is more appropriate to the closing of an Ibsen play than of one by Shakespeare. But it was not for aesthetic reasons that it was never done at Stratford. Ironically, the Board turned it down because there is in it a reference to the abdication of Edward VIII.

But we must return to that revealing summer experience at the University of Washington when I first knew Mr. Payne and when he told me that the production of Shakespeare on an Elizabethan stage was "something to be done and not written about."

The two productions, *Cymbeline* and *Love's Labour's Lost*, were played on the huge proscenium arch stage of Meany Hall. As I remember, there was a platform built in front of the footlights, extending toward the audience and over the orchestra pit. The stage setting was composed of half-timbered, painted flats. There were two entrances, one up right and the other up left, inner stages above and below and a "shade" supported by two pillars between which was strung a curtain drawn by two curtain pages. These pages (pulchritudinous coeds in doublet and hose) after opening or closing the penthouse curtains sometimes sat on stools in front of the pillars, sometimes carried the stools to the extreme right and left of the downstage area; sometimes, for a short scene, they would stand by the pillars or disappear behind the closed curtain or make exits right and left. Occasionally they would become part of the play and take on the chores of a household servant or messenger. They undoubtedly helped to emphasize the presentational nature of the production, but I blush to say that I thought them pleasantly "quaint" and was piqued by the daring exposure of the well-shaped feminine legs.

Though Mr. Payne did not insist on our "taking the tones," that peculiar patterned speech which Poel had insisted on, he did dictate each line and inflection. In fact, his first read-through of the play went like this: first, he read the whole play to us, stopping to make comments and to give information about character relationships, Elizabethan customs, word meanings, and so on. Then he read each scene with more comments, and finally, he read each speech in the scene before it was read by the person cast, correcting inflections, explaining character and meanings. After the first speech was re-read by the actor, the second speech was first read by Mr. Payne, then by the actor, so alternating through the scene.

This process disturbed some members of the cast, but I was not upset by it, as my grandmother, in following the principles of Delsarte, had used much the same process in the days of my childhood when she first taught me to "speak pieces" and later when she prepared me for declamation contests.

It may be of interest to note that Jim Beard, now a famous gourmet and chef, was in the cast. He was then a big rotund young man out of Carnegie Tech, and I was much impressed with his performance as Cymbeline. Other than Jim, we were a pretty lightweight cast.

While I was impressed by Mr. Payne's wealth of knowledge and his command of background material which made the plays immediately more meaningful, I did not, at the time, understand the value of the scholarly materials he brought to bear on the history of the theatre, the philosophy, politics, folklore and mores of Elizabethan times. A full appreciation of the importance of these values did not come until my Stanford days, which brought me under the influence of Dr. Margery Bailey.

I was perhaps prejudiced by my current exposure to two disparate approaches to Shakespeare's plays. In the Theatre Department we were taught that the end product of a Shakespearean play script was a stage production. In the English Department, it seemed to me, the end product of the play script was considered to be a scholarly paper. The term papers in the English classes were, for the most part, regurgitations of these scholarly writings, analyzing the plays as if they were history books, giving the characters a life of their own apart from the life Shakespeare had given them for his own purposes.

I graduated from the University firmly convinced, in my ignorance, that there was little or no connection between scholarship and theatrical production.

My understanding of what Mr. Payne was trying to do was severely limited by my youth and inexperience. But two things impressed me and exhilarated me tremendously. They were his insistence upon a smooth rapidity in tempo and his encouragment of actors to contact the audience directly, especially in soliloquies and asides. Each performance started with the entrance of the curtain pages, who met in the center of the downstage area, bowed to each other and then bowed to the audience. They then pulled the curtains as if to present the production to the audience. This helped to emphasize the atmosphere of a play, on a stage, being performed by actors before each specific audience.

He insisted upon an articulate but swift delivery of lines and seldom allowed pauses between lines. Each actor was forced to pick up cues immediately, which meant that the intake of breath which accompanies the preparation for the articulation of a new idea had to come during the previous speech prior to the word cue. This even extended to the first line of a new scene, which had to come on word cue from the last line of the previous scene. This meant, that the entrance of the new scene must overlap the exit of the former scene.

I have seen this gentle man lose his patience only a few times over the years. But I remember vividly the time when, after trying an entrance over and over, he finally went on stage and lifted a young actress bodily through the doorway upon word cue. She made it on time thereafter.

The inner-above and the inner-below stages were both curtained. These curtains and the curtain between the pillars of the penthouse were used to indicate change of place. That is, one or another of them was either opened or closed to signify such a change. Frequently there were changes of setting in the inner stages, formal hedges in the inner-below in *Love's Labour's Lost*, a bed and hangings along with Iachimo's chest in the inner-above in *Cymbeline*, and, I believe, a cut-out curtain in the inner-below for the "cave." If I remember correctly, there was some indication of the "narrow lane" for the battle scene. The penthouse curtain, when closed, made it possible to set up platforms, furniture or props in front of the inner-below curtains. This location provided much better sight lines than were possible in the inner stages. And because the audience sat in straight rows in front of the proscenium, these changes in furniture and props did not distract from the action on the forestage.

Payne called for two intermissions, though he explained to me, as stage manager, that the scripts were written to be played without intermission. Modern audiences, accustomed to such breaks, he feared, would not sit through a full production without them. Other than these two intermissions, the productions went through without a pause.

To say that the processes and techniques that I have just mentioned were all that I carried away from those two productions would be a dreadful oversimplification. There were many less tangible things which were to shape an approach to the production of Shakespeare in Ashland. I do not refer to the values any young actor receives from contact with a great director and teacher, but to those impressions, attitudes, prejudices (if you will) toward Shakespeare's scripts in relationship to their presentation on an Elizabethan stage garnered from my association with Iden Payne.

To analyze those facets of the bias Mr. Payne induced toward the scripts as instruments of production is difficult for me, viewing, as I do, the experience of those two productions from a distance of over 40 years. Many impressions did not become fully meaningful until my first Stanford stint fifteen years later. But the seeds were planted, though they did not foliate for many years. As I remember, some of them were as follows:

1. a preoccupation with meanings of words, ideas, acts, as they would apply to an *Elizabethan* audience;
2. an insistence that a modern editor's script must be read with a knowledge of the earliest printed versions of the plays and with a firm rejection of all those stage directions, especially scene descriptions inspired by eighteenth and nineteenth century productions;
3. attention to the close relationship of prosody and meaning; and
4. above all, the study of the script to discover and put to use in a twentieth century production what must have been seen and heard in the original sixteenth and seventeenth century productions.

In September of 1931, a little over a year after my experience with Iden Payne, I came to Ashland as an instructor at Southern Oregon Normal School. As I look back, I am amazed at the extent to which accident, coincidence, fate, if you will, played a part in the shaping of the Oregon Shakespearean Festival. President Churchill chose me to join his faculty on the recommendation of Miss Henrietta Challis, of his Music Department, who also happened to be a distant cousin of mine.

In the spring of 1926, having graduated from Bellingham Normal School, I lived with the Challis family in Seattle while attending the University of Washington for the first time. I earned my board and room with them by removing the sod from their lawn, excavating about two feet of dirt, and replacing the sod. I don't remember the exact size of the lawn, but I still recall aching wheelbarrow muscles at the end of the day—especially after those long Saturdays.

One summer before this, I had toured with the Challis Family Orchestra as a dramatic reader, rendering comic and dramatic numbers between their musical selections. I remember some of these readings were delivered in full costume and makeup, and some of them were of my own composition. (God help me!) Mrs. Challis played the piano, Dr. Challis the cello, Sarah played the harp, Mary the flute, and Henrietta the violin. The impact of the ensemble was, as I recall, that of uninspired technical proficiency. I suspect my performance did not add inspiration to what must have been a rather dreary evening. A glimmer of the truth descended upon me one night in a ghost of a town, the name of which I have long ago forgotten. We were playing in an old abandoned movie house. The audience was sparse enough to begin with, but by the time I came on to give my mid-program reading, its members could be counted on one set each of fingers and toes. When I finished, there was loud applause from only one man. I peered into the darkened auditorium and spotted my enthusiastic friend. He was alone in the house and he was very drunk.

We traveled over most of central and eastern Washington, playing one night stands wherever Dr. Challis could find booking. We drove two decrepit Fords. Henrietta and I drove the one with the camping gear and musical instruments; the rest of the family rode in the other. Over the rough roads we frequently encountered, the big Italian harp strapped to a rack on the rear of our car tended to lift the front wheels off the ground, so that driving was a bit tricky.

When we drove into a campground, we pitched our tents, made the beds while Dr. Challis drove to the nearest town to make arrangements for our appearances. Sometimes this meant that we would stay several days in one camping spot. When curtain time approached, we got dressed in our best, rode to the theatre, and returned to the camp after the performance. The meals, cooked on the campground stoves, were inexpensive but nourishing.

This mode of traveling, cheap as it must have been, cost more than we garnered with the concerts. Dr. Challis was a capable dentist, but in those depression times paying dental bills was a luxury most of his patients could not afford. Thus it cost him very little to leave his practice for this wild summer tour, and it was a diversion from the tensions of trying to maintain a home in the University district, support a family of five and eke out an existence by holding off creditors until his patients paid their bills. I remember that my compensation for the summer tour was a blue serge suit!

He was kindly and generous to a fault, considering his financial limitations. But I remember that I thought him extremely quixotic. Like Alice's White Knight, he tended to ride off in all directions at once, but always with the air of having thought out every move in advance according to the latest scientific theories. At one time, he was at work on a novel about a prehistoric tribe. I remember that he explained to us how he had arrived at a detailed description of the position they assumed when they sat in the rain. He had us look at the way the hair on our arms grew in a pattern to shed water from the elbows, when our hands were clasped over our heads. He designed a "revolutionary" boat which he had built to his own specifications. One day he took us all out for a ride on Puget Sound. I was frightened when I first looked at his creation. It was top heavy, and I was sure it would turn over at the first wave. But the weather was calm and we set out, only to be overtaken by one of those sudden squalls which are common on the Sound. When the waves got so high that I was sure we would swamp, the engine began to sputter. Dr. Challis seemed completely unconcerned about the whole thing, but finally decided to go to attend to the motor. With casual instructions to keep headed into the wind, he left me with the wheel to battle the elements. I have never been so green with fright in my life.

In the Challis home, the one budgeted item was the girls' music lessons. There was always money for that, somehow. And the one regularity in the home schedule was the daily practice sessions for each of the girls. Mrs. Challis was a wan, ineffectual person whose plaintive nagging had no effect upon the two younger ersatz music students. Henrietta was always conscientious in her practicing and joined in haranguing her two younger sisters when they shirked. The day's practice schedule was reviewed each night by Dr. Challis and the punishment for skimping or omitting practice was the re-assignment of the housekeeping duties of those who were virtuous to those who shirked. So between the sound of endless scales on the various instruments, the quarrelling over musical duties and the arguments over whose turn it was to wash the dishes, there was little peace in which to pursue my own studies.

Each morning before he left for his office, the good doctor would open for discussion the matter of the evening menu. The final veto of most requests was the emptying of his purse to disclose a dollar bill or two and some small change. He always managed to bring home something satisfying. I do not remember going hungry. Frequently he would deliberately create suspense on his return home by making us guess the contents of a package or sack contributed by one or another of his patients (in part payment of a bill), fruit or vegetables generally, but sometimes fish, rarely meat. I do remember the excitement when he brought home six big crabs. They were quickly rinsed off after the backs were removed; a plate, fork, a nutpick and a block of wood were found for each of us. A bowl of mayonnaise was placed in the center of the table and a hammer was passed around so that we could take turns cracking the shells on the block of wood, remove the meat, dip it in the mayonnaise and gorge ourselves on that most excellent of all seafoods.

And so it came about that six years later, Henrietta recommended me to President Churchill for a position on the faculty of Southern Oregon Normal School. All this does not explain, however, why it was that I was interested in a position with a Normal School. In order to understand that, you should know about other people and circumstances.

One of my instructors at Bellingham Normal School was Victor H. Hoppe. He taught what was then called "Expression" courses similar to those now listed as "Speech and Theatre" courses. He also directed the extra-curricular plays, one of which was produced each quarter. If we don't count Rosalind and we certainly shouldn't, which I played as a high school student for a student assembly, my first Shakespearean role was Adam in *As You Like It*. The production was staged on a wooded knoll on the Normal School campus. Professor Hoppe directed and played Jaques. I remember that he provided a tremulous fiddle in the wings for my "big" scene in which Adam collapses. The next summer he produced *Romeo and Juliet* and played Friar Laurence. I stage-managed that show and played Tybalt.

It was the latter production that provided an experience which I still recall so vividly that the memory induces a cold sweat. The costume house had provided me with a costume complete with a black, shoulder length wig, a wonderfully "sweepy" cape, and a beret with a dashing feather. Romeo was played by my very good friend Oliver Nelson. Neither one of us knew anything about fencing, but the young man who played Mercutio was a fencer and he laboriously taught us every thrust and parry of each of the stage duels. We conscientiously learned every move by rote and rehearsed them endlessly. I prided myself on my ability with stage makeup. There was always makeup around our home, and I had been experimenting with my face since I was ten years old. Taking the black wig as my cue, I made up very dark with a neat mustache and beard. With my doublet and hose, feathered beret and cape, I thought that I cut a very dashing figure, all fiery and Italianate.

I had worked out very precisely the business of Tybalt's entrance for the fatal duel. (Enter, swaggering, listen to Romeo's challenge with a villainous sneer.) "THOU, WRETCHED BOY," (carelessly toss beret aside) "THAT DIDST CONSORT HIM HERE," (suavely sweep cape up over left shoulder to free sword arm) "SHALT WITH HIM HENCE." (Out sword and into carefully choreographed fight.)

Dress rehearsal went well, but on opening night I got as far as "THAT DIDST CONSORT HIM HERE," when I realized to my horror that my wig had gone with my beret! Like a lightning flash, the ridiculous figure I must have presented was seared into my brain. All in a split second I could see the ring where my very dark makeup left off and my pale forehead and blond hair must have shrieked out for attention. I knew that if the audience laughed I would die! I would not let them laugh. I would die first, or somebody would die. "SHALT WITH HIM HENCE" My sword was out and I started toward Romeo. Oliver told me afterward that he could see the whites of my rolling eyes and that he was sure that I was going to kill him. Of course the choreography went out the window. I do not remember what happened on stage, but the audience did not laugh. Oliver finally was able to insert his sword under my upstage arm, and so put an end to Tybalt's madness but not to my agony. After the scene in the dark backstage, I wept.

I suppose those productions must have been pretty bad, romanticized never-never Elizabethan—costume rental house period, mood music in the wings, oratorical delivery, untrained actors, in fact, a hodgepodge of elements gathered together almost accidentally. But I thought Mr. Hoppe was a superb actor and his classes were the most exciting in the school. I thought that sometime when I got to be an old man like him (he couldn't have been over 35) perhaps I, too, could be a teacher of speech and theatre in a Normal School. I still remember the chills up and down my spine as I listened to him one day in class give Shylock's "How like a fawning Publican he looks...." speech. I am sure it was the memory of that experience which persuaded me in 1935 to choose *The Merchant of Venice* as the first Festival offering and to launch on the series of 11 Shylocks I have played over the years. In fact, I suppose it was from him that I inherited the idea of playing in the productions which I directed. In the early days of the Festival this practice was an integral part of the operation.

You can understand, then why it was that in 1931 when I saw my master's degree within reach, I asked the University of Washington Employment Bureau to find me a job in a drama and speech department of a Normal School. And if you remember that 1931 was in the depths of the depression, you can understand why I received an indignant refusal. I was told that I would be fortunate to get a job of any kind, even teaching English in a country high school. With that beneficent ignorance which it has always been my good fortune to possess, I replied that they should trouble themselves no further for I would find my own job.

As a matter of fact, I discovered only two vacancies in Normal Schools in the entire country: one in eastern Washington at Ellensburg, and the other at Southern Oregon Normal, of which my cousin Henrietta informed me. I applied to both institutions and was elated when I was asked to come to Ellensburg for an interview. The interview went well enough, but I was asked to submit a list of the plays I had directed. Because of the weakness of that list I lost the job, and made up my mind that any play I produced from then on would look good on a list. This was what you might call a backdoor to good taste, but it was a valuable lesson. It was agonizingly late in June before I got the telegram of acceptance from President Churchill. And so it was that I came to Ashland in September of 1931.

III

Exercises

I N COMING TO ASHLAND I faced the most bitter disappointment
I had experienced in my young life. Southern Oregon Normal
School did not have a drama department or a speech department.
What is more, there was little prospect in policy or in facilities for the
development of either one. The school was only six years old and
boasted a student body of less than three hundred. The two-year
curriculum was designed for the purpose of training grade school teachers, and all the courses had a "professional" slant. Liberal arts courses
were strictly the province of the University of Oregon. Courses such as
geography, English literature and music were taught so the student
might gain a practical knowledge of the subject matter he was to teach
when he became a grade school teacher.

I found myself assigned to the traditional freshman English composition courses and several one-quarter (three hours a week) courses
in public speaking. The single crumb that was tossed my way was a
course called "Play Production." It was offered once a year for three
quarter-hours of credit. Strangely enough it was this course that got
me into trouble and almost wrote finis to my Ashland career. What a
shame it would have been if the Festival had been aborted before it was
conceived. But more of that later.

When I first saw the auditorium, I was horrified. I decided that it
must have been designed by a genius, for no one but a genius could
have known so many rules of theatre architecture to break in order to
make it impossible to produce a play in the place. The school was
housed in one building, and the auditorium took up the entire depth of

39

the center section of the second floor, with major classrooms on either side. This meant that the room had to be used as a hallway by the entire faculty and student body. Twice a week the creaky folding chairs were removed from the resonant, polished, flat floor so that Virginia Hales (a wonderful gal who doubled in brass as the Dean of Women) could teach folk dancing, which was the physical part of women's physical education. Over this hard surfaced floor the architects had hung a plaster dome suspended on wires. I have never been inside a bass drum but if I ever were, I am sure the acoustics would be much the same. The stage was equipped with red, white and blue foot lights matched by a monstrously heavy set of red, white and blue strip lights counterweighted by a chunk of cement. The plastered stage ceiling was about two feet above the proscenium arch, which was 15 feet high and 28 feet wide. The two dressing rooms, one on each side of the stage, were barely out of sight lines back of the proscenium opening. The stage itself was only 10 feet, six inches deep, and there was a steam radiator in the middle of the back plastered wall.

You can well understand why I was disappointed, and you can also realize that the very blow to my ambition became a stimulus to hunt for alternate ways of satisfying my urge to do things theatrically creative.

The Festival was not to start for almost four years, but these were very important years spent (unknowingly) in preparation for what was to be the most important venture I was ever to undertake. In those four years I was to discover a potential audience; key people (with appropriate talents, interests, information and enthusiasms), a congenial environment (both climatic and cultural) and, perhaps most important of all, a way to achieve something of significance in American theatre in spite of all the handicaps of academia.

One policy which I started out with and which has proved basically sound over the years is an insistence that every professional action should be special and not routine, every production important and not trivial. Everyone does his best work when he feels, not that he, himself is important, but that what he is doing is important and will result in something of lasting significance.

I realized that, if I were going to develop an extensive extracurricular theatre program, my first task was to convince faculty, student body, and townspeople of the importance of that project. I decided to start with the faculty.

Then, as now, it was taken for granted that varsity athletes were helped by being allowed to make up missed classes and examinations, sometimes by special coaching when necessary. I knew, of course, that such a policy with regard to students concerned with extra curricular theatre had never been considered. I therefore decided to produce as my first theatrical venture in Ashland a play, cast completely from the faculty. I chose for a vehicle George Kelly's classic, *The Show-off*. This realistic comedy is the best play Kelly ever wrote, but it is far from an easy one to perform satisfactorily. But I had several interesting personalities among the faculty who I thought could carry the show, with proper coaching. I cast myself in the title role of Aubrey Piper for several reasons. First and most obvious: because I am a ham and, like Bottom, have always wanted to play all the parts. Second: because I thought that if I displayed my ability as an actor impressively, the faculty cast would be more likely to accept my direction. Third: I had played the role the year before at the Seattle Repertory Playhouse under the expert direction of Florence Bean James. I will never forget the ecstasy with which I read the note from Burton and Florence James in which they asked me to play Aubrey in the University production at the Playhouse. I had done Sir Christopher Hatton, a bit part in *The Critic*, for them the quarter before and I remember that they said they were attracted by my "ability to make a comic comment on the role." I have had a warm regard for that term ever since.

I am sure that my faculty cast considered me a very brash young man, but they were fortunately amused rather than offended by it. I worked them very hard and we eventually all proceeded from the premise that this was not to be just another faculty fun show. It was to evolve into an aesthetic object representing the very best creative work which it was possible to achieve as a result of their combined individual artistic contributions. The production was successful, not only because we had surprisingly large audiences of townspeople and students for three nights, but also because the comedy stemmed rather more frequently from George Kelly and his characters than from the incongruity of staid faculty members behaving in an unfamiliar way. If you want to get to know a person rapidly, go camping with him, serve in the army with him or be in a play with him. In any case, I am sure that we all felt a bit closer as a result of our association in *The Show-Off*.

I have said that I was fortunate in the people I was able to cast in the show, but I didn't know how fortunate I was in one particular

instance. The casting of Walter Redford as the father in this production
may well have saved me from being fired at the end of my first year at
Southern Oregon. I promised earlier to tell how the Play Production
class got me into serious trouble.

As I have said, the course was a three credit-hour course which
was offered for one quarter a year. Later I was able to make it a
laboratory course with only one hour lecture a week with six hours of
lab which allowed the students to learn by doing. Also it provided a
way to get my scenery built. But this first year I had not learned how
to change from the customary three hours of lectures a week. The
course consisted of tidbits of information designed to be useful to the
neophyte director: "How to build a flat," "How to design a rehearsal
schedule," "How to mix scenepaint," and so on. Indeed, in the time
allotted, it was barely possible to skim the surface of the load of information I was eager to impart concerning the aesthetics, techniques,
psychology, of a very complicated process.

I was fortunate to have an exciting group of youngsters in the
class. There were, as I remember, about 25 registered for the course.
This was approximately 10 percent of the student body. They were a
very sharp group, including three who were included in Terman's
famous study of genius. It also included William Cottrell, an extremely talented sixteen year old, who was later to play an essential
part in the developments which resulted in the emergence of the Festival. They were a stimulating group, and I believe it was in this class
that I learned to throw away my lecture notes and to discuss pertinent
problems with the students.

At the end of the quarter I was asked by some of the students in
the class if it was possible to offer an advanced class in the subject. I was
naturally complimented that I had generated enthusiasm in the class.
At that time it was possible for the president of each state institution to
make all decisions concerning curricula. But I thought that it would be
better if the request for an advanced course came to President Churchill
from the students, rather than from me. I therefore suggested that a
delegation from the class call in at his office and state their case.

Mr. Churchill was a little bantam rooster of a man with a grizzled
head and a rugged face featuring sparkling eyes that could dance with
amusement or shoot fire according to the occasion. It was known that if
you were one of his faculty family, he would defend you fiercely
against outside criticism of word or deed. It was also known that he
could flay you alive in the privacy of his office, sometimes in criticism

of the same word or deed. However, it was with a clear conscience that I answered the summons to his office following his conference with my student delegation. I was therefore completely unprepared for the blow to my psychological solar plexus which followed.

"Mr. Bowmer, sit down. I have a serious matter to discuss with you." I was puzzled by his tone, but still felt no warning of what was to come.

"I am sadly disappointed in you as a teacher!" That hurt, but the knockout blow was to follow!

"I have just had a talk with some of your students from your play production class. They feel that they have learned so little from you in that course that they would need to take another whole quarter of the subject matter to make up the deficiency!"

The unfairness of the accusation, the stupidity of the misinterpretation of my students' motives, the hopelessness of the future development of theatre in the institution, all hit me so hard that I completely lost control. I don't remember what I said, other than to shout that people spent their entire lives learning about the production of plays. I must have said much more, and most of it was pretty violent and only stopped when I stomped indignantly out of the office.

The next day was Saturday. In the morning sometime I received a telephone call from Walter Redford, who asked me if I would take a hike with him. I was surprised, but not unwilling, so early that afternoon we took one of the many paths near the campus that led up into the hills. When we had gone some distance, Walter suggested that we sit down for a breather. We found a convenient log and I looked expectantly at him. He was a big, pleasant soft-spoken man of more than ample height and girth. I always thought that the expression around his eyes seemed to say that, if the next thing you said was funny, he would not be unprepared. He wasted no more time with preliminaries, but spoke at once to the point.

"Angus," he said, "I'm going to tell you something that nobody else at the Normal School knows. Next year I am going to be president of the institution and I want you on my faculty. But you won't be here unless you go and make your peace with President Churchill."

Well, that was that. The following Monday, I got an appointment with the president and told him that if I had said anything that I shouldn't have said on our previous meeting, I was sorry and I apologized. I stressed the importance to me of making a success of my first year of college teaching and sincerely hoped that I could be given

an opportunity to "make good" at Southern Oregon. As a consequence. I stayed on the next year under Dr. Redford and somewhat
more liberal policies toward theatre. But there were still three more
years of preparation before the Festival started.

Throughout all this I frequently wondered why President Churchill had ever hired me in the first place. But of course it was because of
my six years of teaching in the elementary schools of Washington.
That was a big mistake on his part. But then, he couldn't know that the
only reason I taught in grade school was to earn money which would
enable me to pursue theatre courses at college. I think I was a good
teacher, if an unconventional one. I never did go all the way with the
professional educators. In fact, some of the dullest college courses with
which I have come in contact have been the capital E, Education
courses, and some of the dullest people I have ever known have taught
them.

It was a near thing, my going into education. Up to 24 hours
before I was to have entered the University of Washington after
graduating from Oak Harbor High School, I assumed that I was going
to major in journalism. Not that I wanted to be a newspaper man, for
my father had always discouraged that. He and his own father were
both country newspaper men but he had actually discouraged me from
learning the cases, making up forms, feeding press or any of the other
skills involved in the print shop. Looking back on it now, I can see that
the fact neither his father nor he had been able to accumulate any
money must have made him wish for something different for me.
However, I was sublimely unconscious of the fact that we were underprivileged. I must must have assumed that being without funds was
the natural state of Man. As a matter of fact, I gave it very little
thought.

I had been interested in writing as a means of satisfying the vague
creative hunger that I felt but couldn't identify. I had written some
poetry and I had received a very encouraging letter from Sid Sydell, the
editor of *American Magazine*, to which I had sent a short-short story
before that form had emerged. I thought (mistakenly, of course) that
majoring in journalism at the University was the way to get started in
the writing field.

It was the Saturday before Labor Day, I remember, that my parents came to breakfast with unaccustomed solemn faces expressing
their dismay and disappointment as they explained to me that there

would not be money enough to see me through four years at the University. The expressions changed to puzzled relief when I announced that in that case I would like to go to Bellingham Normal School. The quick switch in plans actually came as a sort of relief to me for several reasons.

The most immediate argument for Bellingham was one that I kept to myself: a girl friend was going there. The next and most practical reason was that I could earn a teaching certificate in one school year, and I was sure that I would be able to sign a nine-month teaching contract before the end of that time. Also, the expenses at Bellingham were reported to be much less than at the larger University. Thus it was decided that we would make a trip to Bellingham to inquire about the costs and registration requirements.

There were two other reasons why the sudden change in plans was not difficult for me. These seeds had been planted much earlier, and had been lying dormant, but now they blossomed forth so vigorously as to make the change seem almost providential. The previous winter Professor Victor H. Hoppe had come to our school to present an evening's entertainment in which he performed a full length play, portraying all the characters himself. I have spoken previosuly of his influence over me and of my tremendous admiration for his ability as an actor. I still remember the thrill of that performance, including his appearance in full evening dress, the first white tie and tails I had ever seen.

Then there was Grace Eccles. Miss Eccles had been my teacher for the three years I had attended Oak Harbor High School, from which I had graduated the previous June with a class of eight. She could have sat for a cartoonist as a model for the caricature of the old maid school marm so popular with the humorists of the day. She had extraordinarily long front teeth, shiny nose and forehead topped with a pile of blond hair from which wisps continually strayed in such a way as to threaten the collapse of the entire structure. She had, however, earned the affection and respect of all of us and we trusted her judgement in academic and other matters excepting only those in which the young always think they know more than their elders. One of her extracurricular duties was the directing of the annual junior and senior class plays. I participated in these events in various capacities for three years, because the small classes meant that everyone needed to lend a hand. I must have made a nuisance of myself, giving advice where it was not needed. But instead of being offended, or feeling that I should be taught to respect protocol, Miss Eccles encouraged me, sought my help and advice, and the last year, I was given considerable directorial responsibilities.

One day, I remember, she asked me what I expected to do when I graduated. I told her of the plans to major in journalism, and she said, "Have you ever thought of majoring in drama? Oh, I don't mean going into professional theatre," she hastened to add. "I mean with the idea of teaching. The first year or two you might teach in a small school like this one and only direct the junior and senior plays. Give it some thought, for I think you have a distinctive flair for theatre." Neither one of us dreamed that she was actually prophesying. For I was to spend my first teaching assignment in the Oak Harbor School system and would direct the junior and senior class plays.

And so I began my career as a potential educator with nine months at Bellingham Normal School. I remember very little of my classroom work that year, outside of Mr. Hoppe's classes. The last quarter I was scheduled for practice teaching, and my sole supervised professional experience before being inflicted on the helpless young was a three hour course in which I taught spelling to a room of fifth graders. This was particularly ironic because I never have been able to spell. Any correct spelling between these covers is, I assure you, the work of the editor.

I remember much more of my extra curricular activities. There were 900 students in the school, 800 of whom were girls! It was very easy to be popular with those odds. Needless to say, my girl friend was soon lost in that mob. I sang in the college male quartet, I was elected treasurer of the freshman class, a member of the student council.

Financial matters were not particularly difficult. My folks sent me $25 a couple of times, and I worked at a variety of odd jobs. The football boys had all the campus jobs, of course, but I let it be known that I was on call whenever one of them wanted a day off, so I was busy several days a week at odd hours, cleaning erasers, sweeping floors, wiping silverware at the dorm. Other jobs included getting up at four in the morning to build fires in a bakery, selling shoes at a department store, and clerking at J. C. Penney's on Saturdays. Before the beginning of the third quarter I had signed a contract to teach for nine months at Oak Harbor. On the strength of this contract I was able to get a student loan to see me through the rest of the year. I was very proud of that contract although it brought me in only $75 a month for nine months, with $15 a month additional for doing the janitorial work. The school was a two-room structure which housed the first four grades, and I taught the third and fourth grades in the same room where I had attended the fourth grade. I also was forced, for lack of other sources, to go back to the same methods used by Miss Smith, my fourth grade teacher.

I have already mentioned that I directed the high school plays, but I must add that I also coached basketball and football. One of the complications to all this was the fact that all the students involved in these activities had known me as a fellow student just a year previously. The task of exerting authority while still remaining on friendly terms was a very good lesson in practical psychology. It was here I first learned how to influence others without seeming to try.

I felt that my students should learn to call me by my last name, and one of my father's favorite stories concerns my success in that endeavor. I had been ill and out of the classroom for several days. One of my fourth graders came by our house on his way to school. Dad was out in the yard chopping kindling, and the lad shouted to him, "Hey, Charlie, is Mr. Bowmer going to be in school today?"

The next year they moved the fourth grade up to the high school building and I was hired again —this time to teach the fourth and fifth grades, the same students I had taught before. At the end of that year my two-year certificate gave out, so that I had to go back to Bellingham. I finished the class requirements for my life certificate at the end of the winter quarter, and then went on to the University of Washington and life with the Challis family, of which I have written in the previous chapter. In the meantime, a couple of summer quarters at Bellingham had provided me with the experience in those two Shakespearean productions under Victor Hoppe.

The next fall, I signed up to teach the sixth grade in Oak Harbor. These, of course, were the same pupils I had taught in their third and fourth years. Before that year began, however, I had married Lois Muzzall, a talented, shy, raven-haired girl I had known and dated throughout my high school days. Without her the Festival would not have been possible. But more of that later.

We settled down into the lap of what fortunately we didn't know was the underprivileged. The tiny two-room house we furnished with a couple of kitchen chairs scavenged from my father-in-law's ranch, a card table and a folding camp bed. Somebody gave us a small flat-topped wood burning stove, which after having the rust sandpapered off, and a good coat of stove blacking, served for both heat and cooking.

Incidentally, I felled a tree and sawed it into stove lengths and chopped it into appropriate sizes to fuel this stove for all that winter. A pump and an outhouse in the back yard were the only plumbing.

That fall Lois returned to Bellingham to finish the work for her teacher's certificate and left me to my rather inept batching. In this little town of about 300 people, there were no restaurants, even if I could have afforded to eat in one. Coffee and dry cereal were no problem for breakfast, and I could put up a passable sandwich for lunch. But it was the problem of those evening meals with the obvious necessity of cooking something and eating it all alone that really bothered me. Lois came home on those weekends when she could get a ride with somebody. This provided a welcome relief from my loneliness and also provided several evening meals for the coming week. I was still hard put to stand my own cooking for at least several nights a week.

I finally came up with what I thought was a clever solution to the problem. The Women's Civic Club was in need of some fund for their community improvement program. I suggested to their president that I could help them raise some of these funds by producing a couple of community plays during the school year. But I explained the difficulty of cooking an evening meal, washing the dinner dishes and conducting a rehearsal all on the same night. So, after due consideration, a committee had an inspired solution for the situation. On each rehearsal night I would have dinner at the home of a club member. The experiment was an unqualified success: I was passed around from member to member for a whole series of delightful evening meals. I had the experience of directing two plays and the women enriched their treasury. In turn the town gained perhaps new sidewalks or play equipment in the park. Whether or not the town was enriched culturally by the productions themselves is a moot question. The first one was, perforce, a non-royalty thing, the title of which I have forgotten. Because there was money in the treasury by the time we chose the second play, it was possible to persuade the ladies to invest in royalty for the production of George M. Cohan's famous spoof of the mystery play, *Seven Keys to Baldpate*.

The operation was a success but the patient died. Because of this very successful venture, I lost my job with the Oak Harbor Schools. When all of my confreres had received their contracts for the next year, I still had not received mine. Somewhat worried but thinking that there must have been some kind of mistake, I went down to the Ford garage to see Dave Judson, the chairman of the school board. He crawled out from under a car and wiped his hands on a greasy rag. Dave was a good man, I knew. He was big and rather easy going, but I missed the usual twinkle in his deep-set eyes, which peered out from under his massive eyebrows.

"Dave," I said, "I'm a bit worried because I haven't received my contract."

"Yeah," he drawled, studiously continuing to wipe his hands.

"Does this mean that I'm not being rehired next year?"

"I'm afraid so," he said with an expression so pained you would have thought that he was losing the job.

"But why, Dave? Have any of the parents complained about my teaching?"

"Nope."

"Any of the board members say that I wasn't a good teacher?"

"Nope."

"Then why, Dave, why?"

"Well, Mrs. X...(She was a member of the school board and of the Methodist church, and I am not changing the name to protect the innocent but simply because I can't remember her blasted name.) "Mrs. X seemed to think that you were spending too much time with those plays and other outside interests."

It is true that my life style had changed considerably, not only because of my marriage, but also because my parents and grandparents no longer lived in Oak Harbor. The Bowmers had always been church-goers. We all sang in the choir and went to church twice on Sunday. In fact, most of our social life had centered around the church. Left to my own devices, my church-going slipped and I no longer sang in the choir. My weekends I spent with my bride, whenever possible, and instead of choir rehearsal, I attended play rehearsal. In one stroke Mrs. X was able to punish me for my back-sliding and also to strike a blow at that worldly institution, "The Theatre." This was my first introduction to the sort of puritanical opposition that I was going to have to learn to deal with before the Festival was ever to materialize.

Thus it was that the next September Lois and I found ourselves the complete faculty of a two-room school at Rosburg. I say "at" rather than "in" for Rosburg was not a town, but merely a spot on the map of Wahkiakum County in southwestern Washington. The region boasted 110 inches of rain a year, so the hills at either end of the 10 miles of graveled road were not navigable for nine months of the year. The slippery clay roads over the hills required three successive days without rain to be passable, and there were not three such days from September to June!

Our approach to Rosburg was by way of Astoria, Oregon, then by boat across the wide Columbia for about 10 miles to the mouth of Gray's River, up Gray's River, up Deep River to Deep River Landing. We disembarked here and hiked several miles to the Rosburg School. For nine months this route was our only access to and from the outside world. Across the road and up a fern-bordered path was the old weather-beaten house that served as our residence. Up the road a few miles was the Rosburg store and community hall, and at the other end of the 10 miles of road there was what was virtually a ghost town, with a big building that had once housed a saloon on the ground floor. Above the old saloon was an old theatre, long ago abandoned and forgotten. It was the only theatre that I have ever seen with the flat auditorium floor and raked stage complete with grooves for the wood wings! Straight out of provincial nineteenth century! For nine months this was (except for one disastrous interlude) our entire world: the school, the Rosburg store and Community Hall, and this old ghost of a theatre.

The inhabitants were mostly Finnish, with a scattering of a few Norwegians. The members of the school board and the other leaders of the Finnish community were soft-spoken, adamant people. Their children, whose grandparents were born in the valley, came to school to learn English. Many of the wives spoke nothing but Finnish.

There was another element, however, who were hearty, outgoing, rough, tough and violent. The principal industry (after bootlegging) was fishing, and there was the same kind of traditional feud between the gillnetters and the purse-seiners here on the rivers as there was between the sheepmen and the cattlemen in the range country. Many a gillnetter had disappeared from his boat in the heavy fog, and many a purse-seiner had fallen victim to the hatred instilled by the perpetual vendetta.

For the most part, they were warm-hearted, generous people, and we found ourselves in the middle of a whirl of community activities. The center of all these activities was the Rosburg store and Community Hall presided over by genial Dan Hall and his attractive wife, Hazel. Dan was the unofficial mayor, judge, doctor and general factotum, a kind of community master of ceremonies. Remember that for nine months there was no doctor, lawyer, minister, just Dan. Once a week there was a meeting of the "Dog" club, so called becuase its raison d'être was an interminable Finnish card game called "dog." This was an exclusively male event and, as you might imagine, pretty raucous and "gamey." If I remember correctly, there were meetings of the women under Hazel's jurisdiction at the Hall residence.

I joined the activities of a kind of wrestling club which was formed when a young Finnish Adonis, whose first name was Milo, returned from a hitch in the Navy with a certain renown as a wrestler. We met for a workout and "lessons" from Milo every week. I religiously did a mile of roadwork every morning before breakfast. In lieu of a cold shower, I had to make do with a galvanized tub filled with water pumped from the well. There were Saturday night dances for which I sometimes played saxophone.

From up and down the rivers and creeks and over the dykes and through the woods, young and old turned out for these activities. No television, only radio, the telephone (when the lines were in operation) and that long circuitous boat trip to Astoria to provide contact with the outside world. But the patrons of the Rosburg store and the parents of the pupils of the Rosburg school were happy to make the most of their own little isolated world.

In fact, when I began to put out feelers about the possibility of establishing a high school, the president of the school board objected very strongly. The world was wicked, he said, and he did not believe in letting his children learn any more about it than was necessary to carry on the business side of fishing or farming.

The first few weeks of school went uneventfully by. Lois taught the first five grades and I had the sixth, seventh, eighth and ninth grades. We found the students very sharp and it was hard work to keep the more intelligent ones occupied in a challenging way so their occupation would be profitable. Most of them came by rowboat along Beaver Creek. Even the little first graders were as much at home in a boat as on land. I was about to say "dry land" but, of course, with 110 inches of rain a year there was no such thing. They all wore big rubber boots, which they removed before coming into the class rooms. Our first effort of mass education was to try to persuade them to bring slippers or shoes to leave at the school to wear during the school day. At the best the air was pretty raunchy by late afternoon. The two rooms were commodious enough to accommodate the thirty or so in each room. Heat was furnished by two big wood-burning stoves.

I was seriously frightened one day to hear a rumor that came to me, (I presume from Dan Hall) that Lois and I had been hired because of my reputation as a "disciplinarian." This news was not only frightening, it was puzzling for two reasons. In the first place, I reflected that I had never had any serious discipline problems, and wouldn't know what to do if I had. Then, too, I had seen no sign of a problem of this kind among the students at Rosburg School. My fears were not allayed by the additional news that the two women teachers the previous year had literally been driven out by a group of older boys. The "Peck's Bad Boy" type of hazing had culminated the day the boys climbed to the belfry and rang the school bell with such a clamor that classes could not be conducted. Then they put a board over the chimney and smoked the whole school out into the yard. The two teachers had left town before the school year was quite finished.

When I inquired as to the whereabouts of these impressarios of mischief, I was told that the older boys did not come to school till after the fishing season was over. This gave me about one more week of respite.

One day one of my young Finns sought me out before school. His dancing eyes showed clearly that he was the bearer of exciting news.

"Tea-chur", he said. (I am sorry that I cannot more accurately indicate the accent which was universal among the young.)

"Yes, Thomas,"

"Tea-chur, do you know who I saw yes-tur-day?"

"No, Thomas, who?"

"I saw Weel-yum."

The name was obviously meant to impress.

"Weel-yum ees com-eeng to school tomorrow!"

My well-controlled lack of emotional reaction to what was supposed to be shattering news was obviously disappointing to my impish little informant.

"Tea-chur, do you know what I heard Weel-yum say?—I heard Weel-yum say, "I theenk I can lick Tea-chur!"

That was approximately the end of the conversation. You can imagine that I looked forward to William's matriculation with considerable interest and mixed emotions. William, I learned, was one of the "big boys" who had been involved in the shenanigans the previous year. When he arrived, I found him to be a pleasant-faced, wiry six footer of fifteen years. He was obviously not interested in school. He was serving time till he was sixteen and could legally leave. In the meantime, however, he had a reputation to live up to. His classmates were constantly distracted by their expectations of his efforts to circumvent the "Establishment."

He could never bring himself to do anything spectacular. but he was a constant gadfly in his efforts to amuse his friends. I was faced with the choice of either being a constant nag, or of finding something of a major nature over which we could cross bats. He was learning absolutely nothing, and he was hindering the other pupils from learning anything.

I suppose because he was bored, he asked to "leave the room" much more often than anyone else. I also noted that he stayed out what seemed an unnecessarily long time at the little outhouse, which my Dutch pupils at Oak Harbor had called the "King house" because of the "throne" inside. I also noted a distinct odor of cigarettes when he returned. I decided that this must be the issue on which "Weel-yum" and I would have a show-down.

I had not forgotten his boast that he could "lick Tea-chur" and I had no doubt that he could do just that if he chose to settle our differences that way. But I had the advantage of surprise, in that I would choose the time and the battleground. So the next time he left the room for an unusually long time, I met him in the cloak room. Carefully closing the classroom door, and trying to keep my voice from trembling, I looked up from my five feet, seven inches, to his six feet, and said in a firm voice, "William, you've been smoking!"

"No, no, Tea-chur, I don' smoke!" His eyes opened wide in innocent surprise at such an unjust accusation.

"Be firm," I said to myself, "this is no time to show hesitation."

Then aloud, "William, don't lie to me."

"No, Tea-chur, I don' lie. See," and he pulled out the contents of his pockets and slapped them to show that they were empty, "I don' have no cigarettes."

I reached out and took his wallet from his hand. Inside were three cigarettes. I shifted my weight to the balls of my feet, ready for whatever might come.

"William," I said with a voice I managed to make sound firm and authoritarian, "you have not only broken the law by smoking on the school grounds, but you also have lied to me! Go in and get your books, and go home. You may not return to school until you bring a letter from the school board saying that you may."

I was prepared for any action that might come, except the one that did. William screwed up his face and started to cry!

"Oh, Tea-chur, don' make me go home!"

I felt like a brute.

The die had been cast, however, and William went home. That

evening after school, I slogged over the wet fields and along the dykes with the children of the school board chairman. We rounded up several members of the board and it was decided, on my recommendation, to get William back into the classroom with a warning that this was his last chance.

When he came back to school we were good friends. We understood each other and he gave very little trouble in the classroom. I believe he actually did some studying. But a few weeks later the whole school board came to the school one morning and, over my protests, expelled William from school. It seems that the night before he had thrown rocks at one of the children of the school board chairman. I felt bad about this turn of William's fortunes.

The next spring, however, it was not without some trepidation that I accepted an invitation from William to spend a Saturday on his fishing boat. I had fleeting recollections of those purse-seiners who had disappeared on the river and wondered, guiltily, if I really knew William as well as I thought I did. I needn't have worried. It was a beautiful day; the sun came out and I think I remember that we caught some fish. I was glad that I knew William after all, and he was obviously elated to be able to show his superiority in his own element and to have me as a pupil in the business of fishing.

The events of that year which some of the Rosburg citizenry will remember most vividly were the two productions we staged in the antique theatre at the end of the 10 miles of road. As usual the inspiration for these productions came as an answer to a community need. The pupils had no place to play outside of the classroom. This meant that during the noon hour and at recess time, they were forced to go out in the rain and play in the mud or stay cooped up in the classrooms. We therefore decided that we would start a fund to build a play shed for the school.

The isolated community was starving for entertainment, so that any theatrical offering was bound to take in a large amount at the box office. We chose as a starter a simple little operetta entitled *Tulip Time*. The songs, stage decorations and dances became the material for our classes in music, art and physical education. The last period of the day, the big folding doors between the classrooms were opened and we would all learn the choruses or cut out construction paper tulips or other Dutch motifs, or make a start in the cramped space to learn the basic dance steps. Community people were cast in the lead singing roles and we rehearsed first in the Rosburg Community Hall and later in the old theatre.

The costumes consisted of blue skirts and white blouses for the women and girls and voluminous blue Dutch pants and white shirts for the men and boys. The skirts and pants were made by the parents and wives out of blue cambric that we bought from Dan Hall at cost. The setting was blue back wall and wings covered with the cut-out windmill and tulip motifs made in our school art classes. Flower boxes filled with three dimensional paper tulips filled the empty spaces.

The rehearsals were energetic, gay, hard-working times for adults and students alike. I believe that not the least benefit from this production was the bringing together of rival factions in the community who had never before had the experience of cooperating with each other. There were some surprisingly beautiful voices among the adult cast, and the children's choruses were sweet and moving as only children's voices can be.

The performances were jammed and we collected several hundred dollars for the play shed. Later in the year we revived *Seven Keys* with an all adult cast and added more to the play shed fund. When we left that spring, we had the satisfaction of seeing a stack of lumber in the school yard, purchased (wholesale) from a school board member who ran a saw mill.

That year was a wonderfully memorable one, and neither Lois nor I would have considered leaving except for the one serious misfortune that befell us. Those of you who remember 1928 may guess as to what it was. We heard that there was a possibility of a run on the Astoria bank where we had our precious savings of $900, which was to start the fund for seeing me through college.

We opened up the big folding doors between the classrooms and Lois took charge of the whole school for the day. I caught the early morning boat at the Deep River Landing and started for Astoria. On the boat was the lumberman member of the school board. I was happy to have his company and decided to follow his advice on what to do when we got to the bank. That was a bad decision. The people at the bank convinced him that there was nothing wrong, and so we both left our funds on deposit. The very next day the bank closed its doors. This misfortune led us to accept higher paying positions in the neighboring Pacific County in the little community of Chinook on the Columbia River.

The next two years were not uneventful, but the life we led was very different from that at Rosburg. I received $1800 a year and Lois received somewhat less. We were able to live on the lesser salary, buy a little car and even put some into the college fund along with my $1800.

The school was a modern little four-room school, complete with plumbing and a large gymnasium. Lois taught the third and fourth grades, and I taught the seventh and eighth and also acted as principal. The town was small, having only a few hundred inhabitants. The chief industry surrounded the fish traps which extended out into the Columbia River. The taxes from these traps and the railroad which ran by the town, made our district one of the richest districts per capita in the United States.

Besides the school there was at least one store. There may have been more than one, but my memory fails me. Strangely enough there was a weekly newspaper. But the biggest contrast with Rosburg was the accessibility of the rest of the world. The landing for the ferry to Astoria was only five miles away at Megler, and a circuitous but passable road of a little over a hundred miles led to Chehalis and Centralia, where it joined with U.S. Highway 99. This meant that during any holiday vacation period we drove to Tacoma, where my parents were living, less frequently to Oak Harbor to see Lois' folks, but most frequently to Seattle and the University of Washington.

Ilwaco, a larger small town, less than 10 miles away boasted a high school, several stores and a movie theatre. Since the Chinook boys who attended school there had to come home by bus, they could not participate in high school athletics. The Chinook school district had no legal obligation to them, but I persuaded the school board to let them use the gym several nights a week under my supervision. The climate was too wet to allow for football or baseball, so the basketball season lasted all year long. We finally organized a club of these school "orphans" and they decided to call themselves "The Yellow Jackets." As you have undoubtedly guessed, there was inevitably a theatrical performance to buy the necessary yellow jackets—a program of one-acts, the only one of which I remember was *A Night At An Inn* by Lord Dunsany.

My first dramatic venture in Chinook came before the Yellow Jacket affair, however. It was a classroom project and, strangely enough, may have been another important influence in the choice of the first play produced for the Oregon Shakespearean Festival. Included in the seventh grade reading book was the trial scene from *The Merchant of Venice*. I must have gone overboard in providing background material for this section, because I remember a terrific uproar of pleading to do the whole play. By this time the whole room was involved and I had to explain the problems presented by having no stage, no money to pay for costumes, not to mention the difficulty of finding potential eighth grade Portias, Bassanios and Shylocks who could sustain the roles through five acts.

We finally compromised by agreeing on the production of a puppet show depicting the trial scene from "The Merchant." One half of the room would build and manipulate the puppets, the other half would learn the lines and be the voices. The puppet stage was built from driftwood scavenged from the beach and the puppets were made from driftwood, plasticine and other school supplies, clothed from scraps of cloth brought from the pupils' homes.

In case you are wondering how we found time to get all this done during the school day, I must explain some things about the measuring of academic achievement in those days. The success of seventh and eighth grade students and their teachers was determined by the number of students who passed the State Examinations at the end of the school year. I had copies of those examinations for the previous 10 years. Anyone who could spell 75 percent or more of all the words on those spelling exams could undoubtedly pass the state spelling examination. Anyone who could solve 70 percent or more of all the arithmetic problems (which were concerned with the number of rolls of wall paper to cover such and such a room or the number of cubic feet in a 30 foot silo 12 feet in diameter) would have no trouble. "Name the wheat states." "What is a legume?" "Name four and their value in —" and so on and so forth. Each student was given a set of questions and did the research in his own text or in the encyclopedias to find the answers. The answer sheets were discussed and passed around and then there was daily drill, drill, drill. I found that this rather dull kind of work was tackled with vigour, if, as a result, they could get at the much more interesting chore of making puppets or staging a scene from a play.

There were many side benefits other than the motivation to work at rather unrewarding tasks. One of these fringe benefits of which I am very proud concerned a boy by the name of Christy. Christy was to my school room in Chinook what William was to the Rosburg school: A big boy, two years behind his contemporaries and saddled with a reputation for mischief. But when he read for the role of Shylock, with his deep baritone voice contrasting with the unchanged voices of his fellow pupils, his efforts were greeted with spontaneous applause from his delighted classmates. The success of the production, which we trouped to a number of schools in the county, was a delight to pupils and parents alike. And Christy tasted the satisfaction of doing something constructive that no one but he could do. He never became a scholar, but he ceased to be a gadfly in the classroom.

The final production in Chinook was *Penrod,* a play based on the famous Booth Tarkington characters. There were a few unusual features of this production. The cast was composed of members of the student body playing the children's parts and the entire faculty and Christy playing the adults. The stage was a platform erected at one end of the gymnasium, composed entirely of driftwood scrounged from the beach. The scenery was made from similar lumber covered with paper, which was ordered through a school supply house and "painted" with colored chalk.

During this time I also coached basketball, and I am rather proud of the fact that my seventh and eighth grade team won the county junior high school basketball tournament.

In the six years that I taught in the public schools of the State of Washington, I do not remember anyone (other than my own students) ever commenting on my ability as a classroom teacher. It was noted, of course, that a sufficient number of my seventh and eighth graders got through the State Examinations and that I kept the big boys out of the belfry. But any promotion or demotion (I was fired once, remember?) I ever received during that time or in the 39 years of teaching since that time were because of my extracurricular work with young people in the community or from the publicity engendered thereby.

Perhaps, after all, it was more my cousin Henrietta's recommendation than my grade school teaching experience that led President Churchill to hire me at Southern Oregon Normal School.

Lois and I had attended the University of Washington two summers during our stay at Chinook. At the end of that time we had saved enough money to enable us to quit teaching for a year and spend five quarters at the University, during which time I finished my bachelor's degree and the residence requirements for my master's degree. I was not able to finish my master's thesis before leaving, so that one of my chores during the first two years at Ashland was to finish that. This circumstance and the nature of that thesis were additional factors in the early stages of the evolution of the Oregon Shakespearean Festival idea.

IV

Instrumentation

T HE FIRST OF THE SERIES of five consecutive quarters I spent at the University of Washington was the one during which I worked under Mr. Payne and was first inspired by Shakespeare on the Elizabethan stage. I have mentioned that John Conway was acting head of the Theatre Department that quarter. John was about my own age and only three years out of Carnegie Tech, where he had worked extensively under Mr. Payne. We all owe John a great deal for his encouragement and his extremely knowledgeable and practical work as a consultant during those years just before and after the start of the Festival in 1935. More of that later.

The next quarter, Glenn Hughes came in as permanent head of the Department. He was a prolific theatrical writer himself, and I took a course in playwriting from him. As a project in this course I wrote a one-act play based on Andrew Jackson's famous duel with Thomas Dickenson. The next quarter I enrolled in Professor Hughes' advanced course in playwriting and launched on a full length play centered around the story of Jackson's relationship with his wife, Rachel. This play, when it was finally completed, was to be my master's thesis. Glenn told me, many years later, that it was the first original playscript to be accepted as a master's thesis at the University of Washington.

The polishing of this playscript was one of my principal preoccupations during my first two years in Ashland. This included its production at Southern Oregon Normal School, for I felt very strongly that I must see it on stage before I could submit the thesis.

As a spin-off from this project, I made two important discoveries. I found a costumer and I learned that people in the Rogue Valley would turn out in large numbers for a Shakespearean production. Without either of these assurances, the Festival idea would never have germinated.

My play, *Andrew Jackson*, was an episodic thing with nine scenes, six sets, 28 characters and there must have been well over forty costumes. Remember, we had no budget, no scene or costume shop and very little room on that 10-foot, six-inch deep stage. Each play was supposed to take in enough money at the box office to pay for its production. But there was no chance in the world for such an extravagant production to pay its own way, so it was decided that a "no expense" event must be staged to raise the money to subsidize Andy Jackson.

Thus it came about that I directed my first production of Shakespeare: a modern dress *As You Like It*. The student cast was augmented by several faculty members. Marion Ady and Lucile Burtis, both of the Art Department, played Audrey and Celia respectively. Loren Messenger, Psychology, played Sir Oliver Martext, and I played Jaques. The setting was designed by the precocious young student, William Cottrell.

Though not at all Elizabethan in appearance, the setting functioned to provide the continuous "story telling tempo" of the script. It was set in front of old grey flannel drapes, parted in the center to reveal a section of the rear plastered wall which we had painted blue, and from which I had managed to have the steam radiator removed. In the center opening of the rear drapes were placed a small silhouette of a castle for the court scenes and, on a wire, a woodland silhouette to be drawn across for the forest scenes. I remember the trees were glued to a scrim made from dust cloth material, a sort of cheese cloth which we were able to scrounge by the bolt from the maintenance department. There were arched entrances at either side and a sort of penthouse supported by two pillars. Between these was strung a draw curtain which Bill Cottrell had painted to resemble a tapestry with two vaguely Elizabethan figures on it. This last was made from beautiful, heavy linen scene canvas which had come to the school from the old Chautauqua stage.

And so through this expedient production, I was able to get my first inkling of the thrill that comes about when you succeed, even in a very small way, in matching the natural rhythms and qualities of young actors with the inherent pulse and flow of a Shakespearean script so that, as if by alchemy, what was old is new, what was ink on paper is alive and vibrant with meaning and excitement for an audience.

The audiences were large and enthusiastic. The income was sufficient to encourage us to go ahead with the plans for the production of *Andrew Jackson*. I suppose the best compliment I received was from an elderly chap sweeping out a grange hall in preparation for a production there some time later.

He said, "Oh, I sure like them college plays. But there was one I liked better than any of 'em. I don't recollect the name, but it was one of them hell-of-a-long-time-ago shows." He was referring to our production of William Shakespeare's *As You Like It*. Certainly no intellectual snobbery there.

The problem of costuming the Jackson play had been a major worry from the first. The scenery we knew could be managed. We had the talent and the man hours available to handle that end. But the expertise and labour needed to design and manufacture over forty period costumes at first seemed an insurmountable obstacle.

To explain how we overcame this obstacle I must go back to the previous year. Those first difficult months in Ashland were made additionally frustrating by my first experience with marital complications. For the first time in our married life, Lois was faced with adjusting to the problems of being a full-time housewife. She had always taught or attended college before, and house work had been something to get over with in as short a time as possible. She was a good housekeeper, but the routine tasks of daily chores at home held neither challenge nor interest. Her efficiency merely meant that she had most of the day with nothing to do. We lived, that first year, on the outskirts of town, several miles from the school and with no near neighbors. I frequently came home to find her in tears of frustration and loneliness. I knew that her unhappiness came principally from her feeling of being out of things, of not belonging and of not occupying her time in some creative way.

She was a good seamstress and made all her own clothes. Her feeling for color was especially keen. With all these factors in mind, it had been arranged for her to design and with the help of a talented student, Maxine Gearhart, to construct the costumes for the robots in Capek's *R.U.R.* which had been our spring production that first year.

This was during the depression, you must remember, and there were both rules and strong feelings against husband and wife teams in the whole field of education. I did not want to do anything that would threaten my job, but as things were at home, I decided to take the risk. The small chore of designing and helping the students to make the robots' costumes was a fairly safe way of getting "the nose of the camel inside the tent."

This experiment was a definite success, both from the domestic as well as the aesthetic point of view. Though she was in no way officially connected with the college, Lois seemed to be welcomed by both faculty and students. Thus it was decided that we would go ahead with the plans for her to design the costumes for *Andew Jackson* and organize a costume crew to help her construct them. There were two provisions. First, we knew that it would take two quarters to produce the play; therefore, no show was scheduled for the winter quarter. Second, and most important, we depended on getting help and advice from John Conway at the University of Washington. I was fairly certain of being able to get his cooperation, for I had admired his work as a teacher over a period of several quarters. I had observed him spend his precious time and talents in helping a country high school teacher organize plans for a P.T.A. Christmas show, and do this with as much concern and enthusiasm as if she had been planning a Broadway opening. It is a quality which I have tried to emulate in my years as a teacher.

Needless to say, we did get John's help, and each vacation saw us making the thousand-mile round trip drive to Seattle to spend every minute possible with John and the library facilities at the University. We learned sources of supplies, period styles, patterns. Lois learned how to use cold water aniline dyes in multiple washes on cheap fabric so as to produce the appearance of expensive textures; learned how to make print fabrics with potato block; in fact, she was able to get a crash course in elementary costuming.

Most of the men's costumes were made from Canton flannel, dyed to resemble various textures: leather, velvet or other suiting materials. Her obvious flair and her ability to get enthusiastic help from students not only contributed materially to the success of the Jackson piece but was the basis for her contributions to the Festival which was to start in two years.

Bill Cottrell's sets were effective and practical, and we received help in their construction from a surprisingly large number of students. Remember that this was in the middle of the depression years, and young people were eager to find entertaining ways of occupying their time without the necessity of spending money.

Re-reading the play now is an excruciating experience, the characters flat and the dialogue crude and melodramatic. My memory of the performance is, therefore, not at all reliable. But I recall that the community was much impressed and delighted by this production which was so unusually spectacular and all "home-grown"—script, actors, costumes, lights and scenery.

One of the exciting features of my life style is that I have so frequently been able to combine business with pleasure. While the production of plays has been of primary importance in my professional life, I still get as much enjoyment out of a good performance as the most enthusiastic amateur. One of the great thrills of my theatre-going life occurred during the Christmas vacation of 1933. Lois and I had planned as usual to drive to Seattle for a conference on the problems in the up-coming Normal School season, but we were especially pleased to have tickets for the three opening nights of Katherine Cornell's repertoire of *The Barretts of Wimpole Street, Romeo and Juliet* and *Candida*. Her company's stop in Seattle, playing through the holiday week, was one of several similar West Coast stops in what must have been the first transcontinental tour by a major star in many years. And in repertory! It was bringing manna to starved people. The wonderfully happy way in which the Seattle audience showed its appreciation is recalled by Miss Cornell in her autobiography as one of the most memorable experiences of her career.

I shall never forget that opening night. The rain had been pouring down for days and it continued to cascade from the sky as we splashed our way to the Olympic Theatre. After curtain time had come and gone, someone made an announcement that there would be a delay in opening, for the train carrying the company and the scenery had been held up by floods. More time passed. There was another announcement, telling of further delay; and another, and another. It was after eleven o'clock when a roar of applause greeted the opening of the curtain which revealed the stage hands bringing on the first pieces of the set for *The Barretts of Wimpole Street*. It must have been after midnight when the play opened to a full house. Who says that the play must go on? The audience, that's who! I have since noted that actors in trouble not of their own making always have a sympathetic audience. The man who sees 2 *Henry VI* in the rain will probably talk about it enthusiastically for the rest of his days.

Miss Cornell and her company were glorious. Understandably, I remember few details after all these years, but I do remember walking away from the theatre each night about six inches above the pavement.

Other than Miss Cornell, there were three members of her company who turned in performances that I still remember. Brian Aherne played an admirable Browning, and it was a treat to see the teen-age Orson Welles swagger as Tybalt. Perhaps the greatest surprise was that Basil Rathbone did an excellent Romeo. It is especially surprising in retrospect because his subsequent casting in the movies has left him typed as a saturnine villain or a Sherlock Holmes. Two years later I produced *Candida* at Southern Oregon, and the year after that, *Romeo and Juliet* became the first of the tragedies to be presented by the Festival.

In the spring of 1934 the State of Oregon celebrated its 75th birthday. Medford was selected as the location for the week-long "Diamond Jubilee." Medford is a town considerably larger than Ashland but located only twelve miles away. The Jubilee Committee gave me what I considered to be my first "professional" theatre job. For a fee of $500, I was to write, produce and direct a pageant which would commemorate the coming of statehood to Oregon. As ex-officio member of the committee, I met weekly with a number of the prominent professional and businessmen of the Rogue River Valley and developed friendships which were valuable in years to come. For many years I sought and received advice of the men that I met during this time.

The pageant I called *Oyer-Un-Gon*, the Shoshone Indian words for "land of plenty," and one of the several possible sources for the name "Oregon." It was staged in the county fairgrounds before a setting designed by William Cottrell. As I learned later, it was not greatly different from other western pageants of which there were legion. It told of the first Indian to predict the coming of the white man, the troubles of the wagon trains, Indian attacks, the first marriage, the conflict between the British and those who wanted the territory to come to the states. It ended in a glorious finale, in which the large mountains split and slid aside to reveal the entire cast on a series of shiny metallic ramps topped by a tower from which arose Miss Liberty with a large windblown American flag! There were over 500 people in the cast, several covered wagons drawn by four-horse teams and twenty or more horses ridden bareback by the "Indians." Each group was led by one or more of my Normal School students, who had practiced the blocking of movement for several weeks. The bulk of the cast was from community groups who came in at the last minute. I sat on a platform on the roof of the grandstand and had telephone communication with costumed runners who could join any of the groups and convey my moment-by-moment directions.

There were a couple of incidents which were to prove valuable in years to come. Both were frightening, each in its own way. In the scene depicting the attack on the wagon train, there was much shooting, of course. It was decided that each member of the cast was to furnish his own gun, and we would furnish the blank cartridges. I have always been afraid of guns, on or off stage, and while I thought I was being overcautious, I arranged to have a member of my staff load the guns. I instructed him to inspect each gun, break it open to make sure that no live ammunition was in the chamber, then to load the blanks himself. He came to me just before the opening night overture was completed and said that he had just checked a deer rifle that had been fully loaded! The man who carried it had been drinking, and would have brushed my man aside if he could. How many people would have been shot but for that extra precaution, God only knows.

The second incident was not without its comic side, and from it I learned a lesson in mob psychology. The grounds in front of our scenic background were being used during the daytime by the men and animals of a rodeo which was part of the celebration. The ground had been scarified so that a man falling from a horse might have a softer landing place than the packed earth of the fairgrounds. Then, on the day before our dress rehearsal it began to rain.

When the cast first started to come in, they were grumbling about the rain, but I told the costume crew to tell them I wanted to see them all in their costumes to check whether or not they were properly worn, fitted correctly, and so on. Then a few of them got a glimpse of the plowed grounds which were being turned into a sea of mud six or eight inches deep. I had already ordered truckloads of sawdust to be dumped in the mud and scattered in an endeavor to soak up the moisture. As a steady parade of trucks emptied sawdust on the grounds, the grumbling rose in intensity and I saw that I was about to have a revolution on my hands. We dressed in the many rooms surrounding a large exhibit hall, which in turn was surrounded on the second floor with a balcony. I had my crew call the cast of 500 together on the ground floor while I mounted to the balcony.

"I don't blame anybody for not wanting to go out in the mud," I explained. "And let me say right here that nobody is going out there unless he wants to. But let me explain the situation. This is the only time that we can possibly time the action of your groups with the orchestra and the narrator. The expense of this pageant has already amounted to many thousands of dollars, but if we do not go through with this dress rehearsal, there will not be a pageant. . . ." At that moment someone in the crowd below shouted, "On with the show!" and everyone started to cheer and applaud. The dress rehearsal went on.

In the fall of that year we produced Tolstoi's play, *Redemption*. We called this play of hopeless idealism by its more popular American title, *The Living Corpse*. As you might have guessed, I played the John Barrymore role of Fedya. I am sure that I was the only producer in the world who would have done that particular bit of casting.

I mention this production, not only because of this wild bit of casting, or because the play required nine sets, but principally because it involved two people who played very different but important parts in the initiation and perpetuation of the Festival.

Without the work of Gordon Claycomb, I believe the Festival would never have started again after the six seasons we were dark just before, during and after World War II. That story comes later, but Gordon and I first met and collaborated because of our production of *The Living Corpse*.

Feeling that he was being stultified by the lack of cultural opportunities in Ashland, Gordon had persuaded his father, who was a prominent Ashland businessman, to send him to Vienna to study music. After five years in Europe, he had come back to Ashland with a very accomplished Bulgarian wife. They were amazed to read the publicity about our Tolstoi production, and Gordon called me on the telephone to ask when we might get together for a chat.

As a result of our meeting, Gordon organized an orchestra, arranged the music and contributed a great deal to the success of that production. His wife, Antoinette, was an excellent concert pianist and for the on-stage music transcribed from memory Bulgarian Gypsy tunes which must have been very close to the music used in the original Russian production.

The orchestra played an overture and transitional music covering each scene change working from the mood of one scene into the mood of the next. This use of music gave the production a unity which it could not otherwise have had.

It was in this production that I learned a lesson which we in theatre too frequently forget. What started as an economy of poverty (lack of money, actors, scenery, costumes, lighting equipment), became an artistic economy which gave me a thrill as an actor-director which I have never forgotten.

In the particular scene to which I refer, Fedya tells the story of his life. He had grown to feel that his marriage was sterile and he himself inadequate and unworthy of the good woman who was his wife. He had come to spend more and more time with the gypsies, eating, drinking, making love and listening with increasing fascination to the lush gypsy music. Falling lower and lower into an aimless life devoted to sensual pleasure, he finally fakes a suicide so his wife can marry the man he thinks is worthy of her.

Tolstoi describes the scene as a dive peopled with numerous low characters eating, drinking, sleeping on the floor, making love in dark corners, and so on. I eliminated all these realistic background figures and limited the furniture to the rough table and two chairs where Fedya sat drinking wine with his confidant of the night. I lit the scene with one candle inside an amber beer bottle. No other light on the stage. The two faces, held close to the candle, were the only things visible to the audience. The innkeeper who was to eavesdrop on the conversation and later betray Fedya, lit a cigarette as he spoke to him and then retired to the darkness. At specific punctuation points, a draw on the cigarette produced a glow which reminded the audience of his presence.

I have never felt the exhilaration of such power. I must explain that the old wooden folding chairs were uncomfortable and noisy. One could measure the attention span of the audience by the shrieking of those chairs. In this scene, during Fedya's long story, I had the power to control these noisy monsters. I could hold the audience without a squeak until I thought they might break away, then I could let them relax and the squawk of the chairs would roll across the auditorium. Then I could bring them back again for a quiet spell of concentration. I am sure that the extreme economy, making our faces and lips the only objects that were visible, forced an attention that would have otherwise been impossible.

At one place, Fedya, speaking of his wife and the man she had married, says, "They are living right here in this city. We are all living here. Last night I walked by their house. The lights were on. Somebody's shadow passed across the blind."

Perhaps the best testimony of the effectiveness of the scene was a comment made by an audience member.

"The scene I liked best was the one in front of the house. You know, the one where the shadow of Fedya's wife passes across the window blind."

You can see why, then, that since the earliest days of the Festival we have always tried to place major emphasis on the imaginative impact of Shakespeare's word, ideas and imagery interpreted by actors for the purpose of influencing members of the audience.

Again I must go back a couple of years. *The Living Corpse* was produced in the fall of 1934. In the spring of 1932, I had been asked to judge a series of one act plays for the state contest sponsored by the Grange. The performance of one young man impressed me very much. He was Robert Stedman, a resident of Phoenix, Oregon. After the performance, I asked him why he didn't come to Southern Oregon Normal School. He was a handsome young man of six feet four, and in addition to his acting ability had, as it turned out, considerable dexterity with tools. His problem was the same as that of many young people in that depression time. He had dropped out of Oregon State College for lack of funds, and he still lacked money to finance even as much as a quarter at Southern Oregon.

By the next January, he had saved enough to come to school for one quarter and I gave him a leading role in Priestley's *Perfect Alibi.* He wasn't in school the following spring, but was of great help to me in the production of *Oyer-Un-Gon.* In the fall of 1934, I was able to get him enrolled in the National Youth Administration program which netted him a small pittance on which he was able to exist. To earn this money, he became my technical director and assisted me in the teaching of my play production class.

By this time I had managed to get permission to offer the play production class each quarter. I taught the classroom part of the course to half of the class while Bob taught the other half in a laboratory section in which all the scenery and lighting equipment were built. This shop was a makeshift affair excavated under Churchill Hall and floored with scrap lumber from an old gymnasium which was being wrecked. This cubbyhole was constructed by students on Campus Day. To paraphrase: It was a poor thing but our own.

Bob Stedman continued in the capacity of technical director for two years at the Normal and for five years at the Festival.

During the years of 1933, 1934 and 1935 Lois and I had an apartment located only a block from the school. It became more and more a gathering place for the young people whose lives centered around the theatre activities at Southern Oregon Normal. I don't know how many pots of spaghetti were consumed there between afternoon classes and rehearsal, after late energy-consuming theatre sessions and on weekends. There were many students who dropped in from time to time, but the "steadies" finally boiled down to Bob Stedman, Bill Cottrell, Bob's girl friend (now his wife for lo these many years), Audrey Lofland and Maxine Gearhart. I remember the food, the planning and dreaming, but most of all I remember the laughter. The breakfast nook was really a "nook," being surrounded on three sides with plastered walls. Bill was the one who dubbed it the "Teensy-Weensy Theatre." It was he also who covered a grease spot on the wall with the sign which read DO NOT LAUGH ON THESE WALLS. Out of the hilarious, carefree atmosphere of the Teensy-Weensy Theatre there emerged the first gleam in the eye which became the Oregon Shakespearean Festival. Only the innocence of youth could have engendered such improbable visions as we had. In my own inexperience I was the blind leading the blind. But out of such unlikely beginnings we now have a theatre whose influence is felt across the English speaking world.

V

First Melody

I T WAS OBVIOUS to all of us who gathered in the Teensy Weensy
Theatre for spiritual as well as gustatorial sustenance that it was
impossible to rehearse and mount two Shakespearean plays at once.
Of course we had a couple of things going for us. We had Lois's experience of costuming *Andrew Jackson* and Maxine Gearhart and her enthusiastic crew. There were indications that some of the ladies in the
town could be interested in helping to sew. Besides this, there was a
tremendous practical advantage in doing the plays on an Elizabethan
stage: one "inn yard" type setting would serve for all plays. Only a
few changes in furniture and properties would suffice.

Nevertheless, we decided to produce one play in the spring on a
portable Elizabethan stage at the Normal School and to revive it along
with the production of another play in the summer at the site of the old
Chautauqua building. For the first play, I chose one that would give me
an opportunity to satisfy an ambition which I had nurtured since I first
heard Victor Hoppe deliver Shylock's "How like a fawning Publican he
looks" speech in my Bellingham Normal School days. We would open
with *The Merchant of Venice*, and I would play Shylock.

Ideas about the second play and the revival of "Merchant" were
extremely vague at this point. As I remember, we discussed the problems of moving the portable Elizabethan stage from the Normal Auditorium to the floor of the old Chautauqua platform, but we did not
worry too much about these problems at this early stage of development. Besides, I have always operated on the principle that, if a project
fulfills an actual need and enough people can be persuaded to commit

themselves to it, ways will be found to solve the problems of its realization.

The stage setting proved to be much less portable than we had hoped. The forestage was made from four four-by-eight foot platforms. These were constructed of parallels, that is, folding frameworks, with lids to them. These would have been portable enough except that the pillars supporting the "shade" stood on them. Remember that the stage in the Normal School auditorium was only ten feet, six inches deep, had very little room above and no rigging at all. In order to provide room for the inner stages and sufficient space in front of them for the main action, the shade, which was a kind of porch roof, had to be nailed to the inside of the proscenium arch in such a way that it extended through the curtain line and rested on the forestage pillars.

I could foresee immediate scheduling problems arising. For the auditorium was used every week for assembly programs and the stage was frequently used for other programs as well. Once we got the platforms built and those pillars in place, the setting had to remain there until the last performance of "Merchant"—a matter of several weeks.

Looking back now, I can see this point as another crucial one in the germination of the Festival. Could I get President Redford to guarantee us that time in the auditorium? I went to his office and explained to him what our plans were in as much detail as so far had been decided upon. Fortunately, he approved the idea and said that other arrangements could be made for conflicting programs.

It was this situation which led to my first head-on conflict with a member of the music department. Cousin Henrietta had long gone and was happily married and living in Seattle. The young woman who took her place had planned a concert and was disturbed when she saw our sturdy setting taking up the space on the stage where she had expected to place her musicians. She assumed as a matter of course that I must have my crew remove it.

I told her of my arrangements with President Redford and explained why they had been made. She was quite naturally furious and stormed down to the President's office. Fortunately for us he kept to his promise.

It would not be inappropriate at this point to say something about the traditional relationship between the music departments and the drama departments of typical liberal arts colleges. It is much the same as that between the purse-seiner and the gillnetter or the sheepman and the cattleman. In each case, conflict of interests makes bitter competitors when close cooperation could be beneficial to both parties. It is no more absurd for a music department director to expect a set dismantled during a difficult rehearsal period than it is for a drama director to expect a good musician to sit backstage for three acts to play four bars of a trumpet call for the king's entrance. This competition for inadequate facilities and talent pools is the fault of administrators, who are ruled by legislators, who in turn are under the mandate of the voters, who live in a society which though they haven't the slightest idea of it is still Puritan. Thank God, I think we can begin to see the light at the end of the tunnel, if I may coin a phrase.

At any rate, the young woman who was so understandably frustrated because she couldn't hold her concert on the stage, after making several frantic trips between the auditorium where we were working and the President's office, finally flounced out the door. Her exit line is memorable: "Some people play with dolls, and some people play with stages."

The first cast for "Merchant" was typical of many in the early years of the Festival. There were a very small number who had some college acting experience, fewer still who had a natural flair, and none at all with any acting training. Remember that I taught no acting classes at Southern Oregon, and I myself, though I had a bachelor's and a master's degree with emphasis in theatre, had had no acting theory in college, only coaching. My studies on the subject in the years since have enlightened, enriched, but never supplanted my grandmother's training in the principles and techniques of communicating the spoken word to an audience.

Bob Stedman, who played Bassanio, was one of the few with a natural instinct for acting, as I had noted when I first saw him in the Grange one-act play contest at Phoenix. His six-foot-four height, combined with a wholesome handsomeness, was carried with the natural grace of the trained athlete that he was. His projection of open-eyed enthusiasm and simple charm gave Bassanio a direct kind of verity that many a jaded professional would have had to work hard to achieve. Helen Edmonson, the Portia, was a tall, graceful blonde with a well-modulated voice that had a whisky huskiness about it which carried chills to the back row. She was also one of the most intelligent students that I have ever worked with. In fact, she was bored with her classes and I was continually having to bail her out of trouble. My ar-

gument for her periodic re-instatement was always that her only genuine interest seemed to be theatre, and that if she was going to profit
by an education, she should be given every opportunity to pursue that
interest.

There were several others who, if memory serves me, gave better
than adequate performances. Beverly Young played Nerissa. Beverly
was the niece of Janet Young, the leading lady for the Moroni Olson
Players, and perhaps had some of the family talent for acting. Her
Nerissa was small and rather pert in contrast to the tall, somewhat
statuesque quality of Helen's Portia. George Francis Smith sometimes
seemed a bit stiff on stage, but had a fine voice and a good sense of
humor and did very well in those roles to which this stiffness could
be construed as a quality of characterization. I cast him as Gratian.
Johnny Chipley played Young Gobbo. Johnny pretended no qualifications for the stage, and every move, inflection and gesture he learned
by rote, a long, laborious process for him, the cast and me. Considering
all his handicaps, he did very well indeed. This was typical of the rest of
the cast, including Salanio, Salerino and the Prince of Morocco. This
last role was played by John Harr, a farm boy who had never been out
of the valley and was not to see a seagoing ship or a streetcar until the
next year when we toured *Candida* to Reed College in Portland. I will
never forget seeing his amazement when he stood for the first time
before the full length mirror in complete make-up and costume. He
looked at the reflection of his dusky face, the regal-looking spade beard,
the flashing dark eyes, all set off by his golden burnoose and robe. His
amazement turned to delight. Then, for the first time, he drew himself
really erect, lifted his chin and said, "So that's what he's like!"

My Shylock, as can be seen from the picture taken at that time,
was pretty scroungy and quite obviously villainous. I suspect that it
was a groping protrayal of a very narrow stratum of that richly human
character and bore little resemblance to my performances of the role in
later years.

It is so difficult to evaluate those early performances after all these
years. Much of the satisfaction that I remember must have come from
the sense of achieving as much or more than could reasonably be
expected from what we had to work with. But our sense of accomplishment was not all imagination, nor our memory of it completely attributable to the mellowing of years, for the public response
was extremely warm and the comments in the press highly complimen-
tary. Some of them read like this:

Klamath Falls Herald:

A splendid performance. . . . The elimination of delays, the colorful costumes and setting, the understanding rendition of lines, all gave evidence of careful thought for the maximum enjoyment of the audience.

—Doris Buxton

Medford Mail Tribune:

I was amazed to see how effectively the play runs its course without resort to scenery. . . .

—Ramsey Benson

Ashland Daily Tidings:

One scene snaps into the next, but without confusion to the audience. . . . Watching the play, with its colorful Elizabethan costumes, one gets the effect of turning through a book of Elizabethan prints. . . .

—Ollie Depew

A production so faithful to the original text is rarely seen and is impossible except on the typical Elizabethan stage.

—Ollie Depew

I especially treasure the following letter written after the first Festival performance of Merchant:

July 5th, 1935

Dear Mr. Bowmer:

We feel, my husband and I, that it would not be right to let pass without recognition, the two very delightful evenings you have just given us.

We felt that both productions were put on with exquisite taste and dignity, and the troupe so perfectly drilled down to the smallest detail it was hard to realize that amateurs were on the board, and the lighting and colorful costumes,—everything blended into a perfect whole.

A resident of San Francisco, I have seen most of the big plays and nearly all the actors whose names are in everybody's mouths, but I say truly and sincerely, without any intention of flattery— that I have never seen as fine an interpretation of Shylock as you yourself gave. I quite forgot it was you, and I was stirred to both anger and pity.

The little love scene between Portia and her lover when he opened the right casket was lovely in its simplicity, and the court scene was strong, colorful, appealing and very natural. Indeed, both productions were of so much charm and so understandingly put, that I could not help feeling Shakespeare would have been very pleased.

And we felt that the absence of scenery and the way the scenes and acts followed without disturbing interruptions was very gratifying—the attention was so wholly focussed on the actors.
We were dreadfully sorry when it was over.

Very sincerely

Mary Thomas
(Mrs. W. J. Thomas)

You notice that all the comments mention the uninterrupted forward thrust of the action. This is what I have come to call Shakespeare's story-telling tempo. Our success with this technique has been caused by two factors. For one thing, I always taught my actors that, even if we were not the world's greatest, we should do whatever we did with conviction, as if we meant to do it that way. Then, if we kept a vigorous and appropriately exciting pace, we could properly take advantage of the fact that we had as a partner the best playwright in the world.

As Miss Depew indicates above, our use of an Elizabethan stage made this story-telling thrust possible. Our conception of this stage, borrowed from Mr. Payne, was based on the theory that players at one time played in the open courtyards of Elizabethan inns. Thus our stage represented one side of an inn yard, modified for the purpose of presenting plays. This use of an architectural facade meant the spaces were non-specific and could, for instance, be transformed by words only from a court (identified by the presence of courtiers) to a forest: "So this is the forest of Arden." There is every reason to believe that Shakespeare did not divide his plays into acts and scenes. This was undoubtedly done by editors when his plays were transformed from working scripts for actors to literary objects by being printed in book form.

I remember that Mr. Payne said there were no indications in the plays that they were intended to be presented with intermissions. He always had used intermissions because he felt that modern audiences were so accustomed to them that they would grow restless during a full length run of a play. I ran an experiment the first three years of the Festival. We knew that being at the bottom, we had nothing to lose by experiment. I noted places for intermissions, but told the stage manager not to call them unless I said to. I then applied my eye to a knot hole every time I was off stage, and for three seasons I found no signs of restlessness to warrant an intermission. For this reason we have not had intermissions in the Elizabethan theatre.

But I'm getting ahead of my story. Before the first Festival opened we had toured the Normal School production to Klamath Falls. Whose idea this was originally I cannot remember, but we were all excited about it. It would give us that much more experience and solidity in the roles, would provide that much more "exposure" through the media of the press and radio and allow that many more people to associate Shakespeare with Ashland.

Aside from some specifically vivid moments in the student matinee, and a general impression of exhaustion, my memory registers a complete blank for that trip. I can't remember, for instance, where (or if) we slept or ate. We couldn't leave Ashland until after four o'clock (I suppose that some of the company couldn't skip classes for one reason or another), which meant that we must have arrived at the Pine Tree Theatre in Klamath Falls sometime after six. We worked all night, or most of it, to get the setting in shape for the two o'clock matinee. If I remember correctly, we had to abandon the forestage, but the stage proper had plenty of depth for the action. The lighting was even more "lamp cord, bailing wire and stove pipe" than it had been at Ashland.

Finally we screwed the last stage brace into place, gummed the last beard on a chin, taped the last electrical splice and sat down to wait for our audience. Unlike most audiences they were to arrive all at once. Every student in the city who paid 25¢ was excused from his afternoon classes to see our production. Finally we heard them coming—three blocks away! If ever I saw true panic, I saw it then in the faces of my cast. It was obvious they had visions of the theatre being torn apart by a hoard of screaming monsters.

It was always my custom in those days to call my cast together just before curtain time so they would be reminded again how each was an important part of the whole, and to give them some few words of reassurance. On this particular afternoon, to draw them together was no problem. No wagon train was ever in a tighter circle in the face of attack. The words of encouragement became, of necessity, words of challenge. I told them:

"None of your audience this afternoon has ever seen this play, and I doubt whether more than a few even know the story. We will never play before an audience so typically Elizabethan. Each has paid money to be entertained. I think they won't object if that entertainment is provided by us. But if we do not provide the entertainment— they will. Above all, don't let their attempts at self-entertainment sidetrack you or disrupt your concentration on your job which is to reach out and grab every last one of them, so that they share Shake-speare's story with us."

When the curtain girls in their tights, pumpkin hose and doublets came out, there were wolf whistles and folded programs airplaned onto the stage. But much to our relief, they calmed down and soon were actually listening! They were vociferous in their reaction to the plot, booing Shylock and cheering wildly when Bassanio chose the right casket.

It was far from a perfect performance, but we felt a sense of victory in that the children had at least listened. Bob Stedman still likes to tell the story about what happened when the lack of sleep finally caught up with me on that afternoon. There is a place, if you remember the trial scene in this play, where Shylock takes out his knife and whets it on the sole of his shoe. This bit of macabre business is the cue for a whole series of lines that follow, the first of which is Bassanio's "Why dost thou whet thy knife so earnestly?" I always took a sight cue for this business from Nerissa's entrance. When my blunted senses failed to register her entrance, there was a slight pause. Bob, who knew everyone's lines, jumped into the breach by ad libbing, "Hast thou thy knife, Jew?" I cast a grateful look upstage to him and said simply, "Hast," and the play proceded.

The evening performance must have been uneventful, for I recall none of it. I do remember that after we got out of makeup and cos-tumes, we went over the border into California to a "place" which my students knew about. There we danced until nearly dawn. I could use some of that energy now. But even if there had been such a thing as an energy bank, I am glad that I was a profligate. For even if I could make a withdrawal from such a bank now, would I in sober maturity, go dancing until dawn? Or start a Shakespearean Festival in Ashland? Probably not.

In planning the details of the Festival for that next summer, I had chosen *Twelfth Night* and worked out a rehearsal schedule for that play and the revival of "Merchant." In this schedule the logical performance dates seemed to fall around the Fourth of July. There appeared to be a number of advantages for us in opening in conjunction with the Fourth. Wouldn't it be a tremendous kick-off for us to have flags, bunting and banners on the street, a parade, bands, fireworks and crowds of people? None of these things could we muster by ourselves, but a good old-fashioned community Fourth of July celebration would automatically include them. Ashland had a long history of such celebrations, but, for some reason there had not been one for the last five years.

Each Tuesday night I met with a group of young business and professional men for dinner and small talk. Gradually they had begun to think of their group as a possible community asset, and there was some discussion of becoming affiliated with one of the national service clubs. I knew that they were on the lookout for some kind of project which would identify our group as one dedicated to community service.

I therefore suggested to them at one of our spring meetings that they become a liaison group to guide the whole community through a revival of the Ashland Fourth of July tradition. I did not neglect to mention that I expected The First Annual Shakespearean Festival to be a part of the plans. My suggestion was received with enthusiasm, for this was exactly the kind of project they had been looking for. It would put our group in the limelight and in touch with the leading citizens and civic groups of the community. As long as I had suggested the whole thing, they were good enough sports to go along with the Shakespeare idea as well.

Another unexpected dividend of associating the Festival with a civic celebration was the fact that the city built, on the old Chautauqua platform, a permanent architectural facade similar to those of Elizabethan theatres. This, we were to discover, was a great deal different from stage scenery which imitated such a facade. In order to help the unemployment situation, a W. P. A. project was established to build the facade with donated materials. I remember drawing the plans on the back of an envelope for Mr. R. Berry, the construction manager. I had not at that time heard of the Fortune Theatre contract which was to provide the dimensions for our later versions. I merely put in the elements that I remembered from the stage setting designed by John Conway for Mr. Payne and which I had helped to build in Meany Hall at the University of Washington. Fortunately, the size of the old Chautauqua stage was quite comparable to that of the Fortune, and consequently, by implication, Shakespeare's Globe. The inner above stage was only nine feet above the main stage floor, instead of the twelve feet which we have since learned is more nearly accurate, and there was no "Musician's Gallery" above that. No roof protected us from sun or rain in the backstage area, and there were no dressing rooms or toilets. Actors had to attend to nature's calls by going to a neighboring building before putting on their tights. Costumes hung on racks under the open sky, and modesty was a luxury we could not afford. We placed the benches and chairs in straight parallel rows, just as the fixed seats at Meany Hall had been, not wrapped around the forestage as we learned to do later. We used a curtain between the pillars of the penthouse, or shade, and I cast shapely coeds as "Curtain Boys" just as Mr. Payne had done.

The cast for the revival of "Merchant" was largely a repetition of the spring production student cast. For *Twelfth Night,* I cast Bob Stedman as Feste and I played Sir Toby Belch. I made an attempt to bring in as many community people as possible to provide a greater variety in ages and a bit more experience. This move, besides giving us a broader base for community interest, brought us some interesting people who played important roles in those development years and beyond.

Maria was played by Jeanne Fabrick, a tremendously energetic personality with a wonderfully zany sense of humour. Her sister Kitty was later to play that role and a splendid Juliet. Fabian, that character who appears, for some mysterious reason, only near the end of the play, was done by Bill Eberhart. You can imagine that it was no handicap for us that Bill was City Editor of the Ashland *Daily Tidings.* Incidentally, he had a very successful career in journalism, becoming in the later years of his short life the head of Associated Press in the Pacific Northwest. John Barker, a high school student, whose instincts led him to use his small thin body and drawn face to project a warm but telling comedy, was Sir Andrew. He played character parts for us at the Festival and the Normal for several years. That this frail, gentle boy should be killed at Anzio beachhead in his first taste of battle was one of the shocking sacrifices which illustrates the idiocy of war.

Dorothy Pruitt played Olivia. Gordon Claycomb had introduced us to Almus and Dorothy Pruitt in the fall of 1934. They ran a music store in Medford in the back of which was a beautifully comfortable studio. Many a winter evening was spent there listening to recordings of the world's top musicians, to Antoinette playing exquisitely on the concert grand piano and to her beautifully broken English. Almus was also a pianist whose music I enjoyed because of its precision and strength. He and Gordon argued over the political situation in Europe, and again I was impressed, for Gordon brought first hand knowledge and could quote from personal conversations with such authorities as John Gunther, while Almus brought the skill of a widely read person with an unusual command of logic. Long discussions of art, music and theatre were carried on over cups of syrupy black Turkish coffee that satisfied the sensibilities if not the senses.

Dorothy is a sensitive person with the artist's yearning for creative communication. At that time she was a fine musician who had done considerable work in ballet. So it seemed only natural for her to try acting as a means of expression. We were lucky to have her as Olivia and later as Ophelia. But in later years she found her true medium in poetry. Her love of nature and her fascination with nature's impact on the human mind and emotions comes through her poetry with a beautiful poignancy.

As you can imagine, that was an exciting summer. Fortunately, though the faculty contracts at Southern Oregon were for twelve months, there were no classes in the afternoon during the summer session. This left us with every afternoon and evening for rehearsal and all the construction and technical work that had to be done. There were a few technicians who did not act, but there were no actors who did not work as technicians. There was material to be dyed, costumes to be cut from patterns and sewn, hooks and eyes to be attached, jewelry and other properties to be made, curtains and lighting fixtures to be made and hung.

I remember that Bob was able to borrow a switchboard from the Shriners. It was equipped with open knife switches and the operator took his life in his hands, especially when it rained. But it had three 2,000-watt dimmers which were a great addition to our little 750-watter. The same old homemade stove pipe and coffee can lights had to serve on stage, but to light the forestage Bob was able to beg two huge 5,000-watt floodlights from Mike Biegel, the City Light Superintendent. We mounted them on a couple of four by fours which we erected out in the audience area, one on the left and one on the right. They were floodlights such as are used to light whole building fronts or to light dams. In order to keep them from lighting the whole lower end of Lithia Park, Bob built three foot long hoods with concentric baffles to corral the light. They must have looked strange indeed, but they worked, if not satisfactorily, at least within the artistic limits we had set for ourselves. The bare circle of cement walls created a very strange echo chamber effect in the very center of the auditorium, so we eventually planted beans that clung to strings stretched up the walls. This helped to break up the reverberation and also provided several messes of beans for the always hungry actors.

On cold June nights a cheerful campfire was built in the center of the weed-strewn slope, and a camp pot of coffee helped to carry us through the evening rehearsals. Afterwards, we sat around the fire, told stories and sang.

We found some old benches that had been built for the

Chautauqua so that they fit the slope of the ground. These were placed
in the rear of the Normal School folding chairs, which were reserved
and sold for $1. General admission was 50¢.

As strangely incomplete and improvised as it was, there was no
doubt, even in those early years, that when you entered this enclosure
you were within the same walls that encircled "The Place," that being
the title in medieval manuscripts given to the special location where
the dramatic action was to happen. It is not an accident that Jimmy
Durante's famous entrance line has always been, "Is dis da Place?"

If there were advantages to having the Festival during the Fourth
of July week, there were also disadvantages. We opened on the second
and discovered that the natural disadvantages of playing in an outdoor
theatre, coupled with the crescendo of noise as the Fourth approached,
were more than a little distracting.

To be on the safe side, each day we staged an afternoon run-
through of the play that was to be performed in the evening. This is a
practice which we followed for many years. We found that it was
difficult to compete with the premature firecrackers and vocal evidence
of holiday spirits even in those afternoon rehearsals. But the opening
performance of *Twelfth Night* seemed to go very well. Our own enthusiasm for this wonderfully varied comedy and our joy in performing it seemed to be communicated to that audience which appeared
large to us, but which was actually pitifully dwarfed by the size of that
180-foot arena.

We thought the background noise was many decibels too high for
that performance and the following night's revival of *The Merchant of
Venice.* But the distractions of the Fourth were many times worse. In
the first place, we were not able to use the stage for our afternoon
run-through for reasons that form the basis of the most frequently told
story about the Festival. I will come to that in due time. You can
imagine what the street noises must have been like that night, with all
the excess adrenalin stimulated by a day of celebrating and of impatient
crowds waiting for the official fireworks display scheduled for ten
o'clock. Since the play ran a little later than that, we had arranged with
the proper officials to hold the fireworks until we sent them word that
we had finished. But the impatience of the crowd became too much for
those in charge and they started the display *before* ten o'clock! This
meant that the last quarter of our production was performed almost
literally in pantomime. For no actor could be heard over the exploding
of aerial bombs and sizzling skyrockets. The glare of the display was at
the actors' backs directly in the eyes of the audience.

This performance was supposed to be the piece de resistance of the run, and the audience was twice as large as the previous two nights. You can imagine how we felt. We thought that the performance was ruined and that all, or at least a greater part of our labors had gone for naught. In one of those strange quirks of fate that sometimes turn adversity to advantage, members of the audience were furious, not at us, but at the stupidity and thoughtlessness of those who had set off the fireworks prematurely. As a matter of fact, we made many staunch friends that night.

Now for the famous Festival story I promised to tell. About two weeks before the Fourth of July I was visited by a delegation from the celebration committee. They opened the conversation by assuring me (with a sort of schoolboy self-consciousness) that they had nothing against Shakespeare, and that furthermore they thought the presentation of his plays was rather a good thing for the community. But they went on to express their concern for a possible deficit in the celebration budget. That this would be a deplorable situation we all agreed. They then came up with a suggestion for a plan that would guarantee the financial success of the whole project. The way they approached the subject made it clear that they expected me to object. Thus it came to them as a great relief when I agreed to allow the use of the Elizabethan stage on the afternoon of the Fourth for a card of boxing matches! I assured them that such an event would be quite typical of the kind of thing that appealed to Elizabethan audiences, though to be sure, their tastes were somewhat more bloody.

This decision resulted in two great benefits for the Festival. In the first place, the boxing match caper introduced us to Roy Craft. Roy was Public Relations Officer for the Civilian Conservation Corps. The C. C. C. was one of the Federal Government's answers to the problem of unemployed youth, and these groups of young men were responsible for building many of the fine trails and recreation areas for which this part of the country is justly famous. It was Roy's duty to arrange the fight cards, pitting the favorite boxers of the various C. C. C. camps against each other. He later volunteered to do public relations for us and put out the Festival's first newsletter. He was eager to take on the responsibility, for he said of the Festival, producing Shakespeare in the foothills of the Siskiyou mountains, "If ever there was a case of 'man bites dog,' this is it." He later became a well-known staff member of *Stars and Stripes* and after the war made a name for himself as editor and publisher of an unusual paper in Alaska.

The second benefit was accompanied by automatic disadvantages, but all in all the benefit far outweighed the disadvantages. The Shake-spearean productions not only paid for themselves, but surprisingly enough, paid for a considerable deficit in the prize fights. Thus Shake-speare was an economic asset from the very first year. This has been a great advantage for us with the average businessman, who lives in a society which is governed by Puritan principles which he does not recognize. One of those principles is that the value of works of art is suspiciously intangible until it becomes a piece of property which can be bought and sold.

I have always believed in the importance of the economic as well as the aesthetic values inherent in art. But the Festival has always been operated on the principle that the economic value of art, no matter how great, is short lived unless the aesthetic values are the result of skill and integrity.

So it came about that at the end of the first short Festival season I found myself in the familiar situation of being the producer of a source of finances for some other community enterprise, and with an empty purse to face the second season. This situation was not to last forever, and after the second season a permanent, if radical, remedy was found.

VI

Variation

AFTER THAT STRENUOUS YEAR, settling down to teaching for the remainder of the summer session was somewhat of a letdown. We did have the first Festival under our belt, however, and that warm thought kept us going. At the end of the summer quarter, Lois and I drove to Hollywood, partly for a vacation, but primarily to try to sell my Andrew Jackson script. The vacation part of the trip was a success. This was my first experience with the movie industry, and I must say that after that bumbling excursion through the Hollywoods, I came home to Ashland a wiser man.

After three days of going from one studio office to another, being alternately ignored and insulted by inferior office help who obviously didn't know nor care what my problem was, I learned, quite by accident, that the studios did not accept original scripts. It finally dawned on me that nobody had ever said flatly that they wouldn't read the play or wouldn't show it to someone who would. But in some mysterious way, I always found myself walking down the street without knowing just how I had been turned down. I was eventually told that I must get an agent if I expected to unload my script.

Where was I to find an agent? The only person I knew in Hollywood was Floyd Crutchfield, the manager of the Los Angeles office of Samuel French, the famous play publishing house. I had met her in Seattle at one of Glenn Hughes' Northwest Drama Conferences. I thought she might remember me. Though she was naturally reluctant to recommend an agent, she compromised by giving me a list of them. So I started on my rounds again. In most cases I did not get past the reception desk, and at the end of a long day I still hadn't seen anyone who would read "Andy Jackson."

But the second day in seeking out one of the addresses given to me by Miss Crutchfield, I arrived at a luxurious office that was in the process of being remodeled. Plaster was still wet in the outer office, carpenters were still busy installing paneling. Unbeknownst to me, this circumstance was most fortunate. It led in some mysterious way to my getting an appointment with the wrong man! The appointment was for the next afternoon and was for the last fifteen minutes before the office closed. That didn't give me much time, but at least I was at last to see a real live agent, and perhaps in fifteen minutes I could persuade him to read my play.

I learned later that this agent's office was run on very tight security, and he couldn't find out how this unknown had obtained an appointment, but he suspected that somehow I had wangled my way onto his agenda sheet by very clever manipulations of some kind. He stayed to see me for the simple purpose of finding out how this mysterious operator had maneuvered it. He was used to dealing with sharp operators, and he was all set for me. His craggy face seemed an appropriate facade for the ruthless strength that had been necessary in his struggle for success in the Hollywood jungle. As I entered his presence, his eyes glared at me from under shaggy eyebrows, and I completely forgot my sales pitch, which I had thought out so carefully. I stammered for a moment and then said in desperation, "Sir, I need help."

The deep lines of his face rearranged themselves into a more pleasant pattern as I told him my frustrating story of trying to get someone to read my play. He was used to dealing with the slyest of operators, but it was obvious that a young, eager college professor was a novel experience. As a result, we talked, not for the allotted fifteen minutes, but for two hours. And, Hallelujah! He agreed to read *Andrew Jackson*.

Of course, he was never able to sell it. And perhaps that was just as well. In all probability, the advice he gave me was a much more valuable asset than the sale of the manuscript would ever have been. After reading the play, he said that my treatment of the material in one or two scenes would be worth money to the studio which bought the rights. But, he reminded me that the story of my play could be found on the history shelves of any library, and that the studios had on their payrolls some of the best writers that money could buy.

"Besides," he said, "It's a screwy business. You never can tell what will sell a property to them. I sold *The Thin Man* only because they fell for that one line where the wife asks the husband if he had an erection when he was wrestling with the girl. And of course that's the one line in the book they can't possibly use. It's a screwy business."

"Look, young man," he said, "do you want to come to Hollywood?"

"Well—yes," I gulped.

"Then don't come to Hollywood. You go back to this Festival you have started. I know you are a modest kind of guy, but even if you have to lash yourself over the back, you must force yourself to realize that you have a commodity as real as the cans of tomatoes on a grocer's shelves: your name. You go back to Ashland and develop that Festival. Just make sure that whenever the Festival is mentioned, your name is also mentioned. Then eventually Hollywood will come to you, you can say 'No' and then you will be sitting pretty."

Hollywood has come to us only once. We didn't say "No," but fate cancelled the appointment. In a later chapter I'll tell the story of Charles Laughton and the Festival.

There was always something a bit heady about a visit to Hollywood in those days. Each time you walked along the street you felt the thrill of adventure. That person you just passed might have been a great star, and you were sorry that you hadn't looked closer. The surreptitious glances cast *your* way were a flattering indication that someone at least for a split second had taken *you* for a celebrity. Along with this proximity to greatness came the intoxicating feeling that somehow the Hollywood magic would transform you from the ugly duckling of reality to some undefined swanlike form that would include riches and fame. Even to this day when the smog clears, the fragrance of eucalyptus trees and flowers, mixed with some other indefinable tropical essence that exists only there, can still conjure up pale ghosts of the old bittersweet euphoria. This still happens in spite of the fact that I lived and worked there during the latter years of the war and learned to look more realistically at the city where they never say "No." But more of that later.

Lois and I came back to Ashland for the start of a very exciting year. We were refreshed and, somehow, inspired by our visit to the film city and took on an ambitious production season at the Normal. The three plays were varied, but each was chosen carefully and each choice was surrounded by its own set of circumstances.

The freshman students at our school came out of high schools in those days with a notable hatred of the classics and a complete lack of experience in attending theatre. I always thought of the student body as the most important section of my audience, and considered that one of my primary educational duties was to expose them to good theatre. On the other hand, I was not anxious to be typed by these young people as a highbrow. Therefore the fall productions were chosen from good theatrical scripts without obvious literary pretentions. It was thus that I turned again to my old friend, *Seven Keys to Baldpate*, by George M. Cohan. There was nothing particularly notable about the production except that it was fun and we were able to use the inner above platforms and the pillars from the "Merchant."

The reasons for choosing the next play and for the radical change from our usual routine of production were more complicated. The Penthouse productions of Glenn Hughes were familiar to me, and I could see several advantages in adopting an arena style for this winter production. In the first place, I wanted to tour a show. I remembered my first lesson in public relations: get to be known outside your own bailiwick. If the Festival were to thrive, Ashland must become known as a center of good theatre. In an arena production there would be no scenery to cart around, and aside from facilitating touring, this style, by limiting the size of the audiences, made it possible to play more than the usual three nights. In addition to all this, such a production would give relief from the abominable acoustics and the hectic and interminable scheduling problems of Churchill Auditorium.

The play was George Bernard Shaw's *Candida*, which you will remember thrilled me so much when I saw Katherine Cornell's company do it. We played it for a total of 17 performances. This gave my cast a chance to have the maturing experience that only playing numerous times before different audiences can give, and which some would need before the demands of the next summer's Festival.

We played in the ballroom of the Lithia (now the Mark Antony) Hotel to a maximum nightly audience of 75. We played there for several weekends, then to a convention and for several rural Granges. Gordon Claycomb had by this time moved to Portland, and he arranged to have us perform at Reed College. I remember I was surprised that the same script played by the same cast was assumed by a rural Grange audience to be about a domestic triangle which ended happily, while the more sophisticated Reed College audience accepted it as a tongue-in-cheek presentation of a conflict of ideas. I suppose one mark of all great drama is that it has something for everybody.

There was an amusing incident which took place during the rehearsals of this production. The cast was discussing the meaning of the poet Marchbank's line: "But I have a greater secret than that in my heart." Because they could not agree among themselves about the nature of the secret, and because I suspected the author was being deliberately enigmatic, I suggested one of them write to Mr. Shaw and ask him what he meant. The girl who was playing Prossy wrote and, in time, received an answer. Mr. Shaw's letters were collectors' items, so it was unfortunate, if not unexpected, that the letter was signed by his secretary. It said simply:

> Mr. Shaw asks me to tell you that it has been such a long time since he wrote the play that he has quite forgot the secret in the poet's heart.

In another attempt to center attention on Ashland as a theatrical center, I organized a drama conference. Samuel French was glad to send Floyd Crutchfield as our main speaker at no expense to us. I was equally glad to have her come and help persuade the high school teachers to choose better plays for presentation by their students. We revived *Candida,* and the University of Oregon production of Sheridan's *The Rivals* was our guest performance. I remember that Ottilie Seybolt, senior director of the University of Oregon Theatre, turned in a beautifully comic characterization as Mrs. Malaprop, and two former Normal School students and active Festival actors were in the cast. William Cottrell played Sir Lucius O'Trigger, and George Francis Smith did Faulkland. I had hoped this would be the first of a series of exchange performances with the University but the return invitation never came.

In working out the publicity campaign for this conference, I hit upon an idea I thought was a good one. At that time Robert Ruhl was the editor and publisher of the Medford *Mail Tribune.* He was a brilliant man who earned a Pulitzer Prize for his paper in 1934. I knew that virtually everyone in southern Oregon read his editorials, and I was sure if I could persuade him to write one about the conference, we would benefit by considerably increased attendance.

Having made an appointment with him by phone, I approached his office with trepidation. He came from a stratum of society that was completely strange to me, and in my eyes represented sophistication, knowledge, self-possession, poise—all those qualities that I had tried to portray on stage but had not mastered off it. The tan of his face emphasized his dapper little white mustache and his bright eyes were noncommittal as he listened to my proposal.

When I had finished, he leaned back in his spring-pivoted office chair and said, without changing expression, "Just why do you think that I should devote space in my editorial column to a drama conference at Southern Oregon Normal School?"

Taking this to be a virtual refusal, I retorted somewhat heatedly, "You may not know it, but this is the first drama conference to be held in the state of Oregon, and it is not being held, as might be expected, at the University of Oregon or Oregon State College or in Portland, but in the little town of Ashland at Southern Oregon Normal School, one of the smallest schools in the state."

I didn't turn on my heel and walk out as I would liked to have done, but nevertheless I left his office thinking that I had lost a battle. Much to my surprise and somewhat to my embarrassment the next issue of the *Tribune* contained a fine editorial extolling the forthcoming drama conference and using much the same "man bites dog" evaluation I had used in my frustration in his office. Lesson number 1001: never underestimate an opponent who may become an ally by assuming that his reasoning is inferior to your own.

The next play after *Candida* was O'Neill's *Emperor Jones*. We had been discussing the possibilities of producing this script for almost two years. Ever since I had first worked with Bob Stedman, I had thought of him as a possible Brutus Jones. I was not sure of his ability to handle the role and I was very conscious of the makeup difficulties. I recoiled from the idea of any semblance of the white man's Negro minstrel in O'Neill's black giant.

It must have been the summer before the first Festival that Lois went to the University of Washington to take a full quarter of John Conway's courses in costuming. Bob batched with me. In the daytime I taught summer school classes and Bob worked at Safeway. At night we spent long hours discussing the play—reading lines and experimenting with makeup. His physique was right and his kinky hair posed no problem. We spent many long sessions experimenting with highlights, shadows and nose putty in an attempt to convert his somewhat aquiline features into what would pass for a Negroid face. When we were not working on *Emperor Jones*, we were talking about life, theatre, the Festival's future. In fact we talked a great deal and slept very little. I remember one warm night of looking up from a tall, cool glass to see a vivid glow in the east of town. We rushed to the window to see what large structure was on fire, only to discover that we had talked the night through and the glow was that of the rising sun.

A year later—after the first Festival—we designed the settings for *Emperor Jones,* using drapery trees in such a way that they could be rearranged in 10 second blackouts for the many jungle settings of the play. We knew the old faded grey outing-flannel drapes had seen their best day and we hated the thought of trying to suggest the limitless depths of the jungle by backing our trees with them. What we needed badly was a set of black velour drapes. We also knew that the Student Council as it had been constituted would never consider allocating money to theatre. This opinion was made no less accurate by our knowledge that the Student Council faculty advisor was the athletic coach. But the previous fall Bob had been given the opportunity to run for Student Body President. He had no particular interest in campus politics, but I felt that the election to this office would be a positive help when listed on an application for a teaching position when he graduated. His final decision, however, was not without certain Machiavellian motivations. He felt that if he were elected he could persuade the Student Council to vote the money for the velour drapes. He was elected, and the money was voted. The black drapes arrived in time for the opening performance of a three night run. Then after playing one additional night in the 1200-seat Medford High School Auditorium, we turned all our energies to the preparations for the second Festival.

We didn't have a souvenir program until the third year, but I still have copies of the cheap little "throw away" programs for those first two years. I have always been proud that the first one read: "The City of Ashland presents—THE FIRST ANNUAL SHAKESPEAREAN FESTIVAL." The second one read: "THE SECOND ANNUAL SHAKESPEAREAN FESTIVAL—Presented by Southern Oregon Normal School." The word "annual" is proof again that we had permanency in mind, even in those improbable and innocent days.

It had been obvious that the advantages of associating the Fourth of July Celebration and the Festival were far outweighed by the disadvantages. Aside from that, there was the need for more rehearsal time, for we were presenting three plays this second year. It is true that two were being revived from the season before, but after a full year, considerable time was necessary to bring them up to performance level. Besides, the later opening date provided an opportunity for Bill Cottrell to take on more acting and staff responsibilities after finishing the spring term at the University of Oregon. While 13 of the previous acting company were repeating, there were many bit parts and a few principals that had to be directed from scratch, and for whom costumes had to be refitted.

Our new play was *Romeo and Juliet,* and we felt adventurous indeed to be taking on a tragedy for the first time. I was very conscious of the danger of scheduling too many performances for fear that our attendance would be thin. Throughout all the early years we tried to ration the number of performances so the audience demand would be just enough to keep our seats filled. In fact, throughout most of the Festival's history we have been able to keep the audience expansion just a bit ahead of the season's expansion. We were anxious, however, to play a whole week that second season. We therefore persuaded Professor John Casteel, from the Speech Department of the University of Oregon, to open the season on Monday, July 27th with a lecture on *Romeo and Juliet.* As recompense we cast him as Friar Laurence. He was not able to come to Ashland until just before his lecture; therefore a student actor, Emerson Pratt, played the role for the opening on Tuesday and the professor played it on the closing Saturday night. On Wednesday and Friday we revived *Twelfth Night* and on Thursday we risked a single performance of *The Merchant of Venice.*

It was a busy summer. Lois had the largest cast she had ever costumed, and with very few part-time assistants. I directed all three plays, played Shylock, Sir Toby and Mercutio, doubling as Friar John. In the morning I taught classes at school, did publicity and supervised volunteer help in the box office. Bob Stedman and his tech crew built furniture, hung curtains, wired the lighting system and planted grass on the sandy slope to the rear of the seats. The latter project also called for spreading fertilizer and constant watering. It was not unusual to see an actor drop a hose with which he had been sprinkling the newly planted grass and run madly for the stage to arrive in time for his next entrance.

Proper presentation of the sword play in *Romeo and Juliet* posed a problem. In spite of the fact I knew next to nothing about it, I was determined to use the rapier and dagger called for in Elizabethan presentation. I realized that the stance of a rapier and dagger duelist must have been very like our modern boxing stance. The dagger in the left hand led and parried with the constant threat of a short jab to a vital spot. The rapier, I knew, must have been held in the right hand, with the right shoulder and leg well back of the left so that the rapier had the weight of the whole body to thrust it home. Because we knew nothing of handling either of these weapons, great emphasis was placed on foot work and the kind of rough and tumble in-fighting we had all seen in westerns. There was much leaping over furniture and the use of acrobatics, the push of feet against torso by a downed fighter to avoid the fatal thrust of an opponent. We had little finesse but lots of activity.

Our principal problem was lack of the proper weapons or even the knowledge of them. For rapiers we used French fencing foils which were much shorter and lighter than the Elizabethan rapier. The problem of the daggers was even worse. For lack of anything else we could think of, we attached wooden hilts to steel rods—God help us! With these lethal weapons, a slight mistake in the timing meant a split scalp and a possible concussion. How we survived I do not know. I remember that for one such piece of bad timing on my part, I paid with a gashed scalp, a few moments of unconsciousness and a headache which lasted much longer.

Actually, I suffered the other kind of headache more frequently. For instance, my Romeo and Juliet were young and eager, but, like all of us, lacked experience. Logan Nininger was a sensitive, intelligent person but really not cut out to be an actor. The only method I could use with him was very careful and meticulous coaching, to which he responded eagerly to the best of his ability. He wanted desperately to please and worked very hard.

The Juliet, Marjorie McNair, was a very attractive youngster whom I had used as one of the two Candidas in the double cast of that play. She was an accomplished dancer, and she, too, worked very hard. However, I had difficulty getting from her the appealing, youthful quality which is so necessary for Juliet. I would keep her after rehearsals and work in long, special sessions. After several of these, I could see some progress. Then at the next rehearsal there would appear in her characterization the authoritative kind of pseudo-maturity which I had been combating the rehearsal before. We would start all over again, and again I would get something of what I wanted, only to have it disappear the next time. It was not until we had been doing this sort of see-saw for about two weeks that I discovered, quite by accident, that she was taking daily "lessons" from Professor Vining, who had been a teacher of Shakespeare at the old Normal School and who had achieved a wide reputation as an orator of the William Jennings Bryan school. When this situation was remedied, and the poor girl was no longer being pulled in two opposite directions, she was happily able to portray the Juliet of which I had thought all along she was capable.

We were fortunate to have several of the best actors back from the previous year. Dorothy Pruitt, with her knowledge of music and experience in dance, brought a grace of movement and a graciousness of manner to her performance of Olivia. This same knowledge and experience contributed a sense of historic time, which, along with the contributions of others, helped to start us on the first steps of a style for which our Festival has become noted.

Bob Stedman repeated his sturdy Bassanio, which contrasted with the surprising sprightliness of his Feste. In *Romeo and Juliet,* for a complete change of pace, he played a gruff but hearty Old Capulet. He also continued as Technical Director and Stage Manager, and without much help constructed all the new props, furniture and such scenery as was essential. The same furniture served for all shows except where specific differences were called for in the action. There were a long table, a small table, long benches and short benches. *Romeo and Juliet* naturally needed the addition of a bed to our store of furniture.

George Francis Smith came back from the University of Oregon to repeat his roles of Gratiano and Malvolio and to play Paris in *Romeo and Juliet.* Bill Cottrell played Benvolio in *Romeo and Juliet* and Fabian in *Twelfth Night.* In "The Merchant," he changed to Young Gobbo, and we were very fortunate to acquire a young actor who proved to be one of the best natural clowns we have ever had to do Old Gobbo. This was Jimmy Baughman, a local boy who knew instinctively how to use his rotund body and round face for the very best comic effects. The scene featuring the two Gobbos became hilariously funny. Jimmy also took on Peter in *Romeo and Juliet.*

Two other new additions to the company were Doreen Leverette and Margaret Knox. The former played a charming Viola and the latter, aside from playing a creditable Nurse in *Romeo and Juliet,* took over the role of Portia at a week's notice, thus converting a major catastrophe into a minor triumph.

The second Festival gave promise in several ways. The casts were somewhat improved, and there were enough of us who had learned something the first year to give a much needed improvement over our first attempts. Then the longer playing season paid off by doubling the first year's box office. But increased expenses, that ever-haunting companion of expansion, left us with a bank balance of only $84.23.

You will remember that the second Festival program read, "Presented by Southern Oregon Normal School." The reason for this credit was our own need for credit. The first year, the cloth, nails, lumber, printing and other costs were charged to the Fourth of July Committee.

For the second year, we still were not sure enough of our potential income to be able to guarantee the local businessmen against possible loss. Therefore we arranged to use the Normal School credit. But we had earned that $84.23, and I felt that it was rightly ours. Therefore I went to President Redford and asked if we might not set up a separate bank account for a nest egg to start the next season. He explained that because we had just become a part of the unified system of higher education of the State of Oregon, the money would have to go into the general fund, but he promised me that it would be "earmarked" so that it would be available the next summer. It was, therefore, with a sense of financial security for the Festival (a false sense, as it turned out) that Lois and I started out for Europe on my first sabbatical leave.

I had been teaching at the Normal School only five years, but my contract was for a twelve month year. Since the sabbatical ruling stated that one was eligible after 18 quarters, it was possible for me to get away for travel and study in less than the usual time. We were to be gone for nine months on half salary. It is an interesting comment on the economy of the time that I was able to put away a hundred dollars each month for two years in anticipation of this trip. This, in spite of the fact that I was getting less than $2800 a year.

This trip to Europe was the realization of an ambition of many years standing. When I was a sophomore at Oak Harbor High School, I had first dreamed of such an adventure. My high school friends thought me a bit touched, and I'm sure my parents wondered what kind of fledgling they had hatched. The good folk of Oak Harbor did not take trips to Europe. Even if they had wanted to go they knew they would never set eyes on money enough to finance such a mad escapade. In fact, we country people seldom saw money even for the necessities. My father and mother must have been relieved to discover my craze took the sublimated form of reading the tour-ship advertisements and writing for travel literature. I don't remember where I got the steamer trunk, but I had it, and it gradually filled with brochures from all the trans-Atlantic steamship lines. I knew every passenger ship that sailed to Europe, knew the deck plans and the fares. Gradually everyone assumed that it was just another collecting hobby—and forgot it. I never did.

It was not until the first year I taught at Oak Harbor that I received any encouragement for the furtherance of my dream trip. I had, for a number of years, been active in the Northwest Boys Conference. Imagine my excitement when I received the program for the annual convention, to discover on the agenda the election of a delegate from the Northwest Conference to the International Youths' Peace Conference in Geneva, Switzerland. I organized all my friends and we campaigned actively for the position. You can picture my delight when I won that election. You can also imagine my chagrin to discover that there was no money allocated to finance the trip.

But I had planned too long, I had imagined myself on that ship too vividly to let the matter drop there. To my mind the Youths' Peace Conference was of worldwide significance. Why, then should there not be a reporter from the Northwest to give to the citizens of our area on-the-spot news concerning this important event? Should not that reporter be a youth; and should not the youth be me?

I was sure that I could persuade one of the Seattle papers to pay my expenses to give them an exclusive day-by-day report. Therefore, I took my courage in one hand and my qualifications in the other and started out for Seattle. By the time I completed the long boat trip to the big city, I realized that both courage and proof of qualifications were meagre indeed. The latter were the letter from Sid Cydell (who, you will remember, said that I wrote well for 16) plus half a dozen clippings from the Oak Harbor *News*—items I had written on reportorial assignments for my grandfather. My courage was not bolstered by my brief encounters with the minor personnel of any of the newspaper offices until I reached the Seattle *Star*. For some reason I passed muster with the outer office people of this rather florid journal and eventually was actually shown into the office of one of the editors. I had a chance to do my sales pitch and show my credentials. After looking over the material and me, he said rather gruffly:

"Yes, we'll hire you."

My spirits soared. I should have known better. He hadn't finished.

"For $75."

So here I was, twelve years later, in 1936, setting out on that long dreamed-of adventure.

VII

Master Class

PART ONE

OUR ITINERARY STARTED OFF with a freighter trip from Seattle through the Panama Canal to New York, a few weeks in New York, then across the Atlantic to London. We traded our car in before we left Ashland and arranged to pick up a new one in Detroit when we returned to the States in May. We then planned to drive to Washington, D.C., and on down to visit the Andrew Jackson country and his home, The Hermitage. From there we were to drive across the southern states to California and home to Ashland.

The only passenger on the *Lillian Luckenbach* besides Lois and myself was a German girl. If my memory serves me correctly her name was Meda Biedefeldt. We watched lumber being loaded into the holds from several ports on Puget Sound, and with quickening excitement felt the slow rise and fall of the ship under us as we emerged from the Straits of Juan de Fuca into the coastal waters of the Pacific. By the time we left San Francisco the deck loads of lumber were 11 feet high.

We ate at Captain Bown's table with the First Mate and the Chief Engineer. The food was hearty, a "meat and potatoes" type of workingman's food, exquisitely prepared. And it was carefully served by a steward whose pleasant black face wrinkled into a warm smile as he came around the deck sounding the ever welcome music of the triangle that called us to meals. Over a distance of more than 35 years, my mouth still waters at the memory of the usual last course of fruit and a sharp crumbly cheddar which Captain Bown called "rat trap" cheese.

Each night, at his invitation, the three passengers joined the captain on the upper deck to watch the changing stars. I suppose the trip was a comparatively uneventful one, as ocean trips go. But aside from the excitement of realizing that this trip really was inevitable, as I had so optimistically predicted all those years ago, there was the surprise of discovering the amazing pleasure in tranquility. After all those years of frenetic creativity there was a sense of recharging my batteries by quietly contemplating the vastness of the sea, the surprising proximity of the countless stars.

There were other sensations too. Fear for one. We crossed the path of what the captain said was the tail end of a hurricane which heaved up mighty waves on the Pacific through which our heavily laden ship stubbornly plowed her way, only to be threatened in turn by the tons of water which cascaded high above our 11-foot deck load and smashed their way across the heavily battened hatches.

Even after the storm abated and the sea became glassy smooth, our fright was renewed by the discovery that the ship was gradually listing to port. We were relieved to learn from Captain Bown that, because of a strike on the docks at San Pedro, we had skipped a scheduled fueling stop there. Thus the oil had been used from the starboard tank, causing the full port tank to pull the ship down on that side. There was no danger, and we were to refuel at Panama. I could not help a prick of fear in retrospect to think what would have happened if we had had that list during the storm. The next day I was doubly thankful for fate's fortunate timing. The *Lillian's* engines came to a complete stop! And we learned that a connecting pin in the propellor shaft had been sheared off. It took the crew the better part of two days to repair the damage. All this time we drifted free, rising and falling on the slow, icy smooth swells of a limitless expanse of ocean. The sensation I remember most was one of detachment from the whole world. And the quiet! Not a sound but the occasional squeak of a spar or the faint rattle of some unidentifiable piece of equipment. It must have been very much like this to have been becalmed in the old sailing ship days.

We finally got under way again and were soon looking forward to seeing a bit of Panama City, for we learned that the ship was to dock to take on fuel overnight before going through the Canal in the morning. We were sharply disappointed, therefore, to hear from the captain that passengers and crew were forbidden by law to disembark. After seeing the fueling gear attached, we went sadly to our berths. Meda was feeling a bit under the weather so had retired much earlier. We had no sooner climbed in than the captain knocked at the stateroom door and asked if we would like to go with him to have a drink at the Port Captain's office. Delighted with the reprieve, we scrambled into our clothes and were on deck in a jiffy. He announced to the Mate in what seemed to be an unusually loud voice that we were going with him to have a drink at the Port Captain's office. He had called for a taxi and as we boarded he repeated again very loudly, "Port Captain's Office."

After a few blocks, much to our mystification, we changed cabs, finally drew up before a large official-looking building, which at first looked completely dark. As we left the taxi and came to the outer entrance, we could see a few dim hall lights burning. But the building was obviously deserted for the night. As we hesitated, Captain Bown said, "Never mind, just leave everything to me." He led us to a door which was labeled, sure enough, "Port Captain." He then pointed to a drinking fountain beside the door. "Have a drink," he said. As all the mystery began to clear in our minds, he told us, "Now if anyone asks you where you have been, all you need to tell them is the truth—you have had a drink with me at the Port Captain's office."

He looked at his watch and said that we were right on time. And as we arrived at the street, an open touring car drew up and the Panamanian driver greeted the captain as an old customer. It must take a great deal of imagination or none at all to be successful at sea. Captain Bown had a truly creative mind, for no one could have dreamed up a more thrilling night's adventure for two country-bred young people. Most of the details have faded behind the veil of years, but the aura of delight remains vivid. The captain had carefully built up the sense of conspiracy and encouraged the idea that we were extremely daring in our first (probably illegal and certainly secret) invasion of a foreign country.

For the rest, it all fades into a glamorous composite of the gliding open car taking us through the ancient parts of old Panama; the tropical moon shining so brightly on the winding jungle road that headlights were turned off; our first view of a land crab scuttling spider-like across the road; spicy scents drifting in from the jungle foliage; two native girls screaming with laughter and lifting their skirts high over their heads after we had passed.

It was very late when we drew up before a dingy cigar stand, and were led by the Captain down a flight of stairs to a Panamanian night club. There we danced for most of the rest of the night, and listened to the native orchestra, which introduced us to new sounds and compelling rhythms which spoke so eloquently of Central America.

It was nearly daylight when we crawled into our berths, but we were up the next morning to see the ship go through the Canal. Lois and I gulped and looked at each other when we saw the Panamanian police bring aboard the bos'n's mate in handcuffs. He had spent the night in jail for jumping ship and being illegally ashore!

The rest of the voyage was comparatively uneventful, and when we arrived in New York, after 32 days on the *Lillian,* we were very eager to start on the next chapter of our adventure: BROADWAY!

In New York and London in that one season, we saw over 40 productions, more than we had seen previously in our entire lives. And what a season! We were able to watch the work of a representative sampling of the very best entertainers and actors of my generation. There is no doubt that all Festival productions since have been influenced by this contact with those great artists. I learned much about all aspects of theatre; I picked up ideas concerning production, makeup, acting methods, comic timing.

For instance, there were Bea Lillie, Reginald Gardiner and Bert Lahr in *The Show Is On.* Bea Lillie had the ability to take a perfectly ordinary idea, attitude or action and so exaggerate it that it became ludicrously funny, and somehow amazingly pertinent. I remember that in one number she came on wearing an attractive costume unusual only in the length of the string of huge pearls around her neck. They hung to below her knees. As she sang and swayed in a natural way to the rhythm of her number the necklace began to swing from side to side. As she became more enthusiastic it moved in a wider and wider arc. At the end of the number it was revolving in a 360 degree circle parallel with the floor. The final pay-off came when she managed to convey the idea that the necklace had done all this of its own accord. And pretending to cover her own embarrassment, as well as to demonstrate that she really had command of the situation, she made her exit using the rebellious necklace as a jumping rope.

Reginald Gardiner, in the same show, did his amazing pantomime portraying the docking of the Queen Mary, and that top banana, Bert Lahr, introduced his famous rendition of "Woodman, Spare That Tree" which was so hilarious that he was forced to repeat it periodically for the rest of his life. In *Red Hot and Blue* we saw the youthful Bob Hope, Ethel Merman and that indestructible clown, Jimmy Durante.

Of course, we also saw many examples of theatre that is so mysteriously called "legitimate." I was introduced to the poetic drama of Maxwell Anderson with a superb performance of *High Tor* with Burgess Meredith. The setting was saved from pedestrian realism by the use of platforms and steps in front of a sky cyclorama. This scenic concept I tucked away for future use. I suppose the best performance I ever saw Helen Hayes do was her portrayal of Queen Victoria from the age of 16 to her death, in Housman's *Victoria Regina.*

It was a special privilege, at this point in my career, to see the wondrous acting of Maria Ouspenskaya in *The Daughters of Atreus,* a production seriously marred by the melange of accents of an otherwise noble cast from Russia, England, Greece, America and some unidentifiable places.

There was *Tovarich* and *Dead End.* Aside from the extraordinarily realistic setting, with the "dead end" kids jumping off the dock into a water-filled orchestra pit, the thing I remember most about the Kingsley play is that line which is so appallingly applicable to young theatre people: "Before you can become an architect, you have to build a building, and before you can build a building, you have to be an architect."

Tickets for *Idiot's Delight* allowed us to discover the Lunts. Aside from the wonder of that evening, that great acting team, Alfred Lunt and Lynn Fontanne have given me many thrilling performances in the years since. I fulfilled a promise made to myself that evening, many years later when I produced the play for Southern Oregon College at the old Vining Theatre. (No, I did not play the Lunt role. I assumed the bit part of Dumpsy, the little waiter.)

The Shakespearean productions were naturally of the most immediate interest, and the ones which exerted the most direct influence upon future Festivals at Ashland. Maurice Evan's production of *Richard II* had received laudatory reviews, and had a longer run on Broadway than any other Shakespeare in a very long time. I was, therefore, hesitant to admit to anyone that aside from the elaborate spectacle, I found the performance over-long and in many places dull. I didn't know why this could be true until many years later when Dr. Margery Bailey criticized our own production of the play. She pointed out that both director and actors had become so enamoured with the poetry that the performances became operatic and the longer speeches, arias. Thus I learned over a long stretch of time that a great playwright produces poetry, not for its own sake, but to bring vitality and point to his characters and ideas. Maurice Evans is a great actor, but to my mind he has always been more effective in vehicles other than Shakespeare's plays because of his conviction that his organ-toned voice is the perfect instrument on which to play blank verse.

We saw three productions of *Hamlet* that year. One was at the Old Vic in London and two were running in New York at the same time. We saw both of the New York productions within one week. Leslie Howard starred in one and John Gielgud in the other. Leslie Howard, a sensitive and appealing actor in motion pictures, had depended upon lens and microphone too long to be able to project from the stage those qualities which suited him for the role. As a consequence, his Hamlet appeared pallid and remote. The settings were beautifully designed. Several I remember were composed of a solid wall of 20 foot-high banners carried on and off by supers. Lois was much impressed by the costumes. Their clean-cut brilliance made the production appear much more colorful to the eye than the costumes of either of the other two productions. We both thought this gave more point to Hamlet's "inky" mourning. The direction was brisk and clear, providing one or two bits of new and effective business. I remember one of these vividly. At the tag line of the play, the four captains, at Fortinbras' bidding, came forward, the scarlet linings of their extremely long black capes flashing bloodily in the lights. As they lift Hamlet's body to their shoulders, only the black of the capes was visible. At the line "Go bid the soldiers shoot!" the body was lifted high to the length of their arms, a cannon fired, and suddenly all was black except for a spotlight shining down on Hamlet's still form. This was a thrilling, frankly theatrical moment, and I lifted it bodily for my own production of *Hamlet* in 1938.

I believe Gielgud's performance was the best acting of that role I have ever seen. I observed for the first time the real meaning of the term "actor relaxation." For instance, in Hamlet's first appearance in the play, you will remember that there is a long bit of exposition during which the king tells of the state of the country before he makes the first reference to the Prince: "And now, my cousin Hamlet and my son." During all this time Gielgud sat far down left, perfectly motionless, with his back to the audience, a white scarf hanging inertly from his relaxed hand. In spite of all the color and movement of the court, the king's speaking, and the stillness of the black back, I could not keep my eyes off this motionless promise of action to come. My memory of the performance was made more vivid and lasting by Rosamond Gilder's book in which she analyzes every movement and speech in that famous production. My admiration of Gielgud as an actor has never diminished, but my personal encounter with him many years later was to teach me (in a not altogether pleasant fashion) something about my duties as Producing Director of the Oregon Shakespearean Festival.

I have never been one to ogle celebrities, but I have always been thrilled to be in the presence of the theatre great. In New York I hit upon a scheme by which I could observe theatre people in their native habitat without being in the least conspicuous. I simply sat in the waiting rooms of casting offices. I used to sit for a whole morning and nobody paid the slightest attention to me. I watched the eager young, waiting nervously until they were summoned, then watched them assume a confidence they did not feel as they entered the inner sanctum, and watched them emerge—so often with a not-to-be-hidden despondency.

Many whose faces were easily recognized went in without waiting and emerged again portraying "confidence" and "success" even to the small gallery gathered in the outer office. On one such occasion the rumor in the outer office was to the effect that a new play about Napoleon was being cast. It turned out to be *St. Helena*, which was produced the following season with Maurice Evans as the star. One of the "successful" ones who went straight in that morning was Peter Lorre, that little fellow with the pop eyes who later made such a reputation for himself in horror movies. It was said that he was being considered for the role of Napoleon. I can think of nothing that would recommend him for the role but his stature. But by his attitude when he came out, no one would have guessed that the part was going to Maurice Evans.

The love affairs which I have had with the two cities of New York and London have progressed in opposite directions. New York, whose glamour and excitement were so stimulating in the thirties, has gradually lost her allure, and I now find her ugly and unattractive. My affair with London, on the other hand, started out inauspiciously. After two months I found that she frustrated and depressed me, and I was ready to, and did, leave her. Thank the Lord it was only a trial separation, for now we get along comfortably, as an elderly couple should. I get a beautiful feeling of muted excitement just being in her presence.

We disembarked at Southampton on Thanksgiving day, and when we arrived in London, we found the city agog about King Edward's affair with Wally Simpson. Not a word had been printed in the British papers, but everyone knew about it. Wherever we went, as soon as our accent was recognized, we were besieged with questions.

"What kind of a person is Wally Simpson?"

"What is she really like?"

"Is it true that she is a divorcee?"

"Was there a scandal?"

It was only a few days later that we listened to the King's abdication speech in the lounge of our little hotel. It was a strange group from all over the world who were drawn together momentarily in that dingy little room, bonded briefly by the emotional suspense into a feeling of fellowhip as we waited for Edward's historic announcement. Besides Lois and me, there was the chronically pessimistic Scotsman who had generously brought his wireless down to make the occasion possible. He was a "civil servant," and as we waited, I remember he predicted the dissolution of the British Empire, much of which has now taken place as he described it. Then there were the two Irish missionaries who looked so much alike they must have been sisters. They had just returned from 20 years in Africa. Sitting primly with hands folded in laps, they looked quite Victorian in their high-necked "shirt waists" and carefully piled-up hair. There was a dark man who obviously must have come from some Asiatic country; and besides several British couples there were a professor and his wife on sabbatical leave from the Massachusetts State Agricultural College. We were joined by the entire staff of the tiny hotel: a competent little Welsh girl, who was the manager; her sister and their two boy friends, refugees from the Welsh mines.

After what seemed like an interminable time, Edward's words came: "At long last. . . ," and we listened, with what must have been a conglomerate mixture of emotions, to his improbably romantic farewell to a kingdom for "the woman I love." There were some tears and some expressions of indignation among the group, but we all felt drawn close in the sharing together of a moment in history.

The next day and for days to come the news vendors' boards were splashed with the sensational and even violent reactions to the abdication. Privately there was some sympathy for the king, as opposed to the official and bitter Church of England denunciation of his alliance with a divorced woman. The sympathetic opinions, which didn't seem to reach the press, appeared to favor the idea that the king had been forced to abdicate because of his tendency to enter into political activities. One illustration I overheard was that he had made a speech in Wales in which he had promised to "do something" about the deplorable economic situation which had thrown thousands of Welsh miners into unemployment and desperate poverty.

I suppose the general opinion of the average uninformed Englishman was best expressed by the toothless little old Cockney woman who ran the tiny tobacco shop across the street from our hotel. Every time I went in to buy cigarettes before the abdication speech, she eagerly plied us with questions and spoke affectionately of "the little king." The morning after his announcement she said with eye-squinting venom,

"The dirty rotter! He let us down."

In the next few days, we got better acquainted with the American couple and learned they were going back to the States in a couple of weeks. We arranged to move into the little cubicle on the fourth floor which they had fixed up as an apartment. There was a two-burner gas plate and an adjacent private bath. They generously left the cooking utensils they had bought for the place; so we were able to save a considerable amount of money on food. The room was tiny, as it was located up under the roof and fitted into odd rhomboidal angles with a ceiling which slanted sharply from about eight feet to no more than three on the outer wall. There were two tiny dormer windows through which the wind whistled freely. In an attempt at do-it-yourself weather stripping, I was able to stuff a whole newspaper, folded over several times, between each sash and sill.

As December wore on, the gloomy weather became bitterly cold, and our spirits sagged with the thermometer. The tiny gas heater, which consumed shillings like mad, gave out about as much heat as an electric toaster. The hotel advertised central heating, but we learned that meant a steam radiator in the hall on each floor, upon which you could place your hand at any time and guess whether the heat was on or off.

We were further depressed by the fact that I accomplished so little in the way of the research that I had vaguely thought about in connection with our stay. As a matter of fact, I was so ill-equipped to do any kind of research and so lacking in the knowledge of what I was looking for that I was ashamed to ask for the proper kind of help. The people at the British Museum terrified me, and we had to satisfy ourselves by wandering through that vast place like a couple of tourists. The London Museum was interesting, but we obtained the most understanding help from the kind people at the Victoria and Albert. I suppose our greatest discovery was the National Portrait Gallery. We spent hours there studying the contemporary portraits of Medieval and Renaissance people. Lois sketched many costume ideas and I was able to study the way the Elizabethans wore their rapiers and daggers, how they stood and wore their clothes and I suppose I was able to absorb a little of the Renaissance feeling. It was, however, many years later at Stanford

University that Dr. Margery Bailey taught me to see, in these portraits, in the stance, the facial expression, the eyes, a reflection of the
ordered world about which Shakespeare wrote.

Not realizing the world of treasure that was there for the asking if
I just went out and "experienced" London, I felt guilty because I wasn't
"doing" anything. I went to the Old Vic and asked about their school,
but I was assured in a very condescending tone that my "American
accent" (it sounded like "Amedic'n acc'nt")would make it impossible
for me to be accepted there. In desperation I started to write a book,
which I facetiously called "A Play Production Pamphlet for Penniless
Producers." I had thought for some time that there was a need for a
knowledgeable book for the school teacher producer who must make do
with little or no money. When I returned to Ashland I found that
during my absence there had been several such books published. But in
our frigid room on the fourth floor of the Alhambra Hotel, I sat with
my bathrobe on over my clothes, huddled over a typewriter when I
should have been outside absorbing the sights, sounds, smells and
historical associations that I have since learned to love so much.

Of course the time did not pass entirely without incident. I read in
the paper of a Shakespeare Fair to be held in one of the old houses on
Berkeley Square. The old house was scheduled for demolition, and
before it came down, they were holding a benefit for The Shoreditch
Housing Authority. As Shoreditch contained the site of The Theater,
where Shakespeare probably first played, it was appropriate for the fair
to be Shakespearean. I went specifically to hear a Mr. Owlete speak
about "A New Globe Theater for London." He spoke in great detail
about the plans for a reconstruction of The Globe on the Bankside near
the original site, a resident repertory company, and a Shakespeare
Library and Museum. The company was already formed, he said, and
they were performing in a building called The Ring, built by an evan-
gelist in an octagonal shape "so the Devil couldn't hide in the corners."
This building was now a boxing arena six nights a week, and the theater company played in it on Sunday, to a "private theater club audience" in one of those dodges that avoided the law which forbade public
performances on Sunday. He explained that half of the square boxing
ring was the forestage jutting out in front of an Elizabethan facade resting on the back half. The audience sat in the half of the octagonal arena
surrounding the forestage. I was greatly interested and determined to
try to see the current production of *The Merry Wives of Windsor.*

After this talk I introduced myself, and after he discovered that I was interested in discussing his fund raising rather than contributing to it, we got along splendidly. I told him a bit about the Festival and we had a great time exchanging ideas about the joys, sorrows and excitement of our mutual problems and accomplishments. I do not know how much money he had raised, but he showed me a check made out to his project for £25 signed by Lloyd George.

As we talked we wandered through several rooms of the old house, looking at the exhibits. We had looked at the costumes worn by famous Shakespearean actors. These had been displayed in one room and we had gone from there to the room featuring Shakespearean theatrical properties. We were in the third room, which was filled with glass cases in which rare books were displayed, when we were approached by a Bobby who told us to go out the exit and come in again by the front rooms we had just left. Queen Mary had just come in and it seems that no one could be in front of her. You can imagine my interest, not to say excitement, as we came up behind the Queen Mother and her party of ladies-in-waiting. Being in the same room with her was a very special experience that I shall never forget. At times, only a step or two separated us and it was easy to observe her rather closely while appearing to study the exhibits. She and her ladies wore clothes that were definitely outmoded, but on her they seemed *right*. Under other circumstances their hats would have been called "frumpy." But hers was obviously what a queen should wear. Whenever I recall that day and see again her erect figure, gentle yet commanding eye, her aura of majesty, I rmember: That is what it is like to be a queen.

The next Sunday Lois and I went to see the "Merry Wives" production. It was a sad mistake. The Falstaff was played by an old gentleman who should have retired in dignity years before. John Conway told me later that he had played Falstaff for many seasons at Stratford and had retired because he was almost blind. The old fellow continually forgot his lines and the show literally stopped several times when his fellow actors were not able to prompt him. At one point, he had to leave the stage without finishing one of his soliloquies. For this and other reasons the performance was interminably long. The remainder of the cast were young and obviously lacking in experience, and they presented a medley of styles, differing from each other as well as from the florid oratorical style of the pathetic old gentleman. It was a uniquely sad experience, and to make an embarrassing situation more embarrassing, the director, Robert Atkins, entered after the curtain call and apologized for the performance! I have never again witnessed anything like that evening in a long lifetime of theatre going.

Fortunately, the rest of our London theatre experiences were highly satisfactory. We saw Edith Evans starring in *The Taming of the Shrew* in one of the West End theatres and in *As You Like It*, which was produced, if I remember correctly, at The Old Vic. I remember thinking that, though she showed a theatrically exciting command of the role, she was, even then, a bit long in the tooth for Rosalind. Her voice, which in her later years was cracked with age, had then an attractive huskiness which still did not suggest youth.

She played a delightful Kate opposite Leslie Banks' Petruchio. I remembered seeing him in American movies and always marvelled at how attractive and effective he was in spite of the fact that one side of his face was paralyzed, a handicap that would seem to be a prohibitive one for an actor.

There were two pieces of entertaining embroidery of Shakespeare's script, one of which was completely extraneous, and one which provided an amusing and inventive alternate to the usual solutions of a problem inherent in the incomplete version of the play that has come down to us. The first was the addition of the wedding bed scene in which the bedding gets tossed around and Kate made generally uncomfortable as Petruchio describes it in the speech which Shakespeare provides. Then Kate's dream was presented by a rather elaborate ballet. It was entertaining, but hardly germane to the plot.

The second piece of flummery was more to the point. You will remember that the body of the comedy is a play within a play presented before the tinker, Sly, who has been brought, in a drunken stupor, to the lord's castle and made to think, when he awakes, that he himself is a lord and that his life with his shrewish wife has been a bad dream. Shakespeare obviously meant for Sly to be on stage observing the action, for he is shown in a scene in which the actors are introduced, and in several places, in the first part of the piece, he comments on the action. But the framework play is never finished, and it cries out for resolution. The two solutions which are generally used are either to omit the Sly sequence entirely, or to adapt the completed framework part of *The Taming of a Shrew*, an anonymous play contemporary with Shakespeare's, the plot of which it resembles closely.

In the Edith Evans production, Sly gets to wandering about the stage obviously looking for what the Elizabethans called the Jakes, the modern English call the Loo, and we call the John. He gets repeatedly mixed up in the stage business. Eventually he makes an entrance at the exact moment when a character called merely the "pedant" is supposed to make one, answers a couple of cues in a way that accidentally makes sense. The "actors" are convulsed with laughter, completely breaking away from their characterizations. They recover immediately, however, and continue the dialogue. As the pedant in the play is actually being asked to impersonate Lucentio's father, it makes a kind of zany sense for Sly to take on this role drunkenly through the rest of the play. One time several years later, I lifted this bit of hocus pocus bodily for a Festival production of "Shrew."

The *Hamlet* at the Old Vic starred the young Laurence Olivier. He was obviously experimenting with a "physical" Hamlet, leaning over backwards to keep from repeating the introverted Hamlet made famous by John Barrymore and many others since the advent of Freud. He stressed the athletic prowess for which he has always been noted. At one point he made a leap of 20 feet or more to the center of the stage from a platform. This somewhat melodramatic approach did not distort the script, nor were the characters any the less believable because of it. It demonstrated for me how legitimate interpretations could differ widely without distorting the intention of the author.

In one piece of business, however, the production demonstrated how a director's cleverness could defeat itself. The death of Queen Gertrude provided the most spectacular moment I have ever witnessed in the theatre. After she drank the poisoned wine, we lost track of her as she wandered up a long flight of stairs, for we were following exciting action below. At the line, "Look to the Queen, there, Ho!" all eyes turned to her at the top of a 20 foot platform. She reeled, turned and fell backwards into a crowd of extras below. There was a tremendous gasp from all of us, and for the only time in my life I saw an audience lifted to its feet from sheer shock. As exciting as it was, it was a mistake, for the preoccupation with this excitement lasted through the end of the play, and Hamlet's death was an anticlimax.

I was much impressed with Olivier's performance, however, as I have always been by the many roles I have seen him enact since then. His straightforward, vigorous portrayal of the prince was to affect me strongly in my interpretation of the role as an actor in 1938 and 1939, but perhaps more in the disastrous production which I directed in 1954.

In the Old Vic production of *Twelfth Night*, the same sort of self-defeating cleverness occurred. Jessica Tandy played both Viola and her twin brother Sebastian. Anyone who knew the play was naturally puzzled as to what would happen in the final scene when these characters confront each other on stage. In fact, we were thinking of this when we should have been thinking about the play. The confrontation was handled very cleverly, however. The actor who played Sebastian was not seen face front, and he was about the same size as Jessica Tandy, and, of course costumed the same. At each exchange of lines between them, there was a surge of the crowd of extras around them, under cover of which they changed stage positions. Thus Tandy was able to speak all the lines for both.

One of the reasons that *Twelfth Night* is one of Shakespeare's greatest comedies is its wonderful variety. It runs the gamut from the melancholy of Feste's songs to the pratfalls of Sir Andrew; from the self-conscious court-of-love postures of Orsino to the pseudo-love missive written by Maria, to the beauty of Viola's "Build me a willow cabin at your gate" and much, much more. I have found that many English productions of this play emphasize the meloncholy thread that runs through it, and do so to the extent of making the piece a muted, sad longing for better days. This does the play a disservice, for Shakespeare has made the play much more than that. In this Old Vic production there was plenty of variety, but the Malvolio-Sir Topas scene was played with Malvolio in a sort of animal cage in the center of the stage. This, I felt, overemphasized the cruelty of the scene; and Malvolio's final exit line: "I'll be revenged on the whole pack of you" was delivered with more tragic than comic effect.

Olivier, surprisingly enough, played Sir Toby Belch and played him very well indeed. Even at that early stage in his career, he had an amazing ability to assume a completely different appearance appropriate to each different character. His Sir Toby was one who had once been very fat but who had lost a hundred pounds or so. Everything about him drooped, from costume to moustache. He and the young actor who played Sir Andrew Aguecheek made a hilarious comedy team. I had seen this other young fellow in several bit parts: LeBeau, in *As You Like It* and Osric, in *Hamlet*. He was obviously just starting to make his mark in London. His Sir Andrew reminded me vaguely of Stan Laurel. He was excruciatingly funny and at one point actually stopped the show. It was during the "gulling scene" where Malvolio is reading aloud the planted letter and the conspirators are listening to him from concealment, making appropriately comic comments to themselves. The scene was a formal garden, complete with shaped shrubs and lots of statuary. At one point Sir Andrew started to tip-toe across the stage to get near Sir Toby. When he was about center stage, Malvolio paused in his reading and turned around as if he had heard something. Sir Andrew immediately arose on one foot and posed in obvious, if ludicrous, imitation of Cupid shooting an arrow. His ridiculous camouflage was evidently successful, for Malvolio resumed his reading. The house rocked with laughter, which grew into applause so loud and long that the pause in the play was obvious and extended. I always remembered this Sir Andrew, though I couldn't remember the actor's name. What is more, I remembered his performances in the two bit parts. Years later, in looking through my old programs, I discovered why my memory of this young actor remained so vivid. His name was Alec Guinness.

As Christmas drew near, the weather became colder and gloomier, and in spite of all the good theatre, we continued to become more and more depressed. We received postal cards regularly from Keith Williams, a young man from Fayetteville, North Carolina, whom we had met on the ship going over. We had said goodbye to him at Southampton, as he continued to the Continent. In his cards, he spoke in glowing terms of his progress across France and down Italy and was now on the Isle of Capri, where he had met and fallen in love with a poetess from Boston. They swam in the blue Mediterranean and basked in the sun every day. He made it all sound very romantic, warm, cheery and perhaps most important, inexpensive.

We had assumed that our meagre budget would prohibit us from traveling, but his insistence upon the low cost of living and traveling in France and especially Italy made us waver in our resolution. Two incidents probably tipped the scales.

The first stemmed from the good feelings we had for the four young people who operated the hotel. They had served us efficiently and courteously, and we knew they worked very hard. We were a bit amused at the solemnity with which the boys changed costumes to fit the particular task of the moment, wearing porter's jackets when they carried luggage and appearing in waiter's black tie and tails when they served at our tables. To show our appreciation, we bought each of them a little gift, a carton of cigarettes for one of the boys, a little potted plant for one of the girls, and I've forgotten what else. On Christmas morning, when we knew they were alone we brought the gaily wrapped gifts down the stairs, singing "We Three Kings of Orient Are." Much to our surprise and dismay, they were not amused. They thanked us, of course, but in frigid tones. We had learned our first lesson concerning British "classes." There are those who serve and there are those who are served. Each should know his place and keep in it.

The second blow to our morale fell that afternoon. We had for some time anticipated Christmas dinner at an interestingly atmospheric restaurant in an old sixteenth century building. We knew it would be expensive, but we felt that this strain on our budget was justified by its expected lift in our morale. We didn't know that on Christmas day most of the population of London either goes to the country or attends a Christmas party at one of the many large hotels. All the restaurants are closed! After reading the "Closed for Christmas" notice on the Red Lion door, we walked for what seemed like miles in search of some place to eat. We finally found one, ablaze with neon lights. It was one of the Quality Inn chain and was really an English imitation of an American glorified hamburger joint. Their big concession to the day was roasted frozen turkey that tasted like cardboard. I remember the waiter, as soon as he heard our accent, asked us if he could be our chauffeur while we were in England. He obviously didn't believe us when we said we didn't have a car. To his knowledge all Americans were rich. He also asked if America was really as Zane Grey pictured it, and whether there were still any wild horses there.

We had tickets for a couple of plays the next week so we decided that right after New Year's we would go and find Keith's paradise. Still one more disappointment was in store for us. Charles Laughton and Elsa Lanchester were starring in *Peter Pan* for the Christmas holiday season, and we anticipated this once-in-a-lifetime opportunity with a great deal of pleasure. It was a good performance except that both the Laughtons were out with the flu, and Captain Hook and Peter Pan were played by the understudies.

Our luck was somewhat better for New Year's Eve. We profited by our previous experience and obtained reservations several days in advance. The dinner was good, and we danced the old year out and the new year in. On our way home as we walked the strangely empty streets, we came upon a sight that stopped us in our tracks at the edge of Piccadilly Circus. The entire square was empty except for two unbelievable, happily grotesque figures. A Scotsman stood on the steps at the base of Eros' statue. He was garbed in complete kilted Highland piper regalia and was squeezing out a wildly lusty tune. On the pavement below him, her skirts held high, her heavy shoes beating out a tattoo accompaniment to the pipes, her spirits inspired by gin and the occasion, a toothless old flower girl was dancing a cockney version of the Highland Fling. It was a hilariously warm picture that made us feel that we were leaving London on an up beat, for in two days we boarded the train for Paris.

VIII

Master Class

PART TWO

K EITH HAD RECOMMENDED a modest little hotel located on the Rue de L'Echiquier in an unpretentious, not to say disreputable, part of Paris. The French I had learned in order to pass my reading knowledge examination for my master's degree was scarcely sufficient to read the signs, much less to converse with anyone. We were excited and somewhat flustered to be in a country where we were truly ignorant foreigners. We managed to fight our way through the porters at the station and find a taxi driver who either understood my English and pantomime, or more miraculously made sense out of my bastard French, for eventually we were deposited at the hotel. As Keith had predicted, we were greeted by the entire family, who had been warned by postcard of our arrival. There was Mama, plump and practical, who never missed anything that went on in the little restaurant, which she ran like a circus ringmaster from her seat behind the cash register. Papa was the chef who came out of the kitchen only on special occasions—one of which seemed to be our arrival. Several of the children waited on table, and fortunately the oldest daughter spoke quite good English. The only member who didn't come out to welcome us was Grandma, whom we glimpsed occasionally through the swinging door to the kitchen as she sat in her black dress and apron peeling vegetables.

Keith had written to them about us. He must have become a favorite in his short stay there, and goodness knows what he had said about us. Whatever it was, it had created a festive welcome for those ''personnes du theatre des Etats Unis d'Amerique.'' The warm smiles, bows and other gestures of welcome seemed to spring from genuine hospitality. All the pantomime was wildly exaggerated, not only because they were French, but also because they realized that we couldn't understand a word of what they said. The English-speaking daughter was a great comfort to us and through her help all arrangements were made without any difficulties. The place was really not a hotel, strictly speaking, but a restaurant with a couple or three rooms overhead.

One of the older boys acted as concierge and porter and took our luggage up and showed us to our room. The stairs were steep and dark, lighted by a single dim bulb operated from switches at bottom and top. We learned to switch on the light and then navigate the stairs at top speed, for with typical Gallic frugality it turned off automatically only seconds later. I don't think we ever made it completely up or down without being forced to fumble the last few steps in the dark.

The restaurant catered to local working people and the food was hearty, nourishing and flavorful. Perhaps the petits-choux came a little too frequently, but I particularly remember the delicious soups, thick with vegetables. I was surprised that they called it "soup-e" rather than "potage," which my dictionary told me was the proper French word.

We stayed only a few days, as we were eager to get to Capri to see Keith and to absorb some of the Mediterranean sunshine. We went to the Louvre and were overpowered by the enormous size of the place. We saw the Winged Victory and the Mona Lisa and far too many more things to remember. We wandered along the Seine, browsed in the book stalls, gazed in wonder at Notre Dame, and picked up a card from Keith at the American Express. I am sure that we did other things I can't remember after all these years. I can't think why we didn't go to the Theatre Francais. Perhaps because of the language barrier we felt the current plays would not be familiar enough to be understood.

At any rate, the language barrier did not keep us away from the Folies Bergere. I was prepared to be shocked at the nudity. I was shocked several times that night, but not at the nudity. I have been back in recent years and I have found that the "Folies" has fallen off deplorably. The last time I went I felt starved for art and cloyed with meat.

In fact I was much impressed that night back in 1936 with the beauty and taste with which the nudes were presented. The star featured that evening was the famous American dancer Josephine Baker, who had just finished a very successful season in New York. I *was* shocked at the dance performed by her and her partner. I still think it was the most lascivious I have ever seen.

The first shock of the evening, however, came when the pert little usherette handed me my ticket stubs and pointed to our seats in the middle of a long row. As I started down the row toward our places, I thought I heard her say, "M'sieu, m'sieu." When I got to my seat, I turned and found that she had followed me in. Her hand was held out toward me, palm up, in an impudent gesture, her face turned up to mine with an unmistakable expression of ridicule. "M'sieu," she repeated in a voice loud enough to turn heads for yards around, "My Teep"! I'm sure I over-tipped her, as she knew I would. How was I to know that you were supposed to tip usherettes in France? Stupid American!

I was somewhat shocked but nevertheless laughed uproariously at a ludicrously funny skit about a sitdown strike in a Cathedral. I suppose I was a bit ashamed at my laughter because the actors were clerical clowns. But that seems strange, for I have never felt reticence about Sir Nathaniel in *Love's Labour's Lost* or Sir Hugh Evans in *Merry Wives of Windsor* or even Sir Oliver Martext in *As You Like It*.

But the real jolt to my ego came at the intermission. It was an incident that further showed up my "innocents abroad" characteristics, and I have been sorry for my actions, or rather my lack of action, ever since. I had gone out to the balcony lobby to smoke, leaving Lois in her seat, as she preferred to rest and watch the audience. The balcony lobby was itself a balcony running around four sides of the upper part of the lower lobby which was a dance floor, where couples were dancing to the lively music of a small combo. I was enjoying the music and looking at the nude murals, when I was startled to see I had caught the eye of a gorgeous blond on the other side of the open square. I suppose my feeling was akin to horror as I saw her coming and realized I was really the one in her gun sights. I was immobolized like a bug on a pin, though there was certainly nothing lethal looking about her. In fact, just the oppostite. Her cream white skin contrasted dramatically with her long black velvet evening gown cut startingly low at what is euphemistically called the neck line. Her walk was a symphony of rhythms. She was in fact frighteningly feminine. As she started to speak to me in French, her eyes sparkled with—what? Enjoyment? Anticipation? Amusement? By this time I was too bewildered to tell. At last I managed to stammer out,

"Je ne comprends pas."

"Oh, Espagnole."

There were in Paris many refugees from the Spanish Revolution, and she had taken me for one.

"No. Americain."

My relief was short-lived.

"Oh, I speak English," she said easily, with only a charming residue of accent.

"I was just asking you if you would like to buy me a drink."

I am sure I blushed as I excused myself,

"My wife is waiting for me inside."

"O, she would not mind. Just a drink. Nothing more."

I wished fervently that I could think of something to say that would make me sound half as sophisticated as she appeared.

"I am sorry, Mademoiselle," I said, with what I hoped was a world weary smile, "but that is one of the pleasures of France that I must deny myself." What an interesting person she must have been. Would that wisdom came before age.

There were several experiences on the way to Capri which are worth noting. The first and most frightening was being dumped, unceremoniously and with only a couple of minutes, notice, into the middle of a maze of railroad tracks at Lyon. This in spite of the fact that we had been assured that our tickets would take us through to Rome without change of train. To add to our confusion, we discovered that we were in the midst of hundreds of people, equipped with skiing gear, milling around seeking their trains either to or from the Alps. The blackness of the night was made even more confusing by the blinding glare of many locomotive headlights, the babble of voices, punctutated frequently by the hysterical shriek of train whistles, and the angry hiss of escaping steam. To make our panic even more frantic was the information that had been conveyed to us from the conductor by an interpreting passenger: we had just four minutes to find the train for Rome!

Dragging our heavy suitcases, we ran until we could intercept someone hurrying in the opposite direction.

"Chemin de fer a Roma?" I would ask, frantically raising eyebrows, shoulders, arms, hoping to indicate interrogation, helplessness and panic. In most cases I would get an unintelligible answer coupled with a directional gesture toward some point on the compass. We would rush in that direction and repeat the process. We thus proceeded in what must have been an exceedingly erratic pattern until at least we joyfully spied a sign on the side of a train which read "ROMA."

We scrambled aboard, but that train never did take us to Rome.

By eight o'clock the next morning, we were so tired and bottom weary from sitting on the third class wooden benches that we got off at Pisa. We stayed the night and the next morning climbed the leaning tower and then caught the next train to Rome. It was on this train that we experienced the incident of the "Captain, the Boor, and the Banty."

The compartment was crowded and the hard wooden benches were uncomfortable. Out of boredom, I suppose, the man opposite me tried to start a conversation. As he spoke in Italian and I in English, there was not much profit in the exchange. I tried my poor French to no avail. He was an oafish sort of clod with a wide grin and malicious eyes. He kept trying to make me understand by shouting, as if my ears and not my tongue were at fault. By his knowing winks to his fellow Italians, I gathered that all this palaver was supposed to be a game of having fun with the "stupid American." He showed me some kind of official I.D. card with his picture on it. It, too, was unintelligible, but he pointed to it and then to himself in a way that was intended to indicate great significance.

At this point a man stopped at the open compartment door and motioned for me to join him in the corridor. He was a large, distinguished looking Italian fellow with the rugged look of an outdoorsman. We introduced ourselves to each other and he told me that he was the captain of a freighter and had for years docked his ship regularly at American ports. He said he was a great admirer of America and Americans. Then he said,

"Do not talk with that foolish fellow in there. He is trying to make a joke with you."

"Thank you very much, sir, for your concern," I said, "but what was he trying to tell me?"

"He was trying to convince you that he was an employee of the government. I am ashamed of my fellow countryman."

He didn't say what kind of employee, but I suspect he didn't like to admit that this stupid fellow was echoing the kind of harassment the average Italian citizen was being subjected to by Mussolini's secret police.

We talked for a long time standing in the corridor, he of his ship and I of the Festival. When he learned we were going to stop only over night in Rome, he offered to show us a modest hotel near the station so we would not have to take a taxi. He explained that his brother-in-law was meeting him and that he could show us the hotel on the way to the car park.

Sure enough, when the train stopped at the Rome station, there he was, waiting on the platform. It had taken me some time to struggle with our bags down the narrow corridor. Expostulating with him for the delay was a little man in military uniform resplendent with officer's insignia, ribbons and other unidentifiable shiny objects. As he stood so erect and elevated his chest so far (either to show off the decorations or to compensate for his short stature) the cock's feathers flying like a flag from the top of his hat were the final touch that have made me think of him ever since as "The Banty Rooster." As he clucked and sputtered in indignation all the way to the hotel, it was obvious he did not share his brother-in-law's admiration for Americans. The captain helped me with the bags, and took us to the desk where he eased the language situation by making the arrangements for the room. I've never forgotten the captain's kindness, and I have often wondered what happened to him in World War II.

The next day we arrived at Naples about noon and dragged our suitcases down to the harbor, pausing long enough to get a bite to eat at a little trattoria. As we approached the dock, the scene was bright and cheerful. The sun shone from a cloudless blue sky and glittered in diamonds from the little waves that danced in the bay. In the distance we could see Capri clearly. The only negative elements in this peaceful scene were the ugly city behind us (Naples is the dirtiest city in all Europe) and the oddly menacing black hulk of a submarine that lurked in the water by the pier.

We boarded the little ship that was to take us on the two-hour trip to the Isle. The decks were crowded with gay clutches of enthusiastic Italian trippers who broke out enormous lunch baskets containing all sorts of native goodies, including horrendously odoriferous cheeses and salami, long loaves of bread, and of course, liters of native wine. There were several others besides Lois and me who were neutral observers of this pleasant, peasant Bacchanalia, and I, for one, did not notice the ship's motion until we were more than a mile from shore. Gradually I began to realize that the rippling wavelets that sparkled so gaily in the sunlight were treachrous camouflage for the increasingly large swells that were lifting the bow of our ship so that we coasted down the far side. Each trip up became more abrupt and each descent more precipitous, until finally, the little vessel, seeming to defy the elements, began to plunge its nose stubbornly into each oncoming roller, sending cascades of water splashing high over the bow and running in torrents ankle deep along the upper deck. Everyone fled, amidst much screaming and laughing, to the lower deck, which was protected by an enclosure at the bow. I suppose it was another half hour before people began to be sick. The motion was not helping my sense of well-being, and there is nothing more empathic than experiencing another person's seasickness. I soon became deathly ill. I rushed below to the rest rooms, but others had all too evidently been there before me, and the enclosed space was not conducive to recovery. I ran back to the deck and with the whole boatload of my companions in misery, hung unashamedly over the rail.

When I had relinquished everything I had, including my will to live, I wandered in a dazed condition to the lounge. If I had been capable of anything but despair, I would have been grateful the place was empty, for there were no sick mamas, no sick papas, and no sick bambinos. I was alone, I didn't know where Lois was, and I wished I were dead. I collapsed into one of the wicker chairs that were lined against the walls and hoped the end would come quickly. A woman entered the room with an aggravatingly un-seasick vigor in her stride. I took no note of her at the moment, but realized later that her high, blond hairdo, rimless glasses and velvet neck band with the cameo at the throat reminded me so strongly of my two Irish missionary friends at our London hotel that I assumed in my semi-comitose state that she, too, had just returned from 20 years in Africa.

The ship was pitching heavily now and as this dignified personage stalked by me one of the wicker chairs was thrown into her path. She was violently catapulted into a full length mirror which shattered into fragments around her. Some measure of my lethargy and lack of interest in life is indicated by the fact that I didn't move a hand to help her. I did wonder vaguely at the lack of blood, but beyond that I couldn't manage to care.

What eventually brought me partially to life was the terrific turmoil which followed. Several members of the crew rushed in, and there was much excited talking in Italian. What really brought me back to life was the jolting realization that the tenor of the hubbub was not that of commiseration or comfort for the dying. Quite the contrary. The captain came to join the fray, and shushing his crew, took a firm stand with the Irish missionary from Africa (for I shall always think of her thus). I thought at first the argument was a religious one concerning differences of opinion as to the nature of the miracle which had brought this woman through a plate glass mirror without a scratch. Without a scratch? I did sit up then for sure enough there was no blood, no broken bones—only a roomful of shattered plate glass. Not only was my "missionary" not bleeding, but she was also not taking any guff from the captain. As I raised my eyebrows in amazement at this puzzling drama, a woman standing next to me translated to her English speaking friend the gist of what was going on. Her explanation solved the puzzle but did not reduce my amazement. The captain was trying to make her pay for the broken mirror! As I watched her standing tall, looking down at the captain as she shouted back at him in fluent Italian (laced I am sure with an Irish brogue), I couldn't tell how the argument was going. But my bet has always been on the Irish.

By the time we landed at the Grande Marina, both Lois and I had recovered sufficiently to gather our luggage together and descend the gangplank. We were greeted by what seemed to be hordes of blue-coated porters, each trying to out-shout and out-shove the others in an attempt to entice us to his particular hotel. Though bewildered, I finally had sense enough to shout out "Ristorante Trieste e Triento." This was the name of the place where Keith was supposed to be staying. A porter came forward, took our bags and ran interference for us through the mob. He led us to the funicular which pulled us up what seemed to be a nearly perpendicular ascent to the little village of Capri.

The Isle of Capri (pronounced *Câ* pri, by the way, the song to the contrary) is shaped roughly like a saddle. The village of Capri, though high above the water, has cliffs lowering over it on both sides. Our little restaurant was perched on the verge of a perpendicular drop to the Mediterranean but was only a few blocks from the funicular and the city square.

There was a great scurry as we arrived and finally a man was produced who, it was alleged, spoke English. He poured forth a spate of words but we understood nothing, except for one sentence that I have never forgotten. He led us down steps to a story below the restaurant where we entered a room that seemed to hang precariously to the cliff side. It was beginning to grow dark, and as he threw open the French windows onto a tiny balcony, we could see the crescent of harbor lights that ringed the Bay of Naples. Brooding above this magic semicircle, faintly outlined against the evening sky, was Vesuvius, with an unmistakable plume of smoke rising perpendicularly to meet the night. To our right and left the unbelievably dramatic cliffs rose high above our heads, marching by giant risers to the sky. A hint of this scene I have experienced on viewing Norman Bel Geddes setting for *The Divine Comedy*.

As he conducted us to the balcony, our little man who "spoke English" pointed to this glory and said very distinctly,

"Da panoram' she is so *very* !"

His expression was so appropriately and delightfully inarticulate that I will always remember it with especial affection. Whenever I view a scene so beautiful that words cannot describe it, I always say to myself.

"Da panoram' she is so *very.*"

Our acquaintance with Keith led to our becoming part of a very strange group of expatriate pseudo-bohemians. Any night of the week some or all of us could be found at one or another of the many small trattorias, talking, arguing, laughing, singing over the excellent Caprisian wine, or noisily drinking the soup or inhaling the spaghetti. Everything was amazingly cheap, and there was a running competition to see who could drive the hardest bargains and live the most economically. Wine was one lira (five cents American) a liter and I found a place where, by guaranteeing to take a liter each day I could get it for the equivalent of about three-and-one-half cents.

This potpourri of self-styled intellectuals and aesthetes included a wide variety of people. There was Vera, Keith's poetess from Boston, and her aunt who owned a convenient nearby villa and whom everybody called "Bunny." The aunt was a tall, handsome widow of middle age whose husband had been in the diplomatic service in the East Indies and who had died there under what was rumored to be "mysterious circumstances."

There were the Dutch artist and his wife (also from Boston) and a little four-year-old son. The wife spoke equally well in English, Dutch and Italian; the artist painted pictures which looked as if he were influenced by both Rembrandt and Dali. One of his paintings, I remember, showed an Oriental figure, beautifully drawn and painted with imaginative, realistic detail—except the neck was about two feet long!

The Swedish writer spoke no English, but his pantomime and facial expression were so graphic that his dirty stories needed no translation.

The English portrait painter was secretly looked down upon because he "painted from photographs." But I suspect he was envied because he was successful and had apparently made a lot of money.

Bunny's boy friend arrived from a vacation in the Alps. The two most startling things about him were first that he was a Bengali, and second that his only luggage consisted of two ski poles and a portable phonograph. He was called "Dada," which, I was told, means "brother" in Bengali. He was a pleasant, dark little man who never missed an opportunity to sing the praises of American women.

They called me "Shakespeare" and even said I looked like Shakespeare. There was considerable gabble about reincarnation, which was no funnier than a lot of their other superficial nonsense. They were not stupid people and I learned a great deal from them, but there was a lot of posing, most of which must have been in fun.

I suppose the most interesting member of the group was a native Caprisian artist whose work I admired immensely. I brought photographs of some of his things back to the States in hopes of getting someone interested in his work. But I didn't know how to go about getting in touch with the right people and my efforts came to naught. He painted in both water color and gouache. Years later I was reminded of the simple, direct strength of his work when I viewed the cave paintings at Lascaux.

Each evening some member of the group would "accidentally" meet him on the street or casually drop in at his home, and by the "merest coincidence" would run across some of the group who would persuade him to join them for a social glass of wine. He would end up by having at least a bowl of soup to fill his empty belly, for he literally had no money. He went hungry in order to buy the materials for his painting. His pride would not allow him to accept charity, and elaborate precautions were taken to keep it from appearing that he was offered any.

He and I used to get together in the afternoons for long talks at a sidewalk cafe on the Square. As I spoke no Italian and he spoke no English, they had to be long talks. It is quite a trick to make a demitasse of espresso coffee last all afternoon, but we did. He spoke a little French but was better in German. My French was pretty poor, but it helped. Coming from New York on the Hamburg I had picked up a few words of German and, surprisingly enough, I found my high school Latin of considerable assistance. We spent a great deal of time staring into our espresso cups, but we did communicate, and I gained much of value from this dedicated young man. The one idea that seemed to recur most frequently was that an artist must never feel that he has "learned" his art. One of the functions of art is to teach the artist as well as the observer. As I remember it, he summed it up simply: "Always esperimentazione."

Keith soon lost the affections of Vera to a young German who was in the throes of composing a Mass which was reportedly to be two hours long. Had I not been a political moron, I could have guessed his political leanings from the fact that he showed me a long letter from Ezra Pound complimenting him on his music, and, I suspect, on his political views. Vera's taking up with a German with far right leanings was puzzling, because her Aunt Bunny kept a picture of Hitler on her mantlepiece into which she solemnly stuck a pin each morning before breakfast. But Vera and her musician were later married, and she spent the World War II years in Germany.

The time bomb was already ticking, but we didn't know how to listen. The Spanish revolution was in full swing, Mussolini's troops occupied Addis Ababa, and the League of Nations was dead. The following year Hitler was to absorb Austria and assassinate Czechoslovakia. The whole world gasped at the calmness with which Mussolini accepted these moves which brought German troops to the Brenner Pass. In a "look there's nothing up my sleeve" gesture Hitler made a spectacular and ceremonious pilgrimage to Italy in that same year. His warm reception by Mussolini was to demonstrate to the rest of the world the solidarity of the Axis. In preparation for his own visit, he sent Hermann Goering to Italy in January of 1937.

In the natural course of things the General was sent to Capri for a few days of relaxation. This time-honored custom had been the standard order of procedure with VIP's since Tiberius Caesar had whiled away his time pushing selected guests off the cliffs there. Goering's arrival created an amusing diversion for us and caused great excitement among the natives.

You can imagine the splash Goering made in this little village, and there was no doubt he enjoyed being the big toad in a little puddle. Each time he appeared in public, he wore a different uniform in which he strutted and postured with unbelievable arrogance and self-admiration. Bonfires were lit in the town square and the little community "oompah" band blatted out patriotic tunes with more enthusiasm than melody.

The day he left I grabbed my movie camera and rushed up to the Hotel Quisisana. The color sequence I was able to get is priceless. Two open touring cars were in the street in front of the hotel! They were the only cars I saw in the month we spent on the island. In the first were the newspaper men who obviously had been liberally entertained. The gathering of spectators was being kept in a wide circle so as to clear a generous path from the hotel doors, across the porch, down the steps and across the street to the cars. The security men who were controlling the crowd were dead ringers for the ones to be seen in the standard "B" movie spy films: black Homburg hats, brims pulled low, shoulders hunched under trench coats, hands thrust menacingly deep into pockets. They might well have been straight out of Warner's casting office, outfitted by Western Costume Company.

Nevertheless, I took the precaution of showing my camera early so that they would have a chance to stop me peaceably rather than be surprised into breaking my camera or extracting my film. In a short time Frau Goering came down the steps and across to the car and took her seat. She was a tall, graceful German actress with a facial bone structure that displayed appropriately dramatic planes and angles. There was a long pause, for the great man was so much of a ham that he couldn't allow her entrance to "fuzz" his own. When the suspense had been built to split-second timing, he made his entrance to silent fanfares.

At this point in the sequence, my film shows a scene which is infinitely more ironic today than it was when it occurred. A little greyhaired lady stepped forward and presented a tiny bouquet of violets to the General. He accepted the tribute with a deep, hat-over-heart bow, and with the violets clutched in his big fat fist, marched, not quite goosestepping, to the car.

A few days before we left the island, our little coterie was invited to a private concert by Vera's German composer. He played a portion of the Mass which he had just finished, and, politics aside, he was a splendid musician. Not being a musician myself I remember little about the music, except that I was deeply moved by the gorgeous tones that came cascading out of the beautiful concert grand piano. Vera had managed to wangle the key to this villa from the caretaker. The owner apparently did not occupy this huge home in the winter and the room was bare of furniture. The walls and domed ceiling were oyster white plaster and the magnificent mahogany grand was silhouetted in a most dramatic manner.

A friend and former student of mine tells a story about that piano, or its twin. Dale Kaegi, who for many years operated the White House

Grocery in Ashland, was a fighter pilot during World War II. He spent some R and R time on Capri and was present when a drunken American G. I. picked up an axe and smashed that beautiful piano into a pile of jangling scrap. One more illustration of the stupid and brutalizing effects of war.

After a month on Capri we mustered up enough courage to make the return voyage across the Bay of Naples to the mainland. The train trip to Rome was uneventful, and as soon as we unloaded our bags at our pensione, we headed for the Coliseum. The day was moving on toward twilight, and we had heard that the ideal time to see that monument was at sunset. After a rather long walk we arrived at the appropriate time to be impressed by the magnitude and sweep of the exterior, but found that time and vandalism had left only a mysterious jumble of walls and tunnels in the interior. My clearest recollection is the sweetly plaintive sound of a solitary bird's song at the moment the sun disappeared.

It was quite dark by the time we came to the Piazza Venezia, but the street lights and the illumination from shop windows made it easy to retrace our steps on the way to our pensione. We cut across that huge square and were in the middle of it when the lights went out. Every light! We looked around and everyone had disappeared. Only moments before, the streets had been crowded with people. Now we seemed to be completely alone in the middle of a square the size of two football fields just opposite that huge snow white monument to Victor Emmanuel. Search lights were now probing the sky, and I could hear the drone of a plane. My God! An air raid! And here we were, of all places in front of the most easily spotted target in all Rome. The Italians had not been allowing the distribution of the Paris Edition of the New York *Herald Tribune* for a week, so we had no way of judging the state of the latest developments in the current tension between Italy and Britain. We were further terrified by a fire truck that came racing through the square with no lights, sirens blaring and bells clanging. We started to run for the nearest sidewalk and were nearly run down by two policemen on a motorcycle with a side car. By the time we got to the sidewalk, we could see that the pedestrians were all huddled in the shop doorways. We made the shelter of one just in time to see a military policeman slap a man with the flat of his sword for moving out along the sidewalk. We didn't dare ask any questions, for if those were English planes overhead our language might get us into God knows what trouble.

Finally, the lights came on and the pedestrians resumed their shopping and we hurried to our pensione. We had never even heard of a practice blackout before.

I must tell of one more incident in Rome that was amusingly paralleled by one in New York. The day we visited St. Peter's was the first day after Mussolini had relinquished the supervision of Vatican City. I suspect the two cockaded officers that stood on either side of the entrance gate to the Cathedral portico were new at their job. The entrance gate was the only opening in a beautiful wrought iron barricade that stretched from pillar to pillar along the whole long distance of the front of the Cathedral. My small movie camera fit snugly into my deep overcoat pocket, so I didn't bother to check it at the booth as I should have done.

Naturally I didn't take pictures in the Church as I knew it was against the rules. But when I came out through the great portals onto the long portico, I was struck with the beauty of the sunlit fountains in the Piazza San Pietro. Shooting from where I stood, on the portico with the wrought iron grillwork silhouetted in the foreground, I secured a striking picture. But as I took the camera down from shooting level, I saw, out of the corner of my eye, that one of the guards at the other end of the portico had taken note and was nudging his companion and pointing in my direction. I had visions of myself in the Vatican jail, and in sudden panic I thrust the camera back into my pocket and started purposefully toward the wrought iron exit gate and the guards. First victory: they stopped where they were. I pulled the brim of my hat low over my eyes, hunched my shoulders under my long overcoat, thrust my hands menacingly deep into my pockets. I stiffened my knees a bit as I walked and just before I got to the grards, I threw them my best imitation of a Nazi salute. Much to my relief, they both came to attention and returned the salute as I marched between them and out the gate.

The companion scene took place in Washington Square in New York City. I had set up my camera on a tripod and had been shooting under my arm at the various interesting characters in the Park. I had changed my location and was setting up again when I noticed a policeman approaching. He had been strolling along the path, swinging his night stick, kidding the nursemaids and chucking the babies under the chin. He spotted me and came over to where I was adjusting my tripod. He looked me up and down, put his hands behind him and teetered back and forth on this heels and toes.

"Hey, buddy, don'tcha know dat its against da law to take pitchers in da Park?"

"No, I didn't know," I said. And as I started to expostulate, he grinned.

"Ya, I know. It's a screwy law, but we got lotsa screwy laws. Y'know my sister up in Maine can't even pick da wild flowers?"

I didn't tell him that I had already taken considerable footage. Then as I started to fold up my tripod, he moved away, waved his stick at me in friendly fashion and said,

"So long, buddy. Just don't take no pitchers in da Park."

Sandwiched in between these two brushes with the law was a lot of theatre going, some of which I have already mentioned. But I must say here that we did get to Stratford for a short visit just before we sailed for the States.

Back in November, when I had first arrived in England I had gone to see Mr. Payne, who was in his third year as producing director at Stratford. I found him in his London office, for the Stratford season doesn't start until Shakespeare's birthday on the twenty-third of April. In the course of our visit, he said,

"Angus, you have had more success with your Elizabethan venture than I have."

In answer to my look of astonishment, he went on,

"In my first years here, they allowed me to do some of my productions in the Elizabethan manner. This year they are not allowing me to do any in that manner."

Mr. Payne's fight to be free from the artistic meddling of the Stratford Board of Directors, while it benefited him little, has resulted in freedom for every artistic head of the Stratford Theatre since that time.

In April our stay in Stratford was cut much too short because of our sailing date. But we did have time to wander through the streets from the birthplace to find a stile and a path across the fields to Shottery. There was a special kind of excitement in treading the path that the young Will must have taken so many times on his visits to Anne Hathaway's cottage.

We also saw an unforgettable production of *King Lear*, directed by Komisarjevsky. The two productions of this play I have directed for the Oregon Shakespearean Festival have been strongly influenced by this production—influenced, I might add, both in their divergences from, as well as their similarities to, that production.

I suppose our eagerness to get back to Ashland started after we had to hurry to the ship from Stratford. Had we known the nature of the blow we were to receive on our return, our eagerness might have taken a different turn. The trip back to the United States was rough and rather dreary. We stopped a short time in New York before busing to Detroit to pick up our new car. Our itinerary then took us to Washington, D. C. for our first visit there, then to Fayetteville for a visit with Keith, and to The Hermitage in Tennessee to pay our respects to Andy Jackson. Only two other memories remain of that seemingly endless flight toward home, an interesting production of Capek's *The Insect Comedy* at the Dallas Little Theatre and the thrilling view of the Grand Canyon at sunset.

We arrived home about the first week in June, and almost my first act was to make a trip to the business office at the Normal School. There I made a heart-sickening discovery, a discovery that was to result in the most important single administrative decision ever made in the history of the Festival.

IX

Re-Orchestration

T HE FIRST THING I learned upon returning to the campus was
that Southern Oregon Normal School had suffered a bad football season and as a result the Festival's money was gone. True,
it was a ridiculously small amount, but we had worked hard for it and
had been promised that it would be "earmarked" for our use. You can
imagine my depression. I could see an endless succession of seasons
stretching into the future, seasons in which the Festival would continue
to exist only for the purpose of providing money to needy boxing
matches, football seasons or other athletic events.

It was obvious that if Ashland was to become "the Salzburg of the
West" the Festival must have control over its own finances. It was
clear, however, that if we expected to keep any possible profits, we
must be prepared to cover any possible deficits.

However, by a bit of judicious inquiry, I discovered that the Festival's local credit rating was very good. Because of our two successful
years, there was a group of key merchants who would extend credit for
long enough to see us through the season. With this assurance in mind
I summoned up enough courage to form the Oregon Shakespearean
Festival Association and to incorporate it as a non-profit, educational
institution. In accordance with Oregon law there must be three incorporators to initiate the application. They were Miss Frances E. Hardy,
Mr. J.W. McCoy and I. The Hardy family operated two of the larger
stores in town and Frances' uncle had been public spirited enough to
offer us credit for much needed merchandise from his hardware store.
Mr. McCoy was the manager of the First National Bank in Ashland.

There were several features of the organization as defined in those incorporation papers that are worthy of note. First, the membership was composed in effect, of those persons who bought season tickets, and the Board of Directors was to be elected from and by these members. The over-all policies were to be determined by this Board, whose duty was also to appoint the producing director. Thus the theatre organization actually belonged to the audience. It was not, as in the case of many community theatres of the time, organized for the amusement of a few talented stage-struck people.

To balance this audience orientation, I insisted on the insertion of a by-law in those corporation papers which stated that the producing director shall have sole authority on all aesthetic matters, including choice of plays, manner of production, appointment of all production personnel and so on. This separation of duties formed the basis for a group of professionally trained and oriented theatre people to produce plays unhampered by the amateur machinations of the laity. It also was to provide a group of solid citizens to keep the artists' dreams tied to earthy practicality, and to assume responsibility in the eyes of their fellow citizens for the impact of the theatre upon the community. I say that it formed the *basis* for such an organization. This did not happen at once, nor has it always worked more recently, nor was the separation of duties always easy to maintain.

I have had to fight to keep Board members on their own side of the aesthetic fence only a few times, and I have always used the only weapon I had: I put my job on the line. The Board's only way of dictating production methods or personnel choices would have been to hire someone else as producing director. That would have been difficult, for I received no salary during those six years before the war. It is an interesting comment on my relationship with the Festival Association that I have never had a written contract with them in all the 31 years I served as producing director.

The initial bout with the board came that first year of its existence, and on unexpected grounds. Bill Cottrell had graduated from the University of Oregon the previous year and had enrolled at the Cornish School in Seattle. He had persuaded two actors from that very fine theatre department to come to Ashland with him and they were both cast in the current productions: Ted Baughn as Romeo in *Romeo and Juliet*, Lucentio in "Shrew" and Orsino in *Twelfth Night*; Morgan Cook as Tybalt in *Romeo and Juliet*, Tranio in "Shrew" and as Antonio, the sea captain, in *Twelfth Night*. Ruth Aston came to us from

North Carolina in response to our advertisement in *Theatre Arts Magazine.*

Some board members objected to this influx of "outsiders." For, as one member of the board put it, "Don't you know that the only reason people come to the Festival plays is to see their friends on stage?" My answer was that, while many community theatres which undoubtedly gave valuable recreational opportunities operated from that point of view, I was not interested in pursuing such a pattern. If they wanted that kind of theatre, they would have to get another producing director. Fortunately, the subject never came up in a Board meeting again.

Our season was a strong one. The leading characters for *Twelfth Night* were all held over from the previous year, with the exception of Orsino. Ted Baughn's training and experience added strength, as did the previous year's experience of the rest of us. In the tragedy, Kitty Ingle played a surprisingly poignant Juliet and Ted Baughn a romantic and dashing Romeo. There was also a number of new company members who had roots in the Valley but who had been other places and who provided more than we could have expected in the way of experience and sensitivity. There was Johnny Reisacher, a music teacher from Medford; Doreen Leverette, a beautiful girl who was home from college; and Richard Sleight, who had been studying art in San Francisco.

But, even so, the company was not as large as we would have liked it to be. I couldn't find anyone to audition for Escalus, the Prince of Verona, so I read the part until I could find someone. I never did find anyone, so I found myself doubling in the roles of the Prince and Mercutio. I remember having them drag the dying Mercutio out, face down, directly up stage so that I could be unbuttoning my doublet in order to make the complete costume and makeup change for the Prince's entrance to stop the fighting just 70 seconds later.

The relative success of various theatrical seasons, measured in aesthetic terms, is always open to subjective interpretations, but there is little chance of misinterpreting the comparison of box office returns. At the end of the third season, then, it was happily reassuring to note that while the second season had doubled the first year's box office, the third year tripled the second.

That season marked the beginning of the souvenir programs of which I have always been very proud. Dorothy Pruitt edited the first two and Dick Sleight designed the first cover.

The next three years were important ones. The last of the three closed the first phase of the Festival's history, and only a miraculous combination of circumstances kept it from being the end of a good try.

The ad in *Theatre Arts Magazine* kept bringing us new people and the number of local people with serious theatre ambitions continued to increase. Notably among the former was Delmar Solem, who later developed such a fine Theatre Department and Shakespearean Festival at the University of Florida. Among the latter contingent was Melba Day (later Melba Day Sparks) who for a number of years has been one of the top teachers of high school theatre in the state of Oregon.

We broke precedent the fourth year by including four plays in our repertoire. *Twelfth Night* and *The Taming of the Shrew* were repeated from the year before, and *The Merchant of Venice* was revived from the first two years. The fourth play was *Hamlet*.

I had studied the play off and on since college days at the University, but in the year since my sabbatical, stimulated by the three great Hamlets I had seen, I poured over the script with a furious concentration. I read every commentary I could get my hands on and promised to forget them all and to approach the script as if I were reading it for the first time.

It was impossible, of course, to rid the production of all the incrustations that had gathered around the script in the three hundred and thirty some years since it had been written. The production did move rapidly. I had only vague and unreliable memories of my playing of the title role. I suspect that it was sentimental, or at least overly romantic. The cast was good. Dorothy Pruitt switched over from Olivia to Ophelia, Bill Cottrell doubled as Polonius and the First Gravedigger. Claudius was played more than satisfactorily by Tom Fairchild from the Cornish School, and an equally effective Gertrude was performed by Grace Forsyth from Washington, D.C. We were fortunate to have Harry Priestly from Cornish to give us expert help with the rapier and dagger and to play Laertes.

Fortunately, the audiences of the time seemed, for the most part, to be happy with the production. Nevertheless, the rate of increase in attendance for the season dropped to only 60% over that of the season before. This in spite of the fact that we were playing four plays instead of three and for eight nights instead of six. This was disturbing, for we were far from the level of attendance which I knew would be necessary to assure the permanency we had all dreamed of.

We hoped to bolster attendance the next season by adding two new productions to the repertoire. We revived the two most popular plays from the year before: "Shrew" and *Hamlet*. To them we added *As You Like It* and *The Comedy of Errors*. In spite of this device there was no increase over the year before. But I am getting ahead of my story.

This was 1939, the year the World's Fair opened on Treasure Island in San Francisco Bay. Everyone knew there would be an unusually large number of tourists on all the roads that led to the Bay Area. I was very much excited, therefore, to receive a letter from Gordon Claycomb concerning a possible national publicity campaign for the City of Ashland featuring the Festival and a possible tour of our company to Treasure Island. Gordon had left the field of music and had been employed by one of the major firms that did public relations for the Fair. He outlined a number of proposed plans, including many alternates, that he would engage himself to undertake if the city would hire him as their public relations representative for one year. His fee was one thousand dollars. The Festival did not have that kind of money, but I learned, soon after Gordon's proposal, that the City Council of Ashland had appropriated one thousand dollars for publicity. The City Fathers, like those of all the cities and towns along highways leading to the Fair, hoped to garner some of those millions of tourist dollars that would be spent by people on their way to Treasure Island.

As you can imagine, I went after that thousand dollars. I appeared before the council to present the best case I could manage. I begged, I pleaded, I cajoled. Afterward, when I got over being disappointed, I realized that I had been lucky to come away with the promise of half of the budgeted amount. But five hundred dollars was not enough. Where was I to get the remaining five hundred? The Festival had five hundred dollars in the bank, but that money was sacred. It was the fund that was essential to our independent continuity. As the Festival expanded, that fund must be increased, not diminished.

The more hopeless the financing of Gordon's scheme became, the more essential it seemed to be to the future of the Festival. Not only was it necessary to increase that box office income rapidly, but it was becoming more and more apparent that, if we were to reach our dreamed-of goals, we would eventually have to enlarge our theatre community from that of the Rogue River Valley to include the entire

West Coast. If this were to happen, the kind of exposure that Gordon's proposal provided for was absolutely essential.

To make a long story short, I borrowed five hundred dollars on the two thousand dollar life insurance policy that I had been paying for since my first year of teaching at Oak Harbor. I paid interest on that loan for several years before I eventually got my insurance out of hock.

Gordon did a splendid job for us. One news release, I remember, was a quarter page illustrated article in matrix form ready to cast and print that went to eleven hundred newspapers throughout the nation. The West Coast coverage was far reaching. One double page spread in *Coast Magazine* caused considerable comment. It featured pictures of our actors in Elizabethan costumes on the streets and in the shops of Ashland. I remember one shot of a boy and a girl in high style Renaissance garb sharing a soda at one of the local drug stores. I flinched a bit at some of this hocum, but it did cause a great deal of interest. The costumes, by the way, were not stage costumes, but Elizabethan clothes made for street wear. Forty of our company wore them in San Francisco and on Treasure Island the entire three days we spent at the Fair. Again I'm going too fast.

One of the first proposals that we explored was a plan by means of which the entire Oregon Shakespearean Festival Company would be brought to Treasure Island to play an extensive repertoire in an especially designed Elizabethan theatre. The first step was for me to prepare a budget including capital outlay and weekly expenditures. Again I went to John Conway for help. I can't remember what the budget was, but I do remember that John came up with detailed sketches for an Elizabethan Theatre patterned after the 1600 Fortune. He had prepared them previously, hoping in vain that Glenn Hughes would build an Elizabethan theatre on the University of Washington campus. He gave me permission to trace the sketches, and these tracings not only provided me with concrete material to present as a basis for suggested capital outlay at the Fair, but they also were the designs from which the second Ashland Elizabethan stage was built in 1947.

Gordon had been able to catch the interest of a group of men who wanted to invest in some kind of money making venture at the Fair. The idea of an Elizabethan theatre at a world's fair was not a new nor an untried one. Iden Payne and T.W. Stevens had operated a Globe Theatre company at three World's Fairs, the ones at Chicago and San Diego being particularly successful.

"Happy those early days."

My first production in the
Elizabethan manner was
Merchant of Venice at Southern
Oregon Normal School, in 1934.
Here is my "pretty scroungy"
Shylock in the courtroom scene.
We remounted the production
the next summer for our
long-remembered Independence
Day opening in the old
Chautauqua shell.

Close up of that first Shylock.

Bob Stedman is come to wive it wealthily in Padua as Petruchio in our first production of Taming of the Shrew.

Twelfth Night *played nine times in our first 40 years. Here's my first Festival Sir Toby, circa 1937.*

It's not exactly true to say that the best part of starting your own theatre is being able to cast yourself in all the good roles. Proof: I only played Hamlet twice, in 1938 and 1939.

We pulled out all stops in 1947, our first post war season: Hamlet,
Macbeth, Love's Labour's Lost *and the ubiquitous* Merchant of Venice.
*Trodding the boards is an accurate description: even the facade was still
raw wood. Here I proclaim as Macduff: "Behold, where stands the
usurper's cursed head." I like the "sophisticated" lighting technique:
one hot spot on the inner above.*

*And as Shylock in 1947. It was many seasons before we felt able to
perform without pulling that curtain between the pillars.*

The 1947 Hamlet, Frank Lambrett Smith, taught me, as
Polonius, useful lessons about performing on the
Elizabethan stage: to upstage an actor, move downstage
and talk to the audience.

Each production taught us new uses of the stage. That
ladder leading to the inner above was our 1947 vintage
solution for the love letter scene where the scholars
spy on each other in Love's Labour's Lost.

Othello *entered the repertoire in 1948 and remained through 1949. Also in their first appearances on stage in those years: Richard Graham, James Sandoe, Allen Fletcher, Philip Hanson, Doug Russell, Bill Patton. Dick Graham played Othello in 1949 and I played (or rather, was cast as) Iago . . . in oxfords, apparently. In 1948 we initiated our presentation of the Chronicle plays in historic order. King John came first.*

Rehearsing is hot work, especially in Ashland's midsummer sunlight. This was 1949 and our first Midsummer Night's Dream. *Nicholas Gilroy is Lysander.*

*I played Nick Bottom.
Alta Wilson is
the beautiful Titania.*

*We mounted five
productions in 1949. Bill
Patton played Paris in
Romeo and Juliet that
year. He left the stage in
1954 to become General
Manager of the Festival,
a role he is still
performing. Ralph
Burgess, Jr. was the
Romeo; Mary Jane Pitts,
now the author Mary
Jane Moffat, did Juliet.*

"The glory and the freshness of a dream."

Allen Fletcher played Oliver to Don Gunderson's Orlando in our 1950 As You Like It. *Nicholas Gilroy was Adam. I directed.*

My Justice Silence in Henry IV, Part Two, 1951 *with George Eckstein as Shallow and Morris Winer as Falstaff.*

The 1951 Twelfth Night *had Bill Oyler playing Orsino and Bill Ball as Feste.*

I was present as Toby Belch, with Ann Guilbert as Maria and Brad Curtis as Sir Andrew.

That's Rick Risso as Henry V before
Agincourt; his "band of brothers" include
Doug Russell, Paul Reinhardt,
Pat Hines, Bill Oyler and Bill Ball.
The year is 1952.

Casca in the center of conspirators
including Rick Risso as Metellus Cimber. A
young scholar named Ellie Prosser played
Portia in that production and Beatrice in
the same year's Much Ado About Nothing.

Bill Ball as Mark Antony delivers the
funeral oration for the 1952 Julius Caesar.
Allen Fletcher, a master of the Elizabethan
stage picture, directed the production.

This was the stage as it looked on a rainy day in 1953. You can tell it was raining; the curtains are swung up to the inner above to keep them dry. Those benches were built by members of the Festival Board of Directors. They were not over-comfortable.

Joyce Womack played Portia in 1953; Bill Larsen, Antonio. This was my sixth version of Shylock. George Peppard appeared as Bassanio; Bill Ball was Lorenzo.

Onstage for the 1953 Taming of the Shrew are Rick Risso, Knox Fowler, Bill Ball, Dick Graham, Bill Larsen and Angus in a nightgown. My mother wondered why I played dirty old men like Christopher Sly; my father understood.

Dr. Margery Bailey made a
memorable Volumnia in the 1953
Coriolanus. *She had played the nurse
in the 1949* Romeo and Juliet *and
served as Academic Adviser to us
through those years.*

The first part of Henry VI, *first
staged in 1953, featured Phil
Hanson as Talbot, Bill Ball as Young
John Talbot.*

The 1954
Merry Wives
of Windsor
featured
James Sandoe
*as Nym (with
the nose) and*
Bill Oyler *as*
Pistol. *Young
John Sandoe
is* Robin. *Not
pictured but
present was*
George
Peppard *as*
Slender.

The 1955 production of All's Well That Ends Well *was directed by Robert Loper. Joan Kugell, now Joan Darling, was Helena.*

B. Iden Payne played Friar Laurence in the 1956 Romeo and Juliet *and directed* Cymbeline. *A young Nebraskan named Dick Cavett appeared in that production of* Cymbeline.

As Sir Nathaniel in the 1956 Love's Labour's Lost; *that's Hal Todd as Holofernes.*

Teddy Seymour as Crab my dog stole Two Gentlemen of Verona *right away from two old hands at the game, Launce and Speed. Nagle Jackson in his first year at the Festival played Speed in this 1957 production.*

Speaking of scene stealers, I learned another valuable lesson: this one in public relations, from Sir John Gielgud, in 1957.

Jerry Turner, who succeeded me as Producing Director, first came to the Festival in 1957; he was Gloucester in the 1958 King Lear; Paul Harper was Edgar.

In the late 1950's Richard Hay designed a pavilion which brought the inner above and inner below action closer to the audience. It was used in the 1958 Merchant of Venice: Shylock is about to gouge Jerry Turner's heart out; Harold Gould is Tubal; other participants include Peggy Rubin, Ted Grover and Hugh Evans.

Michael O'Sullivan as Old Gobbo and Nagle Jackson as his son in Merchant of Venice *that year.*

The '58 production of Troilus and Cressida *marked the completion of all 37 of Shakespeare's works. I'm the one in modern dress. A partial roll call of the Greeks and Trojans: George Vafiadis, Bob Loper, Shirley Patton, Peggy Rubin, Nagle Jackson, Jill Sandoe, Michael O'Sullivan, Hugh Evans, Claude Woolman, Richard Graham, Paul Harper.*

The old theatre was torn down in 1958 and replaced in
time for the next season. Here it is coming down.

And the new one going up.

Spit curls and a Roman nose for poor foolish
Lepidus in the 1959 Antony and Cleopatra.

When Gordon invited me to San Francisco to meet with a representative of the potential investors, I was delighted to learn that I was also to meet Mr. Stevens. I had previously known him only by reputation and because of his long association with Mr. Payne. The meeting took place at a dinner in a private dining room at the St. Francis Hotel, and it was one of the most uncomfortable evenings of my life.

If memory serves me correctly there were only five of us present: Mr. and Mrs. Stevens, Gordon and I and, representing the money men, a man by the name of Pincus. Mr. and Mrs. Stevens were a grey-haired, gentle couple—soft spoken and dignified almost to the point of courtliness. Behind the reserve, there was energy and warmth revealed by sensitive and mobile facial expressions which grew bleak, however, before the evening was over. Mr. Pincus was a gross man whose idea of amusing dinner talk was typified by a long story, telling in loud detail of the numerous complications that occurred when he took Mae West on an auto ride at a time when she was suffering from diarrhea.

I never did learn exactly why Mr. Stevens and I were both at that meeting. The idea of competing against this great man was repugnant to me, but as the evening wore on it became increasingly apparent that I was expected to do so. I spoke only when spoken to, and tried to engage in general theatre conversation with the Stevenses. I remember once when they were telling me about one of the talented young actresses in their company who had performed a brilliant Viola, Mr. Pincus interrupted with scorn,

"Huh! *I* saw Modjeska!"

He seemed determined to belittle the grand old man, and I was embarrassed and humiliated to think that they might believe I was a part of these inexplicable crudities. I was glad when the evening was over. I never saw the Stevenses again, and I never saw Mr. Pincus again. Needless to say we never saw the money to build the Fortune Theatre on Treasure Island.

As I have mentioned before, we did, however, spend three days at the Fair as a part of the important publicity campaign organized by Gordon Claycomb. We did a pre-season performance of *The Taming of the Shrew* in Ashland on the Fourth of July. This was a benefit performance to raise money to help defray the cost of the trip south. There was a caravan of 40 or 50 cars which transported the company and a group of interested citizens at no expense to the Festival. We housed the company in a couple of dormitory rooms at the old Franciscan Hotel.

We made quite a splash on the streets of San Francisco in our colorful costumes. San Francisco was a city of elegant, if conservative dressers. Men wore suits and hats, and a chic woman would not consider her street ensemble complete without hat, high-heeled shoes and gloves. We were noticed.

One day was "Ashland Day" at the Fair and Mayor Wiley of our city was mayor of Treasure Island for twenty-four hours. He valued the medal he received in honor of the event, and for the rest of his life never failed to mention the experience whenever we met. We made a number of appearances during the three days. We played some scenes at the Hall of Western States, and I spoke at the Oregon Pavilion. We performed "Shrew" at the Federal Theatre to quite a large crowd. The production went well considering that we had to do it in a space staging style instead of on our Elizabethan stage. I do not remember that any of the major critics reviewed it.

The big event the company had been looking forward to, however, was the coast to coast, live broadcast which was to be aired from the NBC radio studios on Treasure Island. Bill Cottrell had arranged an hour long script of *The Taming of the Shrew* which we had been rehearsing along with our preparations for the Ashland Fourth of July production. In those days, radio was the home entertainment medium in much the same way that television is today. While hundreds of people saw our production of "The Shrew" at the Federal Theatre, literally millions of listeners all over America would hear our production over the National Broadcasting Company network. It was certainly the high point in the entire publicity campaign Gordon Claycomb had arranged for us.

On the day of the broadcast, LaVelle White, who was playing Kate, showed signs of extreme fatigue, and I took her to the Treasure Island infirmary to get a half day of rest. She was feeling much better when I went to get her just after noon, and we walked back to the NBC studios. We timed our walk to get us to the studios about a half hour before the pre-broadcast run-through that NBC required. We found the place in an uproar. Our radio scripts were nowhere to be found! This was a major catastrophe, for we couldn't go on the air without those scripts. The radio adaptation was very different from the stage version because of the cues for on and off mike voicing and sound effects, but especially because of the extensive cutting required for the shorter 58 minute and 30 second script.

You can imagine our panic. Here was our first chance to break into "big time" and we were muffing the opportunity in a stupidly amateurish way—a way which would embarrass our professional colleagues, and close goodness knew what doors to us in the future.

The next half hour was spent in fruitless scurrying around the Fair grounds trying to trace down every idea and clue as to where the bag with the scripts had last been seen, might have been seen, or should have been seen. I did keep members of the company from wasting time and energy in pointing fingers or flinging accusations of irresponsibility. But the hands of the clock swung in their relentless circle, and when it came time for our required run-through we were still without the precious scripts.

I think it was about this stage of the cataclysm that Dorothy Pruitt remembered that there *was* a script in the studio. It was the one that NBC had required us to send in weeks before for their approval. But there was only one. We needed seventeen.

You can imagine that the NBC management were considerably disturbed by the virtual certainty of a malfunction in their traditionally well-oiled machinery. As he brought his copy of our script to us, the man in charge of the operation said with inexplicable calm and with an amazing generosity, that he would forego the required run-through if we could duplicate the script in time to go on the air.

Someone discovered that there were sixteen typists in our company. Sixteen typewriters were found and rushed to the big work room next to the broadcast booth. The one script was divided equally among the typists and immediately the place was reverberating with the rat-a-tat-tat of sixteen sets of typewriter keys, the uneven tingling of sixteen bells as sixteen carriages ended sixteen lines and were swished back with a bang to repeat the process. No one spoke aloud, and the carpeted floor gave no sound as the non-typist members of the company rushed back and forth with sheaves of finished script pages and copy pages taken from the slower typists to give to the faster ones.

At the time I was only dimly aware of all of this as a hysterical cacophony of sound and a chaos of frantically rushing figures. I was in a state of shock, and for the only time in my life truly paralyzed with panic. When someone thrust a handful of papers at me, I shouted for him to take them away. I was simply unable to cope.

This madness was still going on when the top man in the studio came to me looking at his watch. He said, "I have an orchestra standing by in Los Angeles. In just fifteen minutes we go on the air. But I am required to give them ten minutes notice, if they are to go on the network instead of you. This means that in the next five minutes you must tell me whether you are going to make it or not." Then, as I tried to stutter an answer, he continued, "But before you give me an answer, I want to tell you what it means if you say that you are going on and do not make it. It will cost the network $50,000, and, what is more important to me is the fact that I will unquestionably lose my job!"

As it was obvious that the typists were not going to be through in fifteen minutes, I opened my mouth to say, "Of course, in that case. . . ," when Gordon Claycomb, who had arrived earlier, spoke over my shoulder, and said, "Why, of course we will be on the air on time. Don't worry about it!" I was too confused at this point to object to this blatant over-optimism.

But we did start on time, even though the pages of script were still being typed and rushed to the actors through a good portion of the show. The only bobble was that somehow page 17 was missing from all the scripts. Fortunately, the actors involved at that point were able to get through to the next page from memory!

It was fortunate that this cliff-hanger turned out so well for us. We owe a great deal to the NBC official who was so tolerant and who was willing to risk his job in order to give us a chance to air our show. The broadcast was received well, or at least did not get negative comments. The thing that struck the reporters and columnists as being newsworthy was the fact that among a troup of Shakespearean actors, there should be 16 typists. I must say that since 1952 things have gone much more smoothly in our annual NBC broadcasts from our Elizabethan stage under the deceptively quiet direction of NBC producer Andrew C. Love.

All in all, the public relations chore undertaken by Gordon Claycomb was eminently successful. I am sure that the wide exposure to the public of the name and unique nature of the Oregon Shakespearean Festival made it very much more feasible to open the theatre again in 1947 after being dark for six years.

Ironically, all this publicity did not increase the box office at all for the current season of 1939. This was a shock after the explosive expansions in the previous seasons. Our entire budget was still less than two thousand dollars. We could not afford to level off at this amount of income. And I felt in my bones that all evidence pointed to the fact that we would not merely level off but would go down hill. Remember the time. The World War II syndrome was already upon us. In less than three weeks after the close of the season, Britain and France had declared war on Germany. All the world was troubled and preoccupied with the future.

When the Board met, I proposed that we close the Festival until times were more propitious for its growth. My argument was based on my prediction that we would lose money the next season. We had managed to stow away one thousand dollars in the bank; I did not want to see that fund frittered away in the course of a series of unsuccessful seasons.

When the Board did not see things my way and voted to continue in 1940, I submitted a request for a leave of absence. In my letter I stated that I did not want my name associated with the Festival in a season when it lost money. Bill Cottrell was hired to direct the Festival and Lois agreed to stay on as Art Director. I must add here that there had been increasing domestic difficulties in our home, and later on that year Lois went to Hollywood and I stayed on at Southern Oregon Normal School.

The next summer they did a season of comedies, keeping on *As You Like It* and *The Comedy of Errors;* adding *Much Ado About Nothing* and *Merry Wives of Windsor.* You can imagine that I felt at loose ends that summer. I felt a natural reticence about going to rehearsals, and when I did drop around one night to sit in the back of the auditorium, I was told by one of the Board members in no uncertain terms that I was *persona non grata.*

In a kind of desperation, I turned again to playwriting. I wrote two one acts and submitted them to a contest conducted by Dramatists' Alliance at Stanford University. I was surprised and delighted to receive word that one of them, a farce called *Rogue Rest,* had been chosen as one of the ten best and was to be produced during the annual Dramatists Alliance Conference about the middle of August. I therefore decided to fly down to see my play and attend the Alliance Conference at Stanford. It was thus that I met Dr. Margery Bailey, who was to have such an important impact on the Festival.

My first impression of her, however, was by mail, and was typical of the scholarly rambunctiousness with which all of us were to become so very familiar. She sent to me the two critiques which were written by officials of the contest. They were scathing in their denunciation of my play. But along with these documents she sent her own critique in which she denounced their lack of perception and praised the play in language which would have convinced a much less prejudiced person than I. I have known only one other person who could use the English language with the precision of a surgeon's scalpel. That person was one of her former students, James Sandoe.

My first visit to the Stanford campus was also memorable for another reason. It was there that I received word by telegram that a fire had seriously damaged the Festival stage and completely destroyed the wardrobe.

The company finished the season in modern dress and bits and pieces of costume salvaged from the fire. But my prediction came true. Aside from the damage from the fire, the season lost three hundred dollars, leaving only seven hundred in the bank to be put into a war bond for the duration.

The next two years were negligible dramatically, but two events took place which were to have important effects on my life and the future of the Festival. The first was my marriage to Gertrude Butler, who worked in the Clerk's office at the County Court House in Medford. After all these years she is still my memory, my detail man, my secretary, my other self. The other event was my introduction to a mystique I never understood. I went into the Army. I was a Sad Sack.

X

Intermission

I SUPPOSE I WAS NOT, strictly speaking, a Sad Sack, for inside of three months after being poured into the hopper I rated staff sergeant's stripes. But I was never in anyone's wildest imaginings what you might call a soldier's soldier. I could never remember the ritual I was supposed to recite when reporting to an officer, and my uniforms always looked as if they belonged to someone else.

I used to remind myself over and over that I had, for years, professed to be an actor. I knew how to learn lines and wear a costume. "You're playing the role of Soldier Bowmer," I muttered between my teeth. But it was no good. It is a fact that, while it is common practice for an actor to make pretended personal characteristics and situations seem in his own mind to be very much like reality, it was impossible for me to turn reality into a figment of my imagination.

When I became supply sergeant for Third Battalion Headquarters Company of one of the regiments of the 104th Division at Fort Jackson, South Carolina, I was frequently visited in my supply room by inspecting officers. Whenever a commissioned officer entered the room, I was supposed to spring to attention, salute and say, "Staff Sergeant Bowmer, Headquarters Company, Third Battalion, umpty-ump Regiment reporting, sir." You see I still can't remember it all. So rather than stutter and fumble, I would treat him almost exactly as if I were greeting a visiting college president in my office at Southern Oregon.

I would spring to attention and salute. He would invariably say, "At ease," or "As you were." Then I would smile and say, "I'm Staff Sergeant Bowmer, sir. We're very glad to have you here in Third

Battalion Headquarters Company. Won't you sit down. Is there any-thing I can show you?" By this time he would usually be hiding a grin and be shortly on his way out. I suspect that word got around, for I had an unusually large number of such visits, but very few actual inspec-tions. I'm sure they must have ribbed my commanding officer about his unorthodox supply sergeant, for he would come to me after one of these visits and say, "For God's sake, Bowmer, can't you learn to report properly?" But he never did gig me for it; I suspect he needed me badly. The shortage of non-commissioned officer material stood me in good stead.

Before I went with the cadre which formed the 104th Division, I had been with the 80th in Camp Forrest, Tennessee, having been shuttled there directly from the induction center in Fort Lewis, Washington. My draft number had come up a long time before induc-tion, but I had already applied for a commission in the Army Specialists Corps.

A number of my confreres at the Normal had accepted commis-sions in the Navy, but when I applied they wanted only electronics men or math experts. I showed my letter of application for an Army Commission to the Draft board, and they offered to hold up my induc-tion until I heard from it. But weeks went by and still I didn't hear. The uncertainty of not knowing from one day's end till the next what was going to happen finally got to me, and I told the draft board to let me be inducted. About three months after I arrived at Camp Forrest, I re-ceived a letter asking me if I would accept a commission in the Army Specialists Corps. There was a catch to it, however. It was addressed to me as a civilian and had been forwarded from Ashland. I knew better than to go to my company commander, for I knew he would simply throw it in the waste basket.

There was someone at division headquarters, however, with whom I had become acquainted and I thought he would do me a favor. This was Major James Warner Bellah, G2 for the division. I don't know all of the duties of G2, but one of them is to facilitate public relations. I had first met him when Ted Weems came to Camp Forrest and or-ganized talent from all over the division to produce an original review, which was broadcast as one of Weems' radio series called "Cheers from the Camps." I had done several voices in that show, a feat which seemed to impress everybody. Later, when faced with the necessity of broadcasting a show celebrating the 25th anniversary of a famous battle in which the 80th Division had taken part, he wrote a script for the "voice of the old 80th." The show was, of necessity, very sentimental, and he knew he had to have an actor to "sell" it to the listening audience. I had been pleased when he sent for me to voice his script. He had received a special commendation for it and had not hesitated to let me know that I had shared in the responsibility for its success.

He was a man of broad experience, and we had talked at length in the privacy of his barracks room about Shakespeare, fencing, theatre, Europe in pre-war days, and other topics of mutual interest. In later years, I was to enjoy his stories in the *Saturday Evening Post* about the U.S. Cavalry in the pioneer West.

I took my letter to Major Bellah and explained the situation. In about a week I received a carbon copy of a letter from G3 to the Army Specialists Corps saying that I would be discharged from the Army for the purpose of accepting the proffered commission. I waited for a number of weeks without hearing from anybody on the subject. In fact, the only pertinent thing I ever did hear I read with despair in the newspaper headlines: "ARMY SPECIALISTS CORPS DISCONTINUED."

Gertrude made two trips east to visit me. The first trip was at Christmas time when I was in the 80th Division. The night before she arrived I learned that we were to have a change in company commanders. My two weeks leave was cancelled because there had to be a complete inventory of the supply room before the new captain could take over. The second trip was when I was in the 104th Division. This was also unfortunately timed to coincide with our company's week on the rifle range. Fortunately she was able to stay on. The word had come that all of us over 38 were to be released for work in essential industry. My replacement had come and I had accepted a job with Douglas Aircraft in Santa Monica, California. In typical army fashion, however, I had to stay to "train" my replacement even though he was a transfer from the Quartermasters Corps and knew more about supply than I ever could.

Thus it was that Gertrude and I finally found ourselves fighting the war-time transportation battle to get to California. I was naturally glad to get away from the army, but I didn't know for a long time how lucky I had been to escape going overseas with the 104th. In their first night on the front lines they were entirely wiped out, for it was this green outfit that the Germans chose for their main point of penetration in the disastrous Battle of the Bulge. All those men I knew, all those thousands in the division were either killed, wounded or captured in that one battle.

Douglas Aircraft Company had satisfied the Army that I would be employed by them in some capacity when I reached Santa Monica, but there was no indication of what kind of employment would be offered. Therefore, in a kind of grab bag fashion I became a spot welder in that huge Santa Monica Aircraft factory. The job required a minimum of mechanical skill, and I soon felt that I had mastered the essentials. My efficiency improved and each day saw an increase in the amount of work I could turn out to the inspector's satisfaction.

The work I was doing could, however, be done satisfactorily, perhaps more so, by someone without the years of college training that it had been my fortune to have. My long experience in teaching and community work could surely be made to pay off in the war effort. I talked to my leadman about my concern and he made an appointment for me with a member of the Transfer and Placement Department. It was about six weeks after I started to work for Douglas that I became a member on the so-called "graveyard shift" of that same department.

Now here was a job I could become excited about. It was my duty to interview people who wanted to change their jobs, just as I had wanted to change mine. There were several dozen of us in the department, and each midnight when we came to work there were stacks of files on our desks. These were the files containing the past training, experience and recommendations of all those employees we were to interview that night. They had been placed there by the girls of the filing department who had access to the vast files containing the records of all the thousands of employees in that huge factory.

We had only one directive to guide us in our disposition of each applicant. Each decision was to be made with only one objective in mind. Would it result in increasing the number and/or quality of planes manufactured by Douglas? To this I added my own corollary. It was obvious to me that, whether I granted the transfer as requested, whether I modified the proposal to one more nearly suited to the needs of the factory or the skills of the applicant, or whether I refused the transfer entirely, I must do my best to send the employee back to work with a positive attitude that would result in his using his abilities in a way that would help us win the war. Helping people solve their problems, and doing so in a way that would satisfy them as well as increaseing the output of planes was a challenge that made my job exciting and fulfilling.

Of all the hundreds of people I interviewed during my stay at Douglas, I remember two women most vividly. One, I must admit, was one of my notable failures. The other I list as my greatest success. The first one was a black girl with a master's degree in psychology who worked as a riveter in the plant. She came to me not once, but many times. Her request was always the same. She wanted to be transferred to Inspection. The inspection department was a large and important one. Before a unit of work could leave any department, whether it be spot welding, riveting, assembly, wiring or whatever, it had to receive the okay of an inspector. This was the only way to maintain quality control. This girl had the intelligence, the experience and maturity to be an excellent inspector. This made my decision all the more agonizing, for I knew that there were many men in many departments who would not remain in a situation where their work could be evaluated by a black person. As competent as she would have been, production would have been hindered by her transfer. It was unfair to her, it was wrong, it was humiliating for both of us, but I had no choice. We talked long at each of her interviews, and I think she respected me for my honesty, as I respected her for her intelligence and courage. She knew I was in a dilemma and she pressed me hard. We talked about the whole situation of the black in America. I remember that when I bolstered my argument that the situation for the blacks was improving, by citing the successes of "Rochester," Bill Robinson, Step'n Fetchit, she dismissed them contemptuously with the one word, "Clowns."

The second woman came to me after I had been assigned to the "Hot Spot." This was a little cubicle of an office which hung from the ceiling way out in the working part of the plant. There were no files. Nothing but a desk and a telephone. This office was set up to take care of emergency transfers. A typical example of the sort of situation I had to deal with occurred the first night I presided over the Hot Spot. Two men in one of the departments got into a fist fight. The lead man called me and told me that one of them was on his way to my office. It was up to me to find a spot for him in another department. You can imagine the state of mind he was in when he reached me. It was up to me to calm him down from his wildly belligerent mood, find a place for him and send him to his new assignment in a mood to work. I was tremendously stimulated by the challenge of this new job. I had always heard the phrase, "living by one's wits" applied to confidence men and tricksters, but I know that in this case it could be descriptive of honest labor as well. I have never learned so much in such a short time about the causes and effects of human action.

The transfer of which I have always been proud, came about when a lead man called me in an obvious spate of bad temper. He said, "I'm sending up a stupid old bitch, and I don't care what you do with her as long as you get her out of my hair."

"What's her problem?" I asked.

"She's dumb. She can't follow directions. I don't see how you can get anybody to take her. Good luck. Just don't let her come back here again."

When she arrived she was terribly upset, in tears and embarrassed because of her tears. I had wangled a workable electric percolator and kept it fired up for just such occasions. So while we drank our coffee she had a chance to regain her sense of dignity. We talked about the war news, and I gradually began to inquire into her background. I was puzzled, because I couldn't square my impression of her with the lead man's description. But at last I thought I saw where the trouble was. I detected in her voice and speech the soft monotonous quality I have often noted in deaf persons. Then, although she had arranged her hair in an effort to hide it, I noted a deep scar on the side of her head.

The conversation gradually led around to her problem and she told me that she had been kicked in the head by a horse many years ago. This accident led to her being completely deaf. She was an excellent lip reader, but in the factory it was frequently impossible to stay in a position to see the lead man's lips. She was extremely sensitive about her affliction and this led to her being dismissed. I knew that the lead man in the spot welding department was the son of parents who were completely deaf and dumb. He knew the sign language to communicate with such people, and, as a matter of fact, had several deaf people in his department by choice. I called him and he was only too glad to accept my gal. I saw her frequently after that at lunch breaks and on the way to or from work. She always lit up like a pinball machine whenever she saw me, and the rest of my day would seem brighter in consequence.

Several months after I started working in the Transfer and Placement department there was a sudden drop in the number of applicants for transfer. By this time I was back in the main office, and the entire staff was disturbed by the lack of business in our bailiwick. For months we had been interviewing twelve or fifteen people a night. Suddenly that number dropped to ten, then to half a dozen, and then we were fortunate to find two or three folders on our desks when we came in.

At first we were afraid of losing our jobs. Then it became apparent that the executives were not about to deplete their department for fear of decreasing their own importance to Douglas. The scuttlebutt was that the company had gone off "cost plus" and had stopped hiring new people. This certainly seemed to be the case, and almost everyone suddenly became contented to stay in his own department.

I would have preferred to leave but I could not. I had the choice of staying on or going back to the Army. I had no desire to re-enter the Army and I suspect the Army had no particular need for me.

From a fascinating, worthwhile occupation, my job became a boring, worthless dodge of trying to appear busy. From midnight to seven in the morning is a miserable time to play this kind of futile game. But there were compensations.

Gertrude and I lived with her parents in a little old Spanish style house in the Toluca Lake district, just across Cahuenga Pass from Hollywood. It was a white stucco with red tiled roof and sported a round tower which served as an entry way. Gertrude's uncle had bought it for us to rent, thus solving an otherwise impossible housing situation. Fred and Mame Slagle had no children and Gertrude was like one of their own. Fred owned and operated a deluxe market in Toluca Lake which was in the center of one of the movie colonies which surround Hollywood. Our home was located strategically a few blocks from the market, and excitingly around the corner from Bob Hope's home. Bing Crosby lived farther out in the Valley, but his father and mother were situated in the immediate neighborhood and were close friends with the Slagles. Faces familiar to movie goers were frequently seen in the market. Agnes Moorhead was a steady customer.

Through Aunt Mame's warm friendship with Mrs. Crosby, that marvelous matriarch of the Crosby clan, we were able to get acquainted with her and Bing's delightful, soft spoken, easygoing father. As a result I was able over the years to visit with Bing several times at his home and at work on the movie set.

Mrs. Crosby was an avid and knowledgeable horse racing fan with constant and phenomenal success at the two dallar window. More than once we sat in the Crosby box at Santa Anita, and once Gertrude accompanied Mrs. Crosby to the winner's ring at Del Mar to help her place the floral horseshoe around one of Bing's winning steeds.

Bob Crosby called Gertrude's aunt, "Picnic Mamie" because of her penchant for organizing family outdoor affairs, and when the Slagles celebrated their Golden Wedding Anniversary, he and the Bob Cats cut a special record as a present for them.

All the Crosby offspring had deep love and respect for their mother, but that had never included birthday celebrations. She explained that this stemmed from the days when they had so little that not anything extra could be afforded, not even for birthdays. It was with a sense of giving an appropriate gift to someone who has everything that Gertrude organized Mrs. Crosby's first birthday party and baked her first birthday cake.

I have always had a great admiration for Bing as one of the great artists in motion pictures, and it was pleasant to find that my admiration was enhanced rather than diminished by personal contact. The calm relaxation which had become a trade mark of his work on the screen is a personal resource as well as an artistic one. We observed this characteristic a number of years later when we were able to watch him do the same scene over and over again the morning we spent on the set for "Here Comes the Groom." His mother told us that when there is trouble on the set, Bing just walks away until things are put right. I have tried for years to develop this trait of not getting "up tight," but it is only recently that I have been rewarded with any success.

Another side of the man who is Bing Crosby was revealed to me one Christmas vacation when his mother took us to visit with Bing's wife, Dixie, and to see their Christmas tree. Bing was on the golf course but arrived after a while, greeted us briefly and then set about some duties before sitting down to visit. He first went upstairs to check on the twin who had flunked a course at Washington State, and was spending his vacation being tutored. He then returned a call from Gary who was also having scholastic difficulties at Stanford. Gary was apparently calling to beg for the use of his car which had been confiscated by Bing until Gary's grades came up. I heard Bing say, "Gary, if she loves you, she'll go with you on the bus." Gary didn't get the car.

We had seen the gorgeous Christmas tree and the astounding pyramid of presents that almost filled an entire room, but my eye had immediately been fixed on a beautifully illustrated edition of Shakespeare's *The Tempest* which someone had given Bing. I must admit that it seemed a strange gift to give him, and I thought that perhaps he had not even noted it among all the roomful of riches. Thank goodness my smugness was exposed only to me when I asked him about the gift. He knew a great deal about the edition and the Italian illustrator who is famous in this country for his illustrations of children's books and for his opera sets for the Met. And as if that were not enough, he carried his end of a discussion of the nature of *The Tempest*, its interpretations and the problems inherent in its production.

But again I am getting ahead of my story. I must take you back to wartime Hollywood and my deadly charade each night from midnight till seven in the morning. As boring as those graveyard sessions were, they gave me the freedom to explore Hollywood in the daytime. One of the dividends of this freedom was a chance to act. I joined a company that was playing in a little converted church on Melrose just off Santa Monica Boulevard. This location was ideal for I could go to the theatre at seven o'clock, play the show and drive the rest of the distance to Douglas in time to check in at midnight. I played various supporting and bit parts there in several shows over a period of months.

There was a circumstance concerning stage names that existed while I was at the Melrose theatre that I think is worth recording. I was doubling in one of the productions and used different stage names for the two parts. For one I chose the name of my uncle by marriage, Angus McGinnis, who was my namesake. There were two consequences. The first was that I got two separate mentions in one reviewer's critique of the play. His comments on what he took to be two actors I have forgotten except that they were diverse. He praised the actor Angus McGinnis and damned the actor Bert Livingston.

Because of food rationing, the restaurants were always crowded, and reservations were a necessity. But after having made a reservation, the girl at the restaurant would peruse her list and say, "I'm sorry, Mr. Bemure, but we don't seem to have your reservation," or "No, Mr. Bowerman," or "No, Mr. Bowhunk," or something equally aggravating. One day Gertrude suggested that I use my successful stage name. The result was miraculous. It was an immediate success in obtaining reservations. We were forever after greeted with "Yes, Mr. McGinnis, come right in," or "Yes, Mr. McGinnis, we have been expecting you." I still am Angus McGinnis whenever I make reservations where I am not known.

During all this time, I was able to spend an hour or so each day prowling around Hollywood, looking up agents' offices, being insulted by their office girls, and otherwise experiencing the seamy side of the motion picture capital of the world. By unlucky coincidence one day, while on a search for another address, I came upon an institution called "Stage Nine." It was a private school for the training of young hope-

fuls for television, which was supposed to be the coming thing. I
suppose there were not more than a couple of hundred TV sets in all of
greater Los Angeles, but each week there was a half hour play by
people from this institution experimentally broadcast by the Don Lee
Television station high on the Hollywood Hills. I decided to prepare an
audition for them. It was unfortunate indeed that I could not foresee
that this decision was to result in the near ending of my acting career
and the permanent crippling of that part of my theatre work.

I was accepted into their professional stock company, which, with
the addition of a movie star, performed the weekly television play. My
first casting needs a bit of explanation. The original script was a war
story and opened with a prologue showing first a shot of a hospital
exterior. This was a miniature, set on a trap door. A convoy of miniature ammunition trucks went by and was bombed by a miniature plane
which flew in on a wire. The whole Hospital appeared to go up in
smoke. Under cover of the smoke, the trap (hospital and all) was lifted
and out of the smoke and from the trap arose the god Mars, seeming to
fill the entire sky. It was my full and evil belly laugh and not my
physique which earned for me my first and fatal television casting.

I was given a couple of paragraphs of prologue to learn, and I have
always thought that it must have been the excruciatingly bad script
that led to my downfall. Dress rehearsal came and I crouched down
under my trap door. On cue, I came up with my impressive belly
laugh. Then—nothing. The lens of the camera looked to me as if it
were photographing my tonsils. The director was waving his hands
back of the camera; Ona Munson, the star, was sitting so close that I
could see my reflection in her glasses. I was literally paralyzed. I had
never before realized the privacy one enjoys when playing on a stage.

The director laughed, and said not to worry, that we would do it
again. "Ad lib," he said, "Ad lib." I retreated to my lair under the trap
door and the same scene was repeated, and again, and again. To make a
short story even shorter, I walked out of Stage Nine forever, without
once saying those awful lines.

To pile horror upon horror, the same thing happened to me that
night at the Melrose Theatre, and has happened spasmodically thereafter throughout the rest of my acting career. One of the chief reasons
why I will never act again is because I must avoid the anxiety produced
by the possibility of one of those amnesia attacks.

Meanwhile the boredom caused by the lack of activity in the
Transfer and Placement Department at Douglas Aircraft was becoming

unbearable. I was very much excited when I was offered a way out. I had written a script for an educational film on *Macbeth*, and for several weeks I spent every spare daytime hour scouring Hollywood for someone who would be interested in filming it for me. I finally found a man who said he was. His place of business was a 16 millimeter motion picture processing laboratory, but he had a partnership in a production studio which was a sort of companion enterprise.

"Sure, I'd like to do this picture," he said. "But right now, I'm stuck for a lab man. Why don't you come and run the lab for me and it won't be long before we'll be in shape to film your script."

I told him about my situation with Douglas, and explained that the only way I could change jobs was to move to a job in an industry classified as "essential," and for which my training and education would be more valuable.

He said, "That's no problem. Motion pictures are classified as 'essential' and I'll put you on as educational advisor in our production unit. Then I can teach you the lab work on the side."

Thus it is recorded in the appropriate tomes in Washington, D.C. that I was permitted to leave the manufacturing of aircraft because my education and training made me more suited to be educational advisor for George Spelvin Pictures.

I suppose that it is not necessary for me to say that my script never got filmed, and I spent all my time in the dark developing and printing the 16 mm products of George Spelvin Pictures. But it has always given me a certain sense of distinction to be on record as Educational Advisor for a company which, as I discovered shortly, produced strip tease movies for peek machines and stag parties.

Fortunately, my discharge from the Army came through shortly after this time, and I prepared the application for my old job at Southern Oregon. My very dear friend, Tom Dabagh, called me when he heard that I was leaving and begged me to stay on in Hollywood. Tom was a little guy of Armenian extraction who was head librarian for the Los Angeles County Law Library. I say "little" only in a physical sense, for his heart was ample for two his size. He knew I had made desultory and spasmodic passes at the movie industry, but he protested that my efforts to become a motion picture actor had not been followed through with the proper determination.

What he said was true enough. But my euphoric yearnings had always been vague at the best, and I had been at least partially cured of my sickness by associating for several months with a few of the thousands of star struck young people who constantly believed that their big break would be coming next Tuesday. They never thought of motion pictures as a way to make a living, but always in terms of stardom and millions.

By this time I was eager to get back to Ashland. I told Tom that unless there was someone already inside the industry who wanted me in it, I would never have a ghost of a chance. At that he was very excited. He said, "Look, I have a very good friend who is head of the MGM law department. I'll get in touch with him immediately. Promise me that you won't send in your Ashland application until I call you back."

As a result, on the next Tuesday, I found myself sitting across the desk from Tom's friend with a brief case full of my press clippings, production photographs and a complete resume of my theatrical experience. After a brief talk he said he was going to introduce me to the head of casting for the studio. This was more like it! I was not starting, as was usual, at the bottom, but at the top, where there would be some chance.

His office presented all the space and grandeur one could expect. He was a huge man, heavy of paunch and jowl—type cast for his position. His eyes were judiciously neutral as he stood and offered me his hand over the corner of his desk. After Tom's lawyer friend mendaciously introduced me as "My very good friend," and after a few banal words, I handed over my materials.

After he read my resume, he took off his heavy horn-rimmed glasses, leaned back in his chair and said, "Y' know, young man, you've got two important things in your favor. In the first place, Sid has never asked me this kind of a favor before, and in the second place, anyone who has worked with Iden Payne is good enough for me."

At this point, Ashland was fading away. Those miasmic wisps of fantasy began to shape themselves into the standard celluloid mirage, which in Hollywood was so frequently mistaken for reality and truth.

"So," he went on, "the next thing is for me to set a date for an audition with our studio drama coach." This he proceeded to do, and I met with her on the following Tuesday. In the meantime, Gertrude and I were invited to the Dabagh home for dinner. Our fellow guest was Tom's neighbor, who happened to be the head producer of all "B" pictures for MGM. He invited me to meet him at the studio the next week for a trip around the stages and to meet some of the studio personnel.

The next week when I finished my audition, the drama coach said to me, "You know, I seldom tell anyone what my report on them will say, but I don't mind telling you that I am recommending that you be hired as a member of our studio stock company."

I was delighted and amazed, and I told her so. I thought a motion picture stock company was made up of handsome young leading men and beautiful starlets. "No," she said, "I think you are a very versatile actor and should be of considerable value to the company."

Another week went by before I could get back to the casting office. I was told that my audition was successful, but that there were unfortunately no openings at that time in the stock company. "Of course we never hire directly, but Sid has an agent lined up for you."

The agent was an impressive one who represented some of the top stars in Hollywood. A date was arranged with him on the same day I was taken through the studio by the "B" picture producer. He was dreadfully sorry that his office was such a small one, geared only for the handling of a few top stars. He thought I should get what he called a casting office agent.

The next day I called Sid's office to find out what to do next, but he was on another phone. I called the next day and he was out. The next, he was in conference. I began to get the idea. Every friend had satisfied his friend that he had done all possible for his friend's friend, but somehow when all was over the circle was closed and I was on the outside, with no recollection of anyone saying "No" to me. This is the real Hollywood Magic!

Looking back, I can only feel deeply grateful that, when the winter quarter started, I was back teaching at Southern Oregon. That was January of 1945, two-and-one-half years before the rebirth of the Festival.

XI

Ensemble

I T WAS GOOD TO BE HOME. There was a kind of contentment in it, but no excitement, no fizz. There were just 50 students at the college and more than enough faculty. Theatrical activity seemed to be impractical, but I had bought 16 mm motion picture equipment before I left Hollywood, and I turned out my first and only educational film. This was a 400-foot color sound film entitled "Makeup in the Making." I soon discovered that the machinery for marketing a product is frequently more complicated and remote than the machinery for its manufacture.

Don Darneille, a teacher and administrator of distinction in the Medford school system, was a former student of mine who had acted in many of my productions. He and I started on a series of films to serve as aids in the teaching of grammar. But the marketing difficulties began to become evident about the same time school duties began to catch up with us. Those films are still in the cans.

Of course I had gone down to the old Chautauqua shell to view the ruins of the old stage. It was a depressing sight. Where our Elizabethan stage had stood there was a great gaping hole. The bare circular walls without the stage platform and facade produced a wrenching melancholy as painful as would the sight of the lifeless body of a dear friend.

"Well," I thought, "It was a great idea and a noble experiment." When I walked away, I thought it was forever.

The following January, Walter Redford resigned and Elmo Stevenson became president of Southern Oregon College of Education, as it was now called. I was sorry to see Walter Redford go, for I owed

157

him a lot. He was an easygoing, soft-spoken man, the direct antithesis
of his successor. Elmo Stevenson seemed to be constantly propelled by
a compulsive kind of frenetic energy. He was a fighter and seemed to
require controversy. If controversy did not happen by other means, he
went out of his way to create it. He spent 25 years of his life in
complete dedication to the thesis that Southern Oregon College must
become the biggest, most successful institution in the State of Oregon.
When he called it "the Little Harvard of the West" he was not joking.

The post war education boom as well as the new President's driving promotion resulted in tremendous and immediate increase in the
size of the student body. In the next year-and-a-half I produced four
plays at the College including one each by O'Neill, Coward and
Shakespeare. The Shakespeare was an off-beat, lab production of *Macbeth*. For obvious reasons we were back to modern dress. The most
memorable feature of the production was the music, composed by a
very gifted, odd-ball student. I remember one number was entitled
"Fugue for Strings and Bagpipe."

Those two-and-a-half years between my return to Ashland and
the rebirth of the Festival seem in retrospect to have been a kind of
limbo. My professional life was not dull, but neither was it particularly
exciting. I suppose my own activities lacked direction. I was treading
water. It is possible that I could have spent the rest of my life in this
contented cow existence had it not been for a conversation with Bill
Healey, the secretary of the Ashland Chamber of Commerce. Bill asked
me if I would be willing to start the Festival again.

Bill Healey was an unusual, active, perceptive and considerably
more progressive secretary than the Ashland Chamber had been used
to. His policies and tactics were so aggressive, in fact, that he made
enemies as well as friends for the Chamber. However, I have always
credited Bill for having sparked the fortunate move to start the Festival
again. What I did not know until recently was that he was pushed!
Well, prompted at least.

Robert Dodge had been a member of the Festival Board all during
the pre-war years since the forming of the Festival Association. Bob
and his wife, Rae, had invited Bill and Mary Healey to their summer
cottage at Lake of the Woods for a weekend. Bob came from a family which, for several generations, had been sired by successful and
public-spirited businessmen. Bob tells me that his grandfather was instrumental in the establishment of Ashland's beautiful Lithia Park.
Bill had, therefore, reason to listen with interest to the history of the

Festival and to the estimates of its potential impact on the community, as related that weekend by Bob, whose business acumen Bill had reason to appreciate.

Thus it came about that the energetic secretary of the Ashland Chamber of Commerce asked me if I would start the Festival again. My answer, I suspect, caught him by surprise. It came readily enough, for there had been a lot of time for me to think about the kind of theatre I had dreamed of for Ashland. In the nine years since the start of the Festival I had learned some lessons concerning the nature of that inseparable married couple: the theatre company and its audience. There were certain firm convictions about what a great community theatre should and should not be that shaped my answer.

Perhaps this is a good place to set them down. The list that follows extends far beyond those precepts which shaped my answer to Bill Healey, and some of them may have been conceived *ex post facto*. In any case, here is the list: what might well be called "The Oregon Shakespearean Festival Manifesto."

First, what it should not be:

1. It should not be a plaything for a group of stage struck youngsters.
2. It should not be an exclusive watering place for the socially ambitious.
3. It should not be a platform for the exploitation of any single political, social, aesthetic or religious thesis.
4. It should not be a theatre in which the talents of any one theatrical artist are exploited to the detriment of either the audience's enjoyment or the playwright's intent.
5. It should not have the clinical aura of academia.
6. It should not be a museum.

Then what it should be:

1. It should be a people's theatre, that is, it should belong to its audience.
2. It should be a theatre operated by professional theatre experts.
3. It should have a clear, thoroughly efficient internal organizational structure.
4. It should be a theatre which presents its audience with a wide variety of theatrical experiences, including those provided by the world's great playwrights of all ages.

5. It should be exciting.
6. It should be unique without being quixotic.
7. It should be solvent.
8. Above all, it should be an instrument of communication utilizing trained artists in a theatrical environment to entertain, and at the same time to make clear to its audience, by means of visual and auditory data, ideas and emotions concerning the interrelationships of Man and Man, Man and his environment and Man and his Gods.

This list is far from exhaustive, but I think it presents the nub of the Oregon Shakespearean Festival idea.

But back again to 1947 when Bill Healey asked me if I would start the Festival again. With a few of the above criteria a bit more firmly in mind than they had been before the war, I answered in the negative.

"No," I said, "but if the people of Ashland want to start it again, I am available—for a price." When pushed for a figure, I said I would produce the Festival for five hundred dollars a year. Later that day, I called him and revised the figure to one thousand dollars a year.

This materialistic answer came, not from a newly developed acquisitiveness, but from a firm conviction that the relationship of the Festival to the community must be changed if it were to be successfully revived. Before the war, there had been a goodly number of wonderful, public-spirited people whose help had been essential to the success of the Festival. But I felt there was a limit to an artistic organization which depended upon the help of the community for its success. The reverse should be true. We theatre people should be essential to the success of the community's artistic project. I was also of the opinion that the people of Ashland must want the Festival very much indeed if it were to survive another try. The money yardstick was a measure we could all understand. If they wanted it a thousand dollars' worth, I thought it was worth a second attempt.

Another reason for asking a stout fee for my services stemmed from an experience that had occurred back in 1937 when we were in the process of incorporating the Festival Association. Of the three incorporators, J. W. McCoy was the only experienced businessman, and we depended on him for guidance. He assured us that we would need the services of a lawyer to draw up the necessary papers and see that the application for incorporation was properly filed.

We were able to interest Frank Van Dyke, a fine young lawyer who had been a member of that service club which sponsored the Fourth of July celebration which made the first Festival season possible. He was an enthusiastic Festival fan and later served on the Board. He is now a public figure well known in the state for his services to Oregon. I remember that it came as quite a shock to me when Mr. McCoy said that Frank's services would cost us $75. The amount of our budget at the moment being exactly zero, it was like asking for an arm or a leg. I must have voiced my shock, for I remember Mr. McCoy saying, "Now we must deal with things of this kind in a business-like way. After all, Frank is a professional man, and should be treated like one!" I had been donating my services to the Festival for two years, and I considered myself just as much a professional in my field as Frank was in his. But that was no time to argue on that point, so I kept my mouth firmly shut. When the Festival was reorganized in 1947, I was determined to be a "professional." I suppose it is true that, in general, people value a great deal those things which cost a great deal, and ascribe a lesser value to the things that cost less.

It was understood clearly that President Stevenson must be persuaded to allow the fee, as my accepting money for producing the Festival might be construed by some to be "moonlighting." Holding two jobs at once, or moonlighting, was a practice understandably forbidden to those on full time contract with the State of Oregon. President Stevenson gave his consent to the fee. Who persuaded him or what arguments they used I have never known. Perhaps someone in the Chamber of Commerce, or more likely, one of those who became a member of the new Oregon Shakespearean Festival Board convinced him that producing four Shakespearean plays was comparable to writing a book or a series of articles. Publishing, in those days, was an essential to promotion in almost any institution of higher education. "Publish or perish" was not an entirely humorous phrase. However, I have always suspected that the president considered my Festival fee as part of my salary when budgeting time came around, for I never did receive as much as the average salary for my rank in the state.

A fine, energetic Board was eventually formed and I was hired as the Producing Director. The President was Robert Dodge, whose inspiration had started the move to reopen the Festival. William Healey, whose enthusiastic enterprise had implemented that project, was Executive Secretary. The Vice-President was Walter Leverette, an entrepreneur who operated a fruit packing plant, a chain of movie houses and various other enterprises. The Treasurer was my good friend Marshall Woodell, the Registrar and Dean of Men at the College. It was his forthright insistence on meticulous accuracy and method in Festival business practices for the next five years that laid the foundation for what has always been, and still is, one of our greatest (and for a community theatre) most unusual assets: fiscal responsibility.

Members of the community, especially the college community, became enthusiastic participants in readying the theatre for occupancy. The seven hundred dollars obtained from cashing our war bond would not have finished the job had it not been for the help of those people and that of Mike Biegel and his city crews and equipment. In fact, the community part of the entreprise was, that first postwar season, much more successful than the "professional" aspects which I had been so adamant about. The performances were bad, and some of them excruciatingly so.

Something of the nature of the community spirit that pervaded the preparations for the season are illustrated by a story that Marshall Woodell tells. One night during a rehearsal he was busy at some task, now long forgotten, which required him to be on a ladder in the amphitheatre. He felt a tug on his trouser cuff, and a man he did not know spoke up to him,

"Hey, what organization do you belong to?"

"What?"

"You gettin' overtime for this?"

"Oh," said Marshall, "You mean do I belong to a union? No, I'm the Dean of Men out at the College. You see that man working on the spot light? That's Professor Elliott MacCracken, the head of the Science Department. That man with the hammer is Otto Wilda of our Art Department. The young man digging that hole is Edmund Dews, a Rhodes Scholar, and the man studying his lines over there is Elmo Stevenson, the President of the College."

"Oh," said the man, rubbing his chin, "I didn't know it was anything like that. Hey, have you got your plumbing in yet?"

"No, I don't believe we have."

"Say, my name is John Mills. I'm a plumber. If you get somebody to donate the fixtures, I'll put in your plumbing for you."

I remember my grandmother used to say that if you wanted to make someone your friend you should get him to do something for you, then make sure that he knew how important his contribution had been. This basic principle of public relations was proved a valid one again and again that year. Help came from the most unexpected sources, and many of the people who were active that year became lifelong friends of the Festival.

One of the ways community people were encouraged to take an interest in the Festival was the open rehearsal policy which continues in modified form down to the present day. This unique practice developed quite naturally because people of all ages and shapes and sizes dropped in from the neighboring park or the downtown streets to satisfy a quite natural curiosity as to what all the strange antics and all the loud noises were about. At first they were not shooed out because we were too busy to bother with manning the gates. Then we began to realize that any interest in the Festival was too valuable a potential to overlook. From then on, all comers were encouraged, as long as they didn't make noise enough to disturb the rehearsal. Even dress rehearsals were open in those days. This practice involved a calculated loss. There were many who came to dress rehearsal instead of paying admission to a performance, but over some protest, I insisted that the policy would pay off in the long run. I believe it has done so.

It was after one of those open dress rehearsals or possibly after the opening night that 1947 season that I received a telephone call from a man who identified himself as Jim Allen. He said that the evening before, he and his wife, Eve, had noticed a pile of dirt left over from the excavation of the prompt box pit. I started to apologize for the unsightliness and for the inconvenience to the patrons sitting in the front row. It turned out, however, that Jim had called not to complain, but to offer help. "I wonder," he said, "whether or not you would mind if my wife and I brought in a trailer and some tools to remove that dirt." The fact that he lived 25 miles or so out on the Rogue River amazed me, but didn't seem to bother him. The removal of that refuse was the beginning of a project that lasted a long, long time. It was many years before we could afford to hire a gardener, but until that time Jim and Eve Allen came all the way from their Rogue River ranch many times a season to make flower beds, plant shrubs and bright flowers, to weed, cultivate, mow and otherwise to help us create a beautiful place for our customers to come and enjoy Shakespeare. Jim also served for many years (longer than anyone else) on the Board of Directors, and I am proud to count both Jim and Eve in the circle of my valued personal friends.

As the Festival has grown in succeeding years, our need for community support has expanded greatly. Today, aside from the many unallied volunteers, there are five organizations without whose assistance the Festival would not be able to function. Three of these are community service organizations whose principal project each year is to function in a special and individual way to serve the Festival.

Job's Daughters and DeMolay furnish most of our ushers and the Guardians of the Job's Daughters, assisted in recent years by other community volunteers, do the ticket taking. Soroptimist International, an organization of business and professional women, operates a pillow and blanket concession in one of the booths at the rear of the auditorium, proceeds from which help to swell our scholarship funds. Beta Sigma Phi, a social and cultural sorority, operates a refreshment booth and donates all its proceeds to the company scholarship fund.

In the earliest days the problems of house management were not urgent enough to require more than casual attention. But when on some nights there were large crowds in attendance, someone had to look after the occasional emergency, straighten out ticket problems, answer questions, supervise the ushers, coordinate the closing of the booths and the program of the strolling singers, and in general see that the audience was properly guided from the carnival atmosphere of the Tudor Fair into the opening of the evening's stage performance.

For many years this chore was done almost entirely by two very able men, Rudolf Vest and Ralph McCulloch. They were occasionally helped by other members of the Board. Dr. B.A. Cope, William Moffat and Philip Gates are those whom I happen to recall from the early transitional days.

Today that small number has expanded to 70 house managers. They have a smooth-running organization called, appropriately enough, the "Red Coats" because of the bright jackets they wear to make them easily identified in the crowds. This enthusiastic group has a decided public relations slant to their thinking and before long we shall hear more from them confirming their strong link between the public and the Festival.

The Tudor Guild was organized by community people for the sole purpose of helping the Festival. One of the requirements of membership, when this non-profit organization was incorporated in 1952, was membership in the Oregon Shakespearean Festival Association. Their activities on behalf of the Festival are numerous and varied. They operate the souvenir booth at the back of the Festival dancing green, as well as operating a mail order souvenir business throughout the year for Festival customers. Other money raising activities have been book fairs, style shows, rummage sales and special motion picture showings. They finance a number of company scholarships each year and a non-interest emergency loan fund for Festival Company members. Their housing committee helps the company fight the increasingly difficult problems of finding places to live. Several company parties are hosted each year by the organization. In addition to the $7,000 in scholarships they presently give each year, they have established a plan for three perpetual scholarships: one in honor of Dr. Bailey, the founder of Tudor Guild; one in honor of Margaret Schuler, co-founder of the Guild; and the third honoring Gertrude Bowmer, an honorary member of the Guild, my wife and secretary.

As you can see, it has taken literally hundreds of people working long hours over many years to keep this organization operating. At the risk of offending the worthy people I fail to mention, I would like to pay special tribute to all the members of this grand tribe, but especially to several whom I recall whose contributions have gone on year after year since long ago: Maggie Skerry, Frank Davis, Elsie Butler, Ruth King, Allan Harris, Lou Myers, Shirley Gates, Ella Hendrixson. . . my memory and lack of space, not the number of devoted, stop me.

But back in 1947 in spite of all the help and the combined efforts of company and community people, the theatre plant was a very crude instrument that first year of the revival.

The plumbing backstage didn't get done until the following year, for there was no roof over the backstage area. The only toilet for the cast *and* the audience was located in the nearby YMCA building. In other respects as well, our physical plant was very crude. I remember that the facade was not painted at all that first year, although, I must admit, the raw lumber under stage lights was not entirely displeasing. It was second-hand stuff scrounged from the dismantling of the war-time Camp White, 20 miles away. The uneven weathering of the old boards shaded from various yellow ochre tones toward burnt sienna in the dark corners and cracks.

I wish I could speak as well for the performances. The people of the Rogue River Valley were the real heroes of that season, first as technical assistants and then as audience members. Members of those early audiences were genuine Spartans. I marvel, not only at the effort it must have required to maintain interest and attention, but especially at the endurance of the human posteriors flattened for two or two-and-a-half hours on hard wooden benches or awkward and unstable folding chairs. It was not only that we had no intermissions, but also that we did not cut, except in the case of the *Hamlet* script. I was not against cutting per se, but I believed that if every time we discovered a problem, we simply cut that part of the script, we never would learn how to solve those problems which were solvable.

But our real problem was that there had been a break in company continuity. In those seasons before the war, each year those company members who went away to school had brought back their friends with theatre training and experience. That pipeline had been cut. Our series of *Theatre Arts* ads were just beginning to bear fruit when the theatre closed for the duration. I recall only two names on that 1947 season's program that were brought in by the *Theatre Arts* ad: Frank Lambrett-Smith, and Bill Hernon, both from Vancouver, Canada.

My first contact with Frank posed a serious problem. I knew that I needed mature, experienced actors badly. Frank was no youngster and he had just completed a purportedly successful production of *Hamlet* in Vancouver, B.C. He was also bringing with him Bill Hernon, a younger, experienced actor who was a master of sword play. His price for joining our company was, however, a high one. He stipulated that he direct and play the title role in *Hamlet*. As you will remember, I had directed the play and done the prince twice before the war, and needless to say, I wanted desperately to do it again.

For the first time it began to dawn on me that, if I was to become the producer of a fine, mature company, I would eventually have to give up the practice of pre-casting myself in all the choice roles and directing all the plays. And so it came about that Frank Lambrett-Smith and Bill Hernon appeared in town, and I found that our difficulties had just started.

By the time they arrived we were almost ready to start rehearsals. However, they no sooner arrived than they threatened to leave. At that time Canada was allowing so little money to be taken out of the country, they explained, that they could not subsist on the amount they had with them. I was rescued from this dilemma by the offer to board and room these two for the season. The offer came from that wonderful lady who greets the customers at the main gate of the Elizabethan Theatre each season. Rose Robinette is remembered warmly by thousands of Ashland theatre goers, as she has acted as our hostess for over a quarter of a century.

The repertoire that season included, besides *Hamlet*, *Love's Labour's Lost*, *Macbeth* and a revival of *The Merchant of Venice*. The company was extremely young and, for the most part, completely inexperienced. Aside from our two Canadians, as I remember, there were only three older-than-student actors. One of them was President Elmo Stevenson. Yes, I was trying again the technique that had worked so successfully for me before the war. He was naturally a very busy man, and, as I recall, attended very few rehearsals. But his role of the Duke of Venice was a one-scene part and by its nature allowed me to put him in one place and keep him there so he would not have to learn any difficult blocking. He also managed to keep an official looking sheaf of papers in his hand from which he was able to read a good deal of his lines. As an actor he was in the class of my young innocents, but in spite of that he projected a dominant personality, and his lines rang out with clear resonance and authority.

Two other people with some amateur theatre experience and with their college years behind them were the actors who did the Macbeth and his Lady. Ilene Hull, a young Medford housewife, played a more than acceptable Lady Macbeth, which is certainly one of the things about the production which does not make me cringe to remember. Frank Buchter, a Medford accountant, played the Macbeth. His strongly realistic movement, coupled with the tinge of his New York accent, gave a gangland quality to the role which was quite inappropriately appropriate.

Lambrett-Smith did a very original and very funny porter. But the nightmarish quality of my memories of the show are chiefly due to the deplorable fact that I played Macduff! But it was an accident, I swear it was an accident. I could find nobody at the try-outs to read the role, and I read it in the early rehearsals until I could find someone. I never did. I still challenge anyone to show me how to read convincingly those lines of Macduff after his discovery of Duncan's murder:

> O horror, horror, horror! Tongue nor heart
> Cannot conceive nor name thee,

and all the rest of that horror, down to

> Ring the bell.

A good loud bell starting at the beginning of that speech is what I needed.

There were two other young people who turned in better than student performances. One was Jerry McDougal, a young drama teacher from Medford High School. I think of him among the students

because he had acted several substantial roles for me as an undergraduate at the College. He did a very creditable performance as
Berowne and also played Antonio in the "Merchant." We were lucky
to have him. The other youngster was Eddy Barron, a local boy just out
of the Navy. While he had very little formal training at that time, he
possessed the natural clown's ability to charm your critical faculties
into an amiable, comitose state while performing the most outra-
geously idiotic antics. He did manage to do a warm, straight Horatio in
Hamlet, but his Costard in *Love's Labour's Lost* was the best we have
ever had.

Three girls of the company I remember very well because they
stayed on and played with us for several seasons and I have managed to
keep in touch with them. Each has done some interesting and worthwhile theatre since leaving Ashland. They were all, of necessity, cast in
a staggering load of important parts. Ninon King played a witch,
Katherine in *Love's Labour's Lost*, Ophelia and Nerissa. Suzanne
LaMarre was cast as a witch, Rosalind in "Love's Labour's" and Gertrude in *Hamlet*. Trubee Wetterau played the Princess in "Love's
Labour's," Portia in "The Merchant" and the Player Queen in *Hamlet*.
They were wonderfully charming, intelligent girls, but they were in-
credibly naive theatre-wise. I remember, one exhausting day, stopping
a rehearsal of *Love's Labour's Lost* to have a special conference with the
girls in which I tried to explain to them that the words of the play were
not strung together one after another like pretty beads on a string, but
that each word had a specific meaning which, when put together with
other words having their own specific meanings created ideas. That
these specific meanings and ideas had to be thought out ahead of utter-
ance seemed to come to them as a complete surprise.

You can see that I had a challenging coaching job to do aside from
all my producing duties: supervising volunteer box offic workers,
doing public relations chores, coordinating technical with directorial
staff and performing as plant manager. Aside from these duties, I was
directing three plays and playing five roles: Shylock, Boyet, Macduff,
Polonius and the First Gravedigger.

Out of most disasters a soupcon of good may be gleaned. Such was
the case of Frank Lambrett-Smith's production of *Hamlet*. The style
and what you might call "taste" of that production were so far from
what we were trying to do in Ashland, that, for many years after, I
required from each director a prompt book and a written explanation of
what he intended to do with his assigned script; and I required it be in

my hands long before the director arrived in town. To this practice and, more importantly, to the practice of hiring only those directors who were obviously aware of and in sympathy with what we were trying to do, we owe the evolution of what may truly be called "the Ashland style."

I cannot review for you that production of *Hamlet*, but I can set down some typical events and pieces of business that are still revoltingly clear in my memory. Perhaps the least offensive act was the cueing of a tremolando violin which sobbed in the wings through each of his soliloquies. I suppose the most ridiculous thing was having a page enter at the beginning of a scene and place a throw rug on the spot where, soon after, Hamlet carefully threw himself in hygienic agony upon that covered spot of stage floor.

I hesitate to relate this next anecdote for fear you will think my bite is inspired by professional jealousy. But I will tell it anyway for it "toucheth me nearly." Besides, I think it's funny.

Frank's approach to this production was obviously in emulation of some of the worst practitioners of the nineteenth century "star manager" system. It was a frequent practice of some of these old "hams" deliberately to surround themselves with inferior actors so they themselves would seem to shine more brilliantly. But if by chance some actor by the quality of his performance seemed to threaten the star's dominance, there were many professional tricks of the trade designed to nullify the threat and (at no matter what damage to the play) to keep the attention of the audience fixed upon the star. These tricks were known under the generic name of "scene stealing." They were capable of infinite variation, but usually consisted of either one or both of two practices. One was "up-staging." The perpetrator of this little gem moved farther from the footlights than the person speaking to him, who was thus forced to turn his back to the audience. This move "opened up" the up-stager so that he might continue to charm the audience with pliant facial expression and gesture, while at the same time limiting the upstart to what expressiveness he could muster with back and shoulders. I have been told that, when two oldtimers got into an "upstaging duel" they often started a scene at the footlights, upstaged each other at each speech so the scene usually ended with both backed firmly against the upstage wall.

The other and more nefarious trick was to exhibit some bright, shiny or brilliantly colored object at an important moment in the antagonist's speech or business, literally flashing it in the eyes of the audience, thus blunting the victim's performance and, again, keeping the star as the center of attention.

Perhaps I flatter myself to think my Canadian Hamlet considered me a threat to his artistic dominance of the play, but I can see no other reason for his trotting out this hoary old repertoire of tricks only in those scenes in which he and I shared the stage.

It began on opening night in that scene which leaves Polonius alone on the stage after the exit of the King and Queen. Then Hamlet enters carrying a book: "Reading" says the script. So far from my thoughts was any idea of an artistic contest that I was momentarily stunned by the completely new characterization he presented on his entrance. He was, for the first time, playing the "mad" Hamlet for real, with wildly rolling eyes and grimacing face. It took me a moment to realize that also for the first time instead of a book, he was carrying a Shasta daisy whose brilliant golden center and shining white leaves must have measured four inches across. This he waved on a foot-long stem as he crossed the stage.

We had always rehearsed this scene far down on the forestage close to the audience. But this night he reblocked himself and crossed above me to the stage-right pillar, where he sat on the pillar bench. This was a stupid strategem, for Frank obviously didn't know what, by this time, I had learned about some of the essential differences between the old proscenium arch or "picture frame" stage and the open stage of the Elizabethan theatre.

On the proscenium arch stage, the up-stage positions are more forceful than the down-stage positions. The opposite is true of the open stage, for when far down on the forestage one has the audience on three sides so that he may "cheat" by appearing to talk to someone upstage while facing three-quarters of the audience. This was especially true of the scene in which some of the best of Polonius' lines were "asides" given directly to the audience. At first I was satisfied with this advantage of which Mr. Lambrett-Smith was obviously unaware. But when he began to pluck the white petals from the daisy and throw them into the audience it was WAR! I had only a short cross to make so I stood between him and over three-quarters of the house, blocking him and his silly game from their view.

The funny thing about all this is that he never caught on to what I was doing. I could tell that each night after a performance, he expected me to chide him about his behavior, but I never said a word. If he knew what was happening, he was quiet about it.

I must say here that this is the only time in the history of the Festival that such blatantly unprofessional "scene stealing" has taken place. It is rather the practice among our company members to use their experience and abilities to enhance the performance of the less experienced. The young walk-on who has only one line is made to look his best by the help of his more experienced confreres.

In summing up my memories of the 1947 season, I suppose the more encouraging factor was the wide community interest which resulted in a box office twice as large as that of the most prosperous pre-war season. As I have indicated, there were some successful performances, but artistically we were still blindly groping our way toward the goals inspired by Iden Payne back in 1930 at the University of Washington.

Looking back, I can see what an important decision it was for me to take advantage of the G.I. Bill and spend the academic year of 1947-48 at Stanford University. It was that year at Stanford which began to clear the path leading the Oregon Shakespearean Festival to its present ongoing position as one of the nation's top cultural institutions, widely respected for its integrity and worth.

XII

Etude

ONE OF THE MANY fortunate circumstances at Stanford was the presence of Virginia Opsvig as head of the costume staff. She had been John Conway's assistant at the University of Washington that summer when Iden Payne introduced me to Shakespeare on the Elizabethan stage. She also played Katherine in the *Love's Labour's Lost* production in which I played Boyet. I had taken a class in puppetry and mask making from her and had found her a tremendously stimulating and creative teacher. We had not kept track of each other, so I was surprised and very pleased to learn she had married John Kerr, an old friend of mine who had played Posthumus and Berowne for Mr. Payne in those two 1930 productions. Even earlier, John and I had been in the cast of *Miss Lulu Bett* directed by Victor Hoppe at Bellingham Normal. Now Virginia commuted to Stanford from San Jose, where John was teaching at the state college.

I have spoken before about the important part "accident," "coincidence," or, if you will, "fate" has played in the development of the Oregon Shakespearean Festival. This recrossing of paths was part of a pattern I remember with something like awe. Among all the universities in the country, I chose to go to Stanford because back in 1940 I had written a play which had been produced there, thus leading me to become acquainted with Dr. Margery Bailey. My own pleasure at renewing the friendship with John and Virginia Kerr was personally gratifying, but the impact of the coincidental presence at Stanford of Virginia and me in a teacher-student relationship had far-reaching consequences for the Festival.

The fact that "Miss O," as Virginia's students called her, had worked in costumes under John Conway and in the Elizabethan productions of Mr. Payne made her particularly understanding about what we were trying to do at the Festival in Ashland.

The previous summer, trying to put together the elements that had made our pre-war productions successful, we had not been able to provide a costume department. The rag, tag and bobtail effect of the rented costumes did nothing to enhance our product. Therefore, it was an important part of the miracle when I discovered Douglas Russell among Miss O's undergraduate students, and persuaded him to come to Ashland as our costumer and costume designer. If you will remember that Lois Muzzall Bowmer, our pre-war costumer, had trained under John Conway, you can see how it was possible for Douglas Russell, trained under Miss O, to pick up an artistic direction which he carried on from where we left off in 1940. Carried on, in fact, for thirteen seasons, growing each season, increasing his knowledge and refining his techniques. He spent his winters as a student at Stanford and Yale and then as a teacher and designer at Carnegie Tech, Florida State and the University of Kansas City. For many years now he has been on the Stanford faculty, has trained many of our costume people, including Jean Schultz Davidson, who has been in the Festival Costume Department for 10 years, five of them as costume designer. His recently published book, *Stage Costume Design, Theory, Technique and Style* is an important addition to the literature on the subject.

As you can imagine, I squeezed in as many courses under Miss O as the law would allow. In an effort to relieve the pressure on Doug in his first year (and also to increase my understanding of staff problems) I designed the costumes for the 1948 Festival production of *Love's Labour's Lost*. These designs were submitted to Miss O as a project in one of her classes.

One of the pleasures of being a college student again was that of being able to act without carrying the additional responsibilities of directing and producing. It had been over 16 years since I had last had that opportunity when I played Aubrey Piper in *The Show-Off* under the direction of Mrs. James at the University of Washington. That year at Stanford I was cast in three productions. One was a thesis production in the Little Theatre. I played Esdras in Maxwell Anderson's *Winterset* under the capable direction of the affable Betty McGee. The other two were major productions in Memorial Auditorium. In one of these I got off to a bad start with Professor F. Cowles Strickland who asked me if I would like to play Ragueneau in *Cyrano de Bergerac*. I said I would but that I was still in rehearsal for *Winterset*. He replied that we could work around conflicts and that it would be understood that I would be a few minutes late for his rehearsal that night. Consequently, when I made my way from the Little Theatre that evening, I found the cast of Cyrano already assembled in the huge Memorial Auditorium. As I opened the proscenium door I was transfixed like a bug on a pin by hearing my name. "Mr. Bowmer," said Strick as I was further impaled by the eyes of all that cast who were gathered in the front rows of the auditorium. "Mr. Bowmer," he repeated when he was sure he had their attention, "If you will remember, I said that I *might* cast you as Ragueneau, not that I would cast you. Now come and take a seat, please." How many times have I imagined an appropriate reply: "And, if you will remember, I said that I *might* be interested in taking the role," or, "Thank you very much, that's all I needed to know" or sometimes simply, "Go to Hell." And in all these daydreams my stinging reply was always punctuated by my abrupt but dignified exit. However, none of these things happened. I just meekly closed my sagging jaw and sat down. . .and eventually enjoyed playing the role. I do not know to this day what triggered that humiliating scene. Later, over the years, Strick and I became very good friends, and I always meant to ask him about it. But now it's too late. He was a good director. I learned to admire his professional background and his no-nonsense approach to theatre. My life is richer for having known him.

Roy Pool, who was playing Cyrano, spoke to me one day about the difficulty he was having with the flamboyant style that seemed to be demanded by the play. I told him about the approach used by my grandmother in developing gestures in the grand manner. "In moving the arm, the gesture starts with the intake of breath at the diaphragm, the impulse moves to the arm where the elbow leads the wrist trailed by the fingers." Almost immediately Roy began to loosen up and to move easily in the larger-than-life style demanded by the play and by the huge Memorial Auditorium. Strick said nothing to me about this until seven years later, when I was again spending my sabbatical leave at Stanford. He was again doing Cyrano, and he asked me to coach the young man who was playing the role. It was then that he thanked me for being so much help to Roy.

The first play in which I participated that year at Stanford was *Richard III* under the frenetic direction of a visiting faculty member, Nicholas Vardac. Roy Pool played the title role and I played two small parts, doubling as Ratcliff and The First Murderer. I'll never forget the unhappy experience of Asher Wilson in that hectic show, and how my own fate and his were intertwined in a melange of director Vardac's unpredictable cuts and revisions. Asher has long been one of my confreres in Oregon and is now the head of the Theatre Department of Portland State University. We often laugh together about our unfortunate experience in that production.

Looking back over the script now, I cannot imagine how the situation was possible, but I have a haunted feeling that in Vardac's version of the play anything was possible. After my exit as the first murderer, helping his partner in crime carry off the corpse of Clarence (played by Allen Fletcher) there was a scene in which Ash appeared as Lord Hastings. During this scene I was supposed to change into Ratcliff, ready to enter at the beginning of the following scene. This was not a long scene, but it did give me time in which I thought I could make the costume and makeup change. Then the director began to cut Ash's lines. I still thought I could make the change, but at each rehearsal he came up with new cuts. Much to Ash's disgust and my consternation, his scene was finally cut completely and I was forced to do a complete costume and makeup change in a 10-second blackout!

In recalling those Stanford productions, I am reminded again of the excellence of that group of theatre students. Their measure of excellence should not be gauged by my recollection of their performances so many years ago but rather by the influence so many of them have had on American theatre. Jules Irving played Garth in *Winterset*, and Herb Blau did the Organ Grinder; they both played in *Cyrano*. I remember vividly their animated conversations in the greenroom as they planned the formation of the San Francisco Actor's Workshop, the success of which led to their taking over the artistic and business management of the Vivian Beaumont Theatre at Lincoln Center in New York City.

Richard Egan became a Hollywood star but you would never guess the extent of his acting excellence or his amazing versatility from the long string of mediocre motion pictures in which he appeared. At Stanford he played an impressive Buckingham to Roy Pool's Richard, and I returned the next year to see his moving performance of Othello. It was also a minor miracle to see that huge, muscular, handsome Irishman transformed into a shriveled pantaloon in a production of Moliere's *The Miser*. I had experimented for some time with a method of plastic makeup using cotton and shellac. Richard asked me to "do" his nose for the Harpagon role. And in appreciation for my doing this chore each night of rehearsal and performance, he presented me with a fifth of Irish whiskey. The Moliere was directed by Hal Todd, who had played a chilling Troc in *Winterset* and who later directed for us at Ashland and much later became head of the Theatre Department at San Jose State.

John Hume played Mio in *Winterset*, and I persuaded him and his wife Kathy to come to Ashland that summer. Ann Guilbert did a bit part in "Cyrano", but she will be remembered not only for her Doll Tearsheet and other roles at the Festival, but also for her funny neighbor of Dick Van Dyke in his television series, and for other television roles.

Allen Fletcher, besides acting in the same productions I had, was also doing a projects class in Direction. I dropped in to observe his work and was so impressed with his ability to translate the expressionistic ideas of George Kaiser's *Gas* into meaningful visual patterns, that I started to work on him in an effort to get him to come to Ashland. I have always been proud that this young man, who is now known for his directing from Stratford and New York to Seattle and San Francisco, began his professional career in Ashland.

Though he was not active in theatre that year, Bill Patton was among those Stanford students who came to Ashland that crucial summer. Starting as a stage electrician, he began a career with the Oregon Shakespearean Festival which was to last more than a quarter of a century. In 1974 he completed 20 years as General Manager of our organization.

As I have said, my real reason for going to Stanford was Dr. Margery Bailey of that institution's English Department. Sixteen years of her dynamic presence, rich knowledge and searing dedication have left the Festival qualities bearing her personal hallmark which time has not nor will not eradicate. Trying to recreate the experience that was Dr. Bailey is as difficult as painting a picture of some great natural phenomenon. (I have never seen a picture of Crater Lake that did not look like calendar art.)

The most concise and accurate evocation of her spirit comes from the loving hand of James Sandoe and was printed in the Festival's 1963 souvenir program. A part of that memorial article follows:

> As a lecturer, Miss Bailey was quite simply incomparable. Imperious, incisive, witty, she spoke *ex cathedra*, Minerva in lightning. She was the more persuasive because, with that wonderfully various voice and brilliant sense of gesture, she could evoke the whole range of Shakespeare's characters.

She was fiercely independent and had small patience with fools, along with a very comprehensive view of their incidence. But even those least patient with her impatience would insist that she had that ultimate patience of deep dedication which is selfless and tireless and as surely dependable as anything on earth.

She was incontestably, unmistakably, sometimes exacerbatingly *herself alone*, capable, as she felt it necessary, of being absolutely ruthless or infinitely gentle. My own debt to her as she cuffed me (with deep love) through Stanford, is incalculable. She fixed standards of judgment, of perception and of excellence that will always be powerfully magnetic. And this indeed is what she did (and still does) for all of us.

As Socrates to Athens, she to us:
A gadfly: loving, unambiguous.
Boulder, Colo. June 1963   James Sandoe

At Stanford in 1935 Dr. Bailey had presented a course in Shakespeare production centered upon the actual presentation of *Othello*. Besides the seminar and the production, there were concerts, lectures, demonstrations and discussions. That must have been a rich and memorable summer for those involved, and any resemblance to the activities of The Institute of Renaissance Studies at the Oregon Shakespearean Festival is not accidental.

The next summer the experiment was repeated, but when the Department of Speech and Drama was formed with Hubert Hefner as its head it seemed obvious that the province of theatrical production was in the new department. What a shame that these two could not combine forces. To say that they were like oil and water is an understatement—rather more like the substances that combine to create nuclear fission. He thought her a meddling female, she thought him a pompous ass.

It is quite understandable that he wanted to run his own department. On the other hand, she felt strongly that she had certain (moral if not legal) proprietary interests in the Drama Department. She had been prominent in the campaign that resulted in the building of Memorial Auditorium, that building which still houses the department. She also had been one of those who had recommended Hubert Hefner for the position as Chairman of the Department. She naturally felt slighted when her summer theatrical festival was discontinued. I think, however, the final blow came when Professor Hefner insisted that the drama department secretary, Chester Barker, discontinue his assistance of Dr. Bailey in her administration and promotion of Dramatists' Alliance, that organization she had created and fostered to encourage new playwrights.

I have mentioned before the extent of my debt to Dr. Bailey, and I will take opportunity again and again to refer to the extent and nature of her impact upon me and the Festival. However, I must say that I also owe a great deal to her old enemy, Hubert Hefner. My debts to her and my debts to him are as wide apart as their own personalities from each other. Her gifts were practical and electrically personal, his were theoretic and institutional. But I needed them both.

If you will look at the pictures of Dr. Bailey and of me, you will see in mine, I suspect, a person who is eager to meet the world on its own terms. In Dr. Bailey's you will see, I'm sure, a person who was determined to meet the world only on her terms. I needed some of that assurance, but I would never get it from imitating her in her more autocratic moods. Nor would I be more assured by becoming an expert in a profession whose practitioners were considered, by the preponderance of Americans, to be, at their worst, wastrels and perverts, and at their best, dabblers and dilettantes. I needed to know more about the theatre and its potential audience.

As a teenager I was not, as is the present brood, concerned with discovering my identity. I have always taken it for granted that my proper place in the society in which I found myself would be provided, more or less automatically, if I remained alert and took advantage of those opportunities that society presented. You can sense with me my grandmother's spirit looking over my shoulder as I write this, so I am forced to add a couple of tabus that she would insist upon as corollaries. First: One must never be envious of others whose position is more exalted or glamorous than one's own. ("You get what you deserve in this world—one way or another.") Second: Never get smug; never rest on your oars. I can hear her as she said to me, "Angus, never be afraid to compliment anyone for fear it will give him the big head, because, before the sun goes down, someone else will come along and tell him something that will take it all away."

I am sure I sensed intuitively many things about the nature of my profession and its relationship to the community, but what Hubert Hefner did was to guide me to a vocabulary which I could use to think more clearly about those relationships and to analyze their meanings.

My notes taken during those Hefner classes are a melange of ideas garnered from Hefner's lectures, Aristotle's *Poetics*, Northrop's *The Meeting of East and West*, and a host of other sources now completely lost. Let me sort out some of those ideas which still seem important to me after all these years.

I will never forget the thrill it gave me to hear Professor Hefner say something to this effect: "Since man could first express ideas, he has been trying to communicate with his fellow man concerning the relationships of man and man, man and the Universe, and man and his God (or Gods). And he has been doing it in three ways: through religion, through philosophy and through the arts."

As drama *in performance* is the most explicit of the arts, it became clear to me why I had sensed my work to be important. There was more to theatre, however, than the communication of humanistic, moral, ecological or religious ideas. There was a fundamental difference between the theatre and the pulpit or the lecture platform. In those classes under Professor Hefner I was to learn more specifically about the nature of that difference and why I should not have been surprised that the profits of the Festival in 1936 had been spent on football.

We in America have been profoundly influenced by the philosopher John Locke. We who believe in democracy owe a great deal to our founding fathers who, some two hundred years ago incorporated in our constitution such Lockean concepts as the equality of men, freedom of religion and by implication from Locke, the principle of government by the governed. No matter how slow or inept we have been in implementing these concepts, any progress that has been or will be made toward their fulfillment we owe to their existence in Lockean philosophy.

John Locke was born only 16 years after Shakespeare's death, and his theories concerning the nature of man and his environment were based on the scientific discoveries of Galileo and Isaac Newton. But during my lifetime scientists have discovered more facts about man and the universe than had been discovered in all the thousands of years preceding that time. It should not be a surprise then to find some of Locke's theories incomplete or actually inept.

Let me explain from my memory of Hefner's classes how Locke's theory concerning the basic nature of things has had an unfortunate influence upon the arts in America, perpetuating a basically Puritan attitude long after we stopped thinking of ourselves as Puritans.

First, I must confess that I am no philosopher, and that I am not trying to explain all of Lockean theory. Scholars will point out that I am over-simplifying, but these ideas, simple as they may be, recalled from those Stanford days, have made it much easier to understand my place as an artist in the society in which I find myself.

Locke posited the existence of two (and only two) kinds of things in the universe. One, the observer, or what he called mental substance; and the other, the observable object, or what he called material substance. The discoveries of Newton and Galileo had established the corporeal reality of material substance, referred to by Locke as "the public object in public space." This simply meant that the material "object" was actual and existed for everyone. The observed object exists for everyone, but it does not necessarily appear the same to everyone.

For instance: my desk is two by four feet, finished in walnut and feels cool to my touch. My wife, coming in from the outside, sits opposite me and for her the desk is also two by four feet and for her, as for me, there is only one desk. But as the light comes over my shoulder, the desk appears tan to her instead of brown, and because her hands are cold, it is warm to her touch. So, Locke said, some qualities are the same for all and some are not.

To explain this kind of phenomenon, Lockeans held that the mathematically verified, directly observed object possessed different kinds of qualities or characteristics. The primary characteristics were those which were always the same for everyone, for instance: extension and number. Secondary characteristics were undependable, or what was worse, actually deceitful. These were the aesthetic characteristics: color, movement, sound, heat and cold, and so on. These characteristics are variable, depending on the observer.

Is it any wonder then that for many years now, the man who builds a bridge has, by many people, been considered a more valuable citizen than one who paints a picture? Or that a man who sings for a living has been looked upon with less favor by most of his compatriots than one who manages a bank?

The obvious practical exception to this kind of evaluation comes about when the painter's pictures sell for enough money so that he buys real estate, hires assistants and invests heavily in the stock market; or when the singer develops, as did a member of a little musical group called the Rhythm Boys, into one of the richest men in show business: the man known and loved the world over as Bing Crosby. The change in attitude of the Puritan (who doesn't know he is a Puritan) comes about when the observed object, even though it depends for its value upon those transitory, emotion-evoking, secondary characteristics, that is, colors and sound, and so on, becomes capable of producing wealth, which in turn may be converted into objects like bridges, land or desks, whose value can be measured in terms of the so-called primary characteristics, that is, number, extension and other solid, dependable materialistic qualities.

At this point in Professor Hefner's classes, then, I knew why I had sensed the necessity of making our Ashland theatrical venture a festival, shaping it to fit into the third largest industry in Oregon: tourism. The tourist dollars spinning off from such a venture gave the theatre a value which would be measured and recorded by the most sensitive instrument of the most conservative citizen: his cash register.

I want to mention one other way in which the rigid Puritan concepts began to break down, resulting in the introduction of the study of dramatic literature in the classroom. Before I discuss this point in detail, however, I would like to tell you of another set of ideas gleaned from Professor Hefner's classes which has been a useful tool in clarifying for me the relationship between the playwright's printed text and the production of that text on the stage.

We used to speak jokingly about Mr. Hefner being on an Aristotelian "kick" that year. He was working on a research project which required a meticulous analysis of Aristotle's *Poetics*. In every one of the classes I took from him he brought in material from the *Poetics*. He did not seem to repeat himself, however, but brought Aristotelian thought to bear upon the subject of each class from a different and illuminating angle. Like most people, I have forgotten most of what I was supposed to have learned from my teachers over the years, partly because one's mind can be cluttered with so many ideas, and partly because much of what one learns is never used, and is thus jettisoned. But one swatch of wisdom, carried away from those classes from Professor Hefner, I have used again and again, so that it remains fresh in my memory. It is basically a list of six items, with which you may be familiar.

Aristotle named the six parts of a play in a sequence which indicated their interrelationships. Each item is made up of—or if you will, transmitted by means of—all the items beneath it. Let me explain further first by giving you the list:

ARISTOTLE'S SIX PARTS OF A PLAY

1.	Plot	4.	Diction
2.	Character	5.	Music
3.	Thought	6.	Spectacle

PLOT: The whole sequence and form of the action and interactions in the play. I remember Mr. Hefner referred to plot as the "architectonics" of the play. You can see that the characters, their thoughts, the words, and all that is heard and seen on stage, are all essential in that fabric or structure we call plot.

CHARACTER: The representation of the differing personages in a play. Again our perception of them is dependent upon the rest of the items on the list, the expression and interaction of their thoughts, the words they use, and the sounds of those words being articulated, sounds from · musical instruments, noises, and also what we see them do, their environment, costumes, and so on.

THOUGHT: The expressed thoughts of the characters and also the ideas engendered by the playwright's manipulation of characters and their actions. Those expressed thoughts are dependent for their expression upon the next item in the list—diction.

DICTION: The actual words used to express the thoughts.

MUSIC *and* SPECTACLE: I list the fifth and sixth items in the list together because they both differ from the other four parts in the same way. In a play script the diction is put down by the playwright in black and white, and through diction it is the playwright's job to make clear to us what we need to know of the thoughts and characters and their interrelationships which make up the plot. But the actual sounds that are supposed to be heard and the actual colors, forms and movements that are supposed to be seen can only be implied or described.

Thus it is that there are some "impuritans" in our classrooms who value the printed play because through the symbolic use of plot, character, thought and diction certain ethical, scientific, religious or political concepts may be conveyed to their students. But because of the absence of the waving banners, the blaring bugle and ruffled drum, the beggar's hovel, the king's bright crown, the guttering torch, the flaring skirt, the muscular thigh, the actual kiss, the parried blow, the lover's whisper, the dying scream, the vocal caress of verse, the youth's gay laughter, the crone's evil cackle, in short, because of the lack of the actual spine-tingling, gut-stirring, skin-crawling sounds and sights of the stage (music and spectacle) they consider the printed text as an end product. At the worst, they consider the stage production as dangerous and extraneous; at best they consider the stage presentation as a sort of visual aid to help the student understand the script.

The play ON THE STAGE BEFORE AN AUDIENCE is the end product of the playwright. It was not by accident that Shakespeare's plays had to be highjacked by printing pirates before they escaped into print during his lifetime.

I will have occasion to refer again from time to time to Aristotle's six parts of a play. You can see how it helped to clarify for me the responsibilities of the director, designer and actor in a Shakespearean theatre. The principal responsibility can be briefly stated: The theatre artist must be sure that what is heard and seen on the stage (Aristotle's music and spectacle) communicates, as nearly as possible to a twentieth century audience the plot, characters, thoughts and diction indicated by the author in his script. Reaching outside the script for elements of music and spectacle, such as did Peter Brook and the late Tyrone Guthrie, has no place in a theatre that has a reputation for producing Shakespeare on an Elizabethan stage.

My studies under Professor Hefner had made clear for me many things I needed to know: the nature of the printed play and its relationship to the theatre; the nature of the negative attitude toward it that I had observed in members of my own community; the function of art as a means of communicating ideas concerning man and his place in the scheme of things. But there were questions which had long nagged at the back of my brain, questions that none of this information satisfied.

What was the nature of the joy I felt when I had made a line sing as I sensed the author had intended—or heard another actor do so? Why do I still feel the roots of my hair stir when I remember Don Gunderson, in our early production of *Titus Andronicus* utter the line: "I have not a tear more to shed"? Why does Hamlet's death leave the audience exalted rather than depressed? When Romeo warns Juliet that dawn is breaking:

> Night's candles are burnt out, and jocund day
> Stands tiptoe on the misty mountain tops,

why do Shakespeare's lines convey so much more than the information?

The answers to these questions, which had previously been in the form of isolated little clots of vague convictions buried nearer my solar plexus than my brain, began to take on meaning during those classes at Stanford. The reason those convictions had remained vague and deeply buried was that they were stifled by a vague sense of guilt. My long preoccupation with the theatre had created a conflict with those basic

Puritan concepts which had formed the values of the world in which I
had been brought up. My parents must have also felt this conflict of
values, for they are remembered by literally thousands of people for
their singing. It is true they almost always sang for no fee, considering
the gift of their performances a return to the good Lord who had given
them the talent.

But they sometimes did sing for money. They performed the first
radio program sponsored by Coleman Lamps over radio station KOMO
in Tacoma. And Dad had been a cartoonist on the Bellingham *Herald*
the first few years of my life, and I remember seeing a picture of him
taken a few years later in which he was wearing a flowing artist's tie. I
remember that Miss Eccles, my high school teacher, in advising me to
"go into theatre" when I went to college, had said with firm emphasis,
"Of course I don't mean *professional* theatre."

You can imagine that it was with delighted relief that I discovered
during my Stanford studies that twentieth century scientists, followed
by the later philosophers, followed by some of the great artists, were
demonstrating that the aesthetic component in the nature of things is a
real and positive good in itself. The colors, sounds, motions and
rhythms, lights and shadows, so essential in drama *on the stage* were a
desirable, indeed a necessary part of things. The conclusion was inevitable, then, that art has two functions:

1. The presentation of the aesthetic component for its own sake,
    and
2. The use of the aesthetic component symbolically to present
    theories concerning the nature of man and his society, the
    nature of the material universe in which he lives and the nature
    of his God, together with the interrelationships of all these
    elements.

It was indeed fortunate that I was able to get these more modern
views of the real functions of theatre straightened out in my own mind
at Stanford, for in the next few years in Ashland I was to engage in the
most prolonged and bitter fight in the history of the Festival concerning their application to our operations.

As my association with Dr. Bailey was a close and continuous one
extended over a period of 16 years, it is not surprising that I cannot
isolate that particular portion of my education for which she was responsible that first Stanford year. Her office was in the basement of the
old administration building. Years before, she had somehow wangled
this dark corner of unused space and, like a mother cactus wren, had

succeeded in covering the scars left by previous inhabitants. For 16 years I went there to seek her advice and help.

The walls were completely lined with books, and the ever present mellow scent of old leather was spiked with the acrid smell of mimeograph ink from the little workshop she had created from a walled-off corridor in the rear. I remember little more about the decor, except a few colorful and odd-shaped pieces of pottery, snugged in about the room. Her home on Kingsley Avenue in Palo Alto she called "Friar's Pocket," and there is something about that name that seems also to fit my memories of her office. For here one felt warm and, somehow, secure. The muted reds, ochres and browns of the book-lined walls insulated against a disorderly outside world, and I never quite dispelled the illusion that from them emanated the wisdom of the greatest minds in literature—a wisdom which was distilled and centered in the being of the gracious patrician lady who sat opposite me at her desk.

Later I learned that she was not always gracious; that she was less astute and less judicial in her evaluation of people than she was in her evaluation of literary characters. But I never knew her equal in the precise delineation of what appeared most logically to be the author's intent as to plot, character, thought and diction, and to be precise and most persuasive in terms of line readings, movements and arrangements of characters on the stage, along with the forms, textures and colors of scenery, costume and makeup.

It has always seemed strange to me that she took me under her wing, so to speak, for most of the students in whom she took special interest over the years have been brilliant scholars. Alas, scholarship has never been my forte; and I will never forget my chagrin, when I had finished my first test in her class in Restoration Comedy, and realized that I had flunked it miserably. I wrote a note on the bluebook before handing it in to her. In it I said something like this: "I *would* do this on my first test from you." I don't remember what grade she actually gave me, but I will never forget the return note she penned on my returned test: it read simply "As you said." No, it was not for my brains that she put up with and assisted me and mine.

Something of the answer to that puzzle came the next year. I had persuaded her to write a critique of our season for the private edification of the company. The result was a review so generous and exhilarating that when I wrote to thank her, I said "I feel very humble—like a bush leaguer who has just found himself in the big league." She wrote back and said, "You must not again say that you are humble or I shall be forced to call you 'Uriah Heep.' After all, you have accomplished something I have wanted to do all my life and have never succeeded in doing."

I am convinced that one of the reasons for the Festival's vitality has been the periodic infusions of expertise and talent from the country's great universities and colleges, each bringing fresh points of view and new inspiration without swerving us from our declared and demonstrated artistic path. The most notable of these have been Stanford, Carnegie Tech (now Carnegie-Mellon University), the University of Texas, Southern Methodist University, and the University of Colorado.

But we owe a special debt to Stanford, first, for pioneering the trend, and second, for sending us so many of our top creative people. Steven Maze, our lighting designer, has been with us for 10 years. William Patton has been our General Manager for over 20 years, and Richard Hay, Festival Scenic and Theatre Designer, has created designs for over one hundred Ashland productions and designed our famed Elizabethan stagehouse as well as the stage, auditorium and other aspects of the Angus Bowmer Theatre. All received an important part of their training and experience at Stanford as students and/or staff. That institution has also encouraged literally hundreds of its talented young students to join our company. A notable member of the latter group was Shirley Douglass who joined our company as an actress in 1958. The next year she and Bill Patton were married and because of her charm, versatility and dedication our company has since been the richer.

I would be remiss if I did not recognize the important part Dean Virgil Whitaker played in the development of our Institute of Renaissance Studies. It was through his efforts that Dr. Bailey was authorized to offer the Stanford Field Course in Shakespeare at Ashland, and without his cooperation Dr. Bailey could not have become the Festival's Academic Advisor and the head of the Institute of Renaissance Studies, positions she held with us for the last 16 years of her life.

As a result of that first year at Stanford, I returned to Ashland with a keener sensitivity of purpose and a small entourage of well-trained theatre practitioners. Fortunately, the 1948 season saw the beginnings of a flow of trained people from other parts of the country. Therefore, with some new blood at Southern Oregon joining with the talented newcomers and a few veterans of the previous season, we were to initiate a new era at the Oregon Shakespearean Festival.

XIII

Instruction

I N THE EARLY DAYS of the Festival, the age-old question of whether art should entertain or educate gave us no option. We knew that we must entertain or perish: entertain in its fullest sense, that is, to capture and hold attention as well as, or rather than, merely to amuse. But we nevertheless found ourselves engaged in various aspects and degrees of education, at first inadvertently or by compulsion, but later on, deliberately and systematically. In the mind of the average high school graduate in those days, the plays of Shakespeare were so firmly branded with the stigmata of "Education," that the Festival was assumed by countless numbers of people to be merely an extension of a series of unpleasant schoolroom experiences. One of the most frequently duplicated conversations over the years is one in which a Festival customer having attended one or more performances repeats an all too familiar refrain: "You know, I always hated Shakespeare ever since high school, so I've never been to the Festival before, but . . ." and here the colloquy varies: "My wife made me come," or "We had visitors from out of town," or "Somebody gave me some tickets." The variants are many. At this point, too, the facial expression differs in each instance, running the gamut from wide-eyed astonishment to sheepish embarrassment—"But you know, I liked it!" The discovery that Shakespeare on the stage can be interesting, amusing, exciting, is surely an important educational experience for each discoverer.

From the earliest seasons we found it inconvenient to keep the auditorium doors locked during rehearsals. As a consequence, people began to drop in to see what was going on. Thus it finally came to be a policy for rehearsals to be open to the public. For a long time this was even true of technical and dress rehearsals. This latter policy had to be modified when the huge crowds (sometimes standing-room only) began to interfere with the final readying of the productions. But, as a consequence of this unique practice, there are a number of people in the valley who have not only seen the entire canon of Shakespeare's plays, but have witnessed the long process of staging each one: from actors' auditions and casting through final dress and performance.

The relationship of company members to the Festival has always had a distinct educational bias. The reciprocal responsibilities of any theatrical director and his company are in many ways educational in nature, but remember that the first Festival productions were done in a literal teacher-student situation with me as the teacher and my students at Southern Oregon Normal as the company. Any good teacher must be an active learner, and it is true that a knowledge of my own ignorance made me an avid searcher after any scrap of information concerning the production of Shakespearean plays. At first this search was a desperate attempt to gather practical knowledge, chiefly from John Conway at the University of Washington. How do you dye muslin? Can we make tights out of long underwear? What was Mr. Payne's stage business in the letter scene in *Twelfth Night*? How do you handle the problem of the incomplete sequence of Sly scenes in "Shrew"? Later, Dr. Bailey was to introduce me to the exciting study of the nature of Shakespeare's universe, and to guide us in the profitable application of this knowledge to the interpretation of his plots, characters, thought and diction through appropriate music and spectacle.

I am fully convinced that one of the reasons why so many of our audience members comment about the excitement and satisfaction they feel in our productions is that they have caught the joy of discovery which they share with our company. The discoveries which each company member has worked so hard to find all through long rehearsal periods he reveals to his audience with the same exultant exuberance as the tyro-bicyclist who shouts, "Look, Ma, no hands!" But the more perceptive recognize each of these discoveries as just another step in the endless search for perfection, for they know that the definitive performance of production has not yet and never will be done. It is this never-ending search that keeps performances fresh throughout the entire season. Indeed, an understanding of this process explains why the Festival has been able, over the years, to stage nine different productions of *The Merchant of Venice* without seeming unduly repetitive.

Aside from the various kinds of educational experiences which were an inevitable part of a Shakespearean festival there are other, more formal educational appurtenances which the Oregon Shakespearean Festival has always tried to develop. Both audiences and company members were less sophisticated in the early days so there was a pressing need for the various attempts we made to inform them concerning the interaction of characters, and the ideas engendered by such interaction, in terms of the man-centered, God-created universe in which Shakespeare wrote.

Dr. Bailey was ideally suited to bring such information to our potential audience. Her lectures were informative, perceptive and dynamically dramatic. Her continuing annual series of lectures was probably the most sophisticated and effective long-term public relations project we ever attempted. During those early years she was not on the Festival payroll, and was listed in our programs as "Academic Advisor."

In this latter capacity she was helpful to the company members in clearing up obscure line readings, Elizabethan definitions of words and phrases, pronunciations and prosody. However, when in 1951 I persuaded her to give a series of lectures to the company on the four plays of the season, I found myself in deep trouble. Her powerful personality, together with the juggernaut momentum of her convictions put the directors in an impossible position. In effect, she was re-directing their productions, and in doing so, was literally tearing the company apart at the very time when getting them all to go in the same direction was one of the major concerns of the directors.

Later, trying to take advantage of her amazing knowledge of the plays and her flair for the stage, I tried a series of critiques of the season on the final day. Having her hold her fire to the end of the season, I thought, would avoid the problem of re-directing the plays and confusing the company. This experiment lasted only a few years, for her violent impatience with mediocrity caused her remarks to be so caustic that, like a disinfectant acid, while curing the disease, destroyed the living flesh.

Dr. Bailey's most successful lectures to the company were those which were concerned with Elizabethan concepts of history, religion, philosophy, economy and science, together with the effects of these concepts on the actions and thoughts of Shakespeare's contemporaries. The fundamental nature of the Elizabethan ideas of God's order in the heavens and on the earth has been reflected in our productions since the time of those lectures. It has been one of the strongest of the unifying influences in the Festival productions over the years. As stringent as some of her medication was, it created, in this area alone, the basis for an integrity which we should always try to maintain.

Since the Festival reopened in 1947 there have been frequent if sporadic attempts by both Festival and Southern Oregon College personnel to bring the two institutions together in a mutually beneficial educational program. President Stevenson made it possible for Dr. Bailey and James Sandoe to be members of the College Summer School Faculty for several years, and in 1950 when Dr. Curt Zimansky from the University of Iowa was our Academic Advisor, he also taught at SOC.

These appointments of Festival personnel to salaried positions at the College were of obvious economic advantage to the Festival, but such a "Distinguished Visiting Professor" program was also of great value to the College, especially had it been regularized and continued over an extended period of time. But there was no one with the time and/or imagination to push for such an extension. I suppose I should have been more aggressive in promoting efforts to develop such a program, but I found that teaching my classes, directing College plays, and administering the artistic aspects of the Festival stretched the outside limits of my energy and abilities. In the early fifties I was appointed head of the English Department, a position I refused to accept. My name remained opposite that title in the College catalogue for three years before the position was filled. In later years, Dr. Herbert Childs, professor of English at Oregon State University, came to SOC for several summers to teach Festival-oriented courses in Shakespeare. But this program the College also finally terminated.

In those years before we had developed our present reputation, and when scholarships were non-existent or very small, we found recruitment of company members much more difficult than it is today. One of the difficulties was that the majority of parents was unwilling to support their offspring for a summer of "playing around" with the theatre, but, ironically, were eager to subsidize the same "playing around" if sufficient college credits could be accumulated in the process. To stimulate additional numbers of trained applicants then, we found it advantageous to offer Southern Oregon College credits for participation in the Festival.

There were a number of courses which, with the assistance of a bit of bending, might serve our purpose. There were four courses in Shakespeare, two in acting, two in costuming and our old catch-all tech course, play production. There was no doubt in my mind that a qualified student, registering for any of the above courses, could learn more and remember it longer by participating in the production of four Shakespearean plays than he could by sitting in my classroom for a comparable length of time. I was aware of the vast difference in the minds of most educators of that time between the "academic" respectability of the course taught in my classroom and the bootlegged "activity" course consisting of practical experience in the Festival. For years we sent out recruitment brochures brazenly flaunting our academic irresponsibility, and I "taught" two sections of each Shakespeare course. Those who were accepted into the Festival company and registered at the College received credits for the course. I also taught the course to other registered students who sat in class, listened spasmodically to my lectures, wrote mostly dull papers and took tests. Other courses were taught with sincere gestures toward academic conventionality, but participating in the simultaneous production of four Shakespearean plays is a full time job. Most "projects," papers and tests were generally neglected by mid season.

This double standard was not legitimate and I knew it could not last. But I thought if we demonstrated a need, someone "up there" would see the great potential Southern Oregon had for some kind of program that would take advantage of the Festival's proximity. I had a driving belief that the Oregon Shakespearean Festival would one day be one of the nation's great theatre institutions. Southern Oregon College administrators did not express a consuming faith in the future of the institution in which some kind of theatre department would assume a national prominence. I have mentioned before and will mention again the various ways in which President Elmo Stevenson went out of his way to be helpful to the Festival. But I think he never knew what my motivations were, nor of what value the Festival was to the College. I remember a long period during which he monotonously introduced me to visiting VIPS as "that queer fellow who plays around with Shakespeare."

The College did not get its Theatre and Speech Department until 1963, just 32 years after I joined its faculty. Dr. Leon Mulling, my longtime friend, was chosen as its head. He had come to SOC in 1946 with special training in speech correction, but he also had a background, interest and flair for theatre. He also happens to be one of the most imaginative teachers I have ever known. A number of years after his arrival we were happily joined by Dr. Dorothy Stolp who was able to relieve me of half of my College directing chores. Later still, two other very special people came to join our theatre-oriented group. First there was Edward Fitzpatrick who became our first "tech" man and later, Harriett Tobin who developed a costume division of the department, literally out of nothing. We all taught public speaking courses which, because they were required, generated the necessary numbers of students in our classes to justify our existence.

I don't remember how many times prior to 1963 we presented various detailed proposals for some kind of special department with emphasis on the availability of the unusual laboratory which could be provided by the Festival. For at least 15 years a theatre building was the second on the list of requests to the State Board. My discouraged prediction during my final years at the College was that a theatre for the department would be built the year after my retirement. You may judge how over-optimistic I was since it is now many years since I retired and as of this writing there is still no theatre. The failure to take advantage of the Festival's facilities to provide a dynamic classic theatre program for SOC must not be blamed entirely on the local administration. Oregon's Unified System of Higher Education was the square hole into which the Festival's round peg did not fit.

A significant step in the development of the Festival was taken when, according to the 1953 souvenir program, Dr. Bailey was no longer listed as "Academic Advisor" but was named "Director of the Educational Division of the Oregon Shakespearean Festival." This educational arm of the Festival became the "Institute of Shakespeare Studies" and finally in 1956 assumed its long familiar name, "Institute of Renaissance Studies."

The almost Herculean and completely selfless task of creating and maintaining the multi-faceted aspects of the institute could have been done only by a Margery Bailey. First of all, let me give you a description of the organization in her own words from the 1959 Festival program:

The Institute of Renaissance Studies is not a general school with a system of credits and degrees; it is a program of advanced courses and seminars directed toward the four plays of the Festival's season, which assumes that the student comes first for Shakespeare in production, and attempts only to enlarge and vitalize that experience thoroughly through lectures and discussions on Tudor life and thought and on problems in producing classic drama. The courses are brief, and arranged in sequences so that entire concentration is possible on one subject at a time; the methods of teaching are of a type which has warranted Stanford University and Southern Oregon College in accepting them as field courses in the arts for college credit in their respective administrative systems.

One of the times I was very proud of President Stevenson was in connection with the Stanford Field Course in Shakespeare. Dr. Virgil Whitaker, head of the English Department at Stanford, expressed his concern to me lest the University of Oregon or Southern Oregon College might resent the offering of such a course in Ashland by a California institution. I told him I thought there would be no objection to the course but suggested he write a query to President Stevenson and also to the head of the English Department at the University of Oregon. He did so and showed me the answers. Dr. Stevenson's letter was a dignified welcome which expressed his pleasure to be able to extend further the cooperation which the College had already given the Festival. The letter from the University of Oregon English Department head (now long gone) said in effect, "Who could be concerned about such a trival matter?"

But let me return to Dr. Bailey and the Institute. Aside from the problems of organizing the five short-term classes, assembling her own lecture material for the University course, and arranging for visiting lecturers, there were the weekly Gresham Lectures, each Thursday at 4:00 at the Public Library. Then on each Wednesday from 12:00 to 1:00, Trinity Noons presented readings by cast and staff in Trinity Hall, the Episcopal Parish House. On Sundays at 4:00 in the Festival Theatre, costumed musicians appeared in concerts of Elizabethan and Caroline music. There was a fortnightly change of book exhibits in the Library, and three exhibits of prints arranged in extension of the course on Renaissance art. Arrangements were also made so certain of these prints could be rented by townspeople and visitors.

The Institute's collection of books and prints grew in size and value each year, largely through gifts and primarily by means of Dr. Bailey's private funds, though many acquisitions were made possible by gifts from James Sandoe. In 1959 a grant from the Oregon Centennial Commission made possible a major enlargement of the collection. The book collection consisted of original materials, reprints, facsimiles and reproductions. The rare books included such venerable items as original editions of Holinshed's *Chronicles,* Camden's *Britannia,* Nicholas Colpepper's Englished medical prescriptions, More's life of Edward V, *The Dial of Princes* and numerous early works on courtly manners, heraldry, sport, law, ecclesiastical practices and the infant sciences.

The prints were beautiful reproductions from museums all over the world and represented the paintings of the Italian and French masters, the Lowland painters and such pre–eminent artists as Velasquez, Titian, Rubens, Durer and Holbein the younger. This valuable collection was housed in the Public Library and was principally under the loving care of June Pentzer. When June retired, the collection was given on permanent loan to Southern Oregon College where it is shelved in beautiful protective cabinets in a special place in the College library, which is, nevertheless, available to the student researcher. Commemorative plaques call attention to the fact that this is *The Margery Bailey Collection*. The College has an on-going plan to enlarge and maintain the collection.

Another of Dr. Bailey's major achievements each year was the publication of the *Ashland Studies in Shakespeare*. Let me again quote from the 1957 Festival program her own exposition of the nature and purpose of this publication:

> To serve as a core of essentials for players, students, and readers, the Institute issues annually a privately published volume of the season's plays. This is the *Ashland Studies in Shakespeare*, a bound, mimeographed volume of articles and reprints with illustrative plates from rarities in the library collection and from famous museums. The contents of the current edition include passages from a 17th Century code of manners, chapters on the character and responsibilities of a military commander by a 15th Century authority, and original articles upon the English and American attitudes toward Shakespeare's *Henry VIII*, the mystery of his share in *Pericles*, and the rituals of stag hunting in the 16th Century.

What she does not say is that she not only gathered and edited all this material, but she also literally published it singlehanded. The mimeographing was all done on her little machine in her work room which she had salvaged out of a tiny hall in the rear of her office at Stanford.

Thus it was that Dr. Bailey spent the last 15 years of her life shaping a unique education program which utilized our Elizabethan theatre productions as a laboratory. She also shaped the Festival's concepts of Shakespearean production so that reliable scholarship made a basis for an exciting theatricality inherent in the playwright's stage and script. May it ever be thus!

After Dr. Bailey's death, the directorship of the Institute was taken over by Dr. Dolora Cunningham. Dolora had studied under Dr.

Bailey at Stanford from which institution she received her A.B., M.A., and Ph.D. degrees. Her studies there and elsewhere provided a splendid background in Renaissance literature. For 10 years she continued the arduous and exacting tasks of carrying on the Institute. Her organizational pattern followed much the same form as that developed by Dr. Bailey. However, the entire emphasis of the Oregon Shakespearean Festival's education program was due for a change. But this change could not take place until after the Festival season had expanded into the school year. This expansion must be related in a later chapter.

The first steps toward this change came when we began to realize that our audience members seemed to be getting older each year. As a result of this observation, Gary Aldridge, assistant to Carl Ritchie in the public relations department, was assigned the task of organizing a program of High School Student Tours. This was in 1964, Shakespeare's four hundreth anniversary year. The assignment was a difficult one, because it required teachers to give up part of their summer vacation period. Gary's efforts were quite successful, however, and this year marked the beginning of an exciting school program that burgeoned in the early years of the seventies.

At about the same time as the Student Tour Program, the College and the Festival cooperated in a unique creative program called The Shakespeare Apprentice Workshop. It was open to high school and college students. The format included a full program of lectures and demonstrations too by Festival personnel, and some participation in Festival production activities by those who were qualified. All registrants were privileged to observe rehearsals and shopwork. Course offerings at the College were included as well as a Workshop production. Students were housed in a College dormitory with official supervision. Most of the organizational work of the project fell upon the efficient shoulders of Dr. Dorothy Stolp and both she and Ed Fitzpatrick taught the college classes.

The program lasted for six years. But each year it became more and more difficult for the College summer school administration to give the project sufficient priority to make it financially feasible. After the sixth summer it was terminated.

Cooperation between the College and the Festival is improving in the seventies, but more of that later. I must now take you back again to 1948.

XIV

Augmentation

D URING THE FIRST FEW seasons after my Stanford year the
Festival turned an important corner. Up to this point our
production style had been, for the most part, a fumbling
attempt by one director with limited background to imitate Mr.
Payne's Elizabethan approach to the presentation of Shakespeare's
plays. But with the advent of a number of new theatre artists, directors, actors and designers, new lights were focused upon old ideas.
These people included not only the ones from Stanford, but also those
from a wide variety of other places, providing a rich expanse of experience and training. There were a score or more of them who worked
with us during the next six or seven years—some of them for a much
longer period. Aside from a wide variety of theatre experiences, both
practical and theoretical, the one thing this nucleus group had in common, in various degrees, was training in the classics and a knowledge of
theatre history which made them an exciting team who understood our
objectives and who willingly worked together to develop a theatre
which was frankly experimental without being precious.

There could be no doubt in the minds of this hardy group as to the
pioneering nature of their venture, for the theatre structure itself gave
ample evidence. The facade and stage areas were built from my tracing
of John Conway's plans. But there were no seats on the weed-covered
auditorium floor, except the benches we later scrounged from the Park
or folding chairs borrowed from the College. The facade still lacked its
first coat of paint, and most embarrassing of all, there was no roof over
the backstage area which was consequently innocent of any dressing
room privacy.

The first project the Festival Board tackled that season was to persuade the City Council to provide the several thousand dollars it required to build that roof. I remember a real cliff-hanging sort of suspense while this important step was being considered by the city fathers. I knew that Mayor Thomas Wiley was sympathetic, for he had had a soft spot in his heart for the Festival ever since he had been Mayor of Treasure Island for a day. But I knew a good many of the council members were skeptical.

I stayed in the background as much as possible, for I thought the request should be a community request, not a personal one. We had some big guns going for us, however, as Robert Dodge, a successful Ashland businessman, was our president, Harry Skerry, a brilliant young attorney, our secretary and Marshall Woodell, the Dean of Men at the College, treasurer.

The Mayor appointed a committee to take the whole matter under consideration and to make a recommendation to the Council. I remember vividly the meeting of that committee, called by its chairman, "Billy" Briggs, whose reputation as an astute lawyer made him a formidable opponent, if indeed he were to be an opponent. His ability to keep his position on any matter a secret was, of course, one of the factors in his successful practice. I was invited to attend the meeting, and when I arrived, found that also present were Robert Dodge, president of the Festival and Dr. Elmo Stevenson, president of the College.

The crux of the meeting came when Chairman Briggs turned to me and asked: "If the council invests this money to build the roof, will you promise to remain in Ashland for the rest of your life?"

I couldn't believe my ears, but I said, rather heatedly, I'm afraid, "Of course not. But if the Festival gets the kind of cooperation it should from the Council, I see no reason why I should want to leave."

Billy Briggs then turned to Dr. Stevenson and asked, "If we go ahead with this project, will you guarantee to hire professor Bowmer every summer?" After only a moment's hesitation, Elmo said "Yes." And we got our roof. His was not an easy promise to keep, for the summer faculty was always smaller than that of the rest of the year, and it was necessary for other faculty members to take turns being hired in the summer. But he kept his word for the rest of my lifetime at the College, although it must have caused him many an administrative headache.

The construction of that roof took until just before the season opened. But rehearsals continued in spite of the maddening bang and rasp of hammer and saw, and the teeth-jolting chatter of the jackhammer. This was not a new experience, for we had gone through the same sort of thing the previous season with the reconstruction of the façade.

I remember the shock when a carpenter let a hammer fall 25 feet into the middle of a stage grouping, missing actors by inches. The constant distraction of scrambling workmen, and the physical effort it took to shout above the ceaseless racket of construction would have been unbearable if each one of us had not been young enough and determined enough to will upon himself a sort of temporary lobotomy which kept him from rushing into the hills screaming and tearing his hair.

As I look back now, I marvel that we accomplished as much as we did. It was taken for granted that we all took on several jobs. Doug Russell, with his Herculean tasks, is a case in point. During his 13 seasons with the Festival he developed an approach to costuming Shakespeare's plays for the Elizabethan stage which has been enriched and expanded by him as well as by his successors. Elizabethan clothes are referred to in the plays:

"... what shall I do with my doublet and hose?" *(As You Like It)*

"... *their hats are pluckt about their ears,*
And half their faces buried in their cloakes, . . ."
(Romans did not wear hats)   *(Julius Caesar)*

"Cut my lace, Charmian. . . ."   *(Antony and Cleopatra)*
(Laces kept the Elizabethan woman's torso tightly
cinched within her stiff, corseted bodice.)

In the light of these and other specific references to elements of Elizabethan clothing, it was logical for him to include them in his costume designs. But he never felt called upon to reproduce Elizabethan street dress in any kind of literal fashion. He modified and combined these elements to suit the character, complement the actor and enhance the play. He even pushed the historical period in some productions to much earlier Renaissance years and in others to as late as the Cavalier period. The exception to this practice was made in the History plays, the first time around. That first cycle was costumed in the historical period of the play. Since that time all history plays in the Elizabethan Theatre have been costumed in modified Elizabethan dress.

The meagreness of the budget for those first few years was naturally reflected in the costumes. They were somewhat scant where we would have preferred fullness, and flimsy where they should have been rich and flowing. However, the fact that we played only 16 days in the 1948 season meant the costumes had to stand up for only six wearings: two dress rehearsals and four performances each play.

With no roof until performance time, there was obviously no place at the theatre for a shop where Doug Russell could build his costumes. As it had been arranged for him to teach two classes at the College, a shop was set up in one of the temporary buildings moved in from wartime Camp White and set up on the campus. Even though the backstage roof was completed that season, the arrangement with the College for the costume shop continued. For three years, Doug taught two courses in costuming, designed the costumes for four plays each season, did a major part of the construction himself, assisted by a few students who registered for his classes and a number of community ladies who gave generously of their spare time. Three names come to mind as I think of the invaluable assistance given by this latter group: Mrs. Ruth King, Mrs. Ethel Putney and Mrs. Una LaMarre. With no wardrobe stock from which to draw, the costuming of those plays was something of a miracle—all the more so when you know that Doug played nine roles during those first three years, including Brabantio in *Othello* and Gaunt in *1 Henry IV*.

That any of us survived those early postwar years was perhaps due to the fact that the whole season from tryouts to closing night was only a little over six weeks. I remember that in 1948 I directed *Othello*, *Love's Labour's Lost* and *The Merchant of Venice*; I also played Boyet in "Love's Labour's"; Hubert in *King John*; Shylock in "The Merchant" (of course); and several bit parts and walk-ons in *Othello*. All this was in addition to my duties as Producing Director which included supervising the volunteer box office help and doing a goodly share of the publicity. And of course I carried a full teaching load at the College.

The first three years he was with us Allen Fletcher directed four productions and played six substantial roles. That first season he directed *King John* and assisted me in directing *Othello*. He directed a revival of *Othello*, together with *The Taming of the Shrew* the next year. It was immediately apparent that he was a tremendous asset to the Festival staff, but he made the greatest impact on us when in 1952 and 1953 he directed *Julius Caesar* and *Coriolanus*.

In order to assist in our search for a unity of style, I required the directors, in those days, to send me prompt books right after Christmas vacation. Allen, who had had early ambitions to be a graphic artist, always sent his scripts with all the stage groupings indicated, not with the customary diagrams, but with stick figures arranged in perspective pictures. In both Caesar and Coriolanus I played bit parts, soldiers and citizens, and I spent as much time memorizing the minutely detailed choreography in the crowd scenes as I would have spent on a heavy supporting role. Thus he was able to make a dozen soldiers into two opposing armies and six men and four women into a mob. He led the way for the rest of us to remedy the static quality in our productions which was first called to our attention by Dr. Bailey. We began to punctuate the speeches with movement, and among other things, to discover the three dimensional nature of our Elizabethan stage and to utilize, for instance, the exciting strength of a long movement directly down stage from the inner-below to the front of the forestage. We had, in our Elizabethan stage, an exciting space at our disposal. Allen Fletcher, by example, led us to discover more and more of the infinite number of ways to use it in illuminating the language, ideas, characters and plots of Shakespeare's plays.

James Sandoe is another director who played a strong part during the fifties and early sixties in creating a basis for what may be called the Ashland style of producing Shakespeare on the Elizabethan stage. Dr. Bailey was instrumental in getting us together. Jim agreed to come to Ashland for a summer of observation in 1948, and to make it financially feasible, President Stevenson was persuaded to hire him for the College Summer School to teach English literature and English composition.

Jim had been one of Dr. Bailey's most brilliant students at Stanford and had, for a number of years, been a member of the English Department at the University of Colorado. He had rebelled, however, when they had insisted that he obtain a doctoral degree. Instead, he went for a year to the Library School at the University of California and went back to the University of Colorado as a librarian. For many years he has held the position of Order Librarian there. For several summers he had directed Shakespearean plays in the outdoor Mary Ripon Theatre on the Colorado campus. When Jim left the department this practice was carried on by others and eventually became the Colorado Shakespeare Festival.

Another of those wondrous circumstances that surround the forming of the Festival was the presence of Dr. George F. Reynolds at the University of Colorado. Professor Emeritus from 1945 until his death in 1964, he had been English Department head for many years. He and his wife were principally responsible for the founding of the University

Little Theatre. But what is more unusual, he wrote his doctoral dissertation at the University of Chicago, on The Red Bull Theatre. Written
in 1905, this was one of the earliest scholarly investigations of production methods in use during Shakespeare's lifetime.

One of the most delightful hours I have ever spent was sitting at a
table with members of our company listening to two of the most truly
gentle men I have ever known argue about the use of signboards on the
Elizabethan Stage. Dr. Reynolds was fully convinced they were used,
and Iden Payne was as firmly certain they were not.

Jim Sandoe, though fully aware of the Poel tradition, brought
another point of view to the directing of Shakespeare's plays on our
Elizabethan-type stage. This double approach encouraged him to view
the directing chore as a learning experience. Thus the staging of the
plays became for all of us more of a search for, rather than a proof of,
methods of fitting together the scripts and the stage.

I suspect that Jim brought to us a wider background of reading
than any other director we have ever had. He was also able to use the
English language in a more effective and precise way than anyone I
ever knew—excepting only Dr. Bailey. One of the signs of summer in
Ashland during the fifties was the sight of Jim's slight, wiry figure
striding vigorously down the streets of Ashland with his eyes glued to a
paperback. He reviewed six detective stories a week, first for the
Chicago *Sun-Times* and later for the New York *Herald Tribune*. In
1949 he won the Mystery Writers of America award for work in this
field. My favorite review was his one-liner on the first Mickey Spillane
novel. It read simply: "Boom-lay, boom-lay, boom-lay boom!"

As is customary during rehearsals, directors dictated notes to a
stage manager or secretary. As is also customary, after each rehearsal
we spent a long time going through these notes with the entire cast—
all, that is, except Jim. He seldom kept the cast after rehearsal, but took
his notes home and the next day delivered to each appropriate actor a
typed paper containing a concise evaluation of where his part was going
and stimulating advice as to what should be done to enhance its positive
qualities and correct its negative ones. Thus he was usually able to
spend at least a half hour more on stage with his actors than was
possible for other directors. Besides, the several hours he spent each
night thinking over his notes before he typed their final form meant
they were cleanly articulated, stimulating and germane.

Jim's first directing assignment came sooner than any of us suspected. Actually it was in that 1948 season when he was observing the

Festival and teaching at SOC. He and I came back to the theatre one evening before the rest of the company. We stopped dead in our tracks at the gate, for on the stage were a half dozen boy scouts engaged in some kind of dramatic activity. They were not strangers, for these same youngsters often wandered in from their meeting place next door to observe rehearsals. We could see they had picked up some scripts we had left on stage and were laboriously stumbling through some lines. It took us some time to realize these boys, who hadn't been born before the first Festival year, were seriously attempting to enact a scene from *Othello*. They were doing it very badly, of course. But there was no mistaking their earnestness and the fact they even entertained the idea took Jim and me by the throat. I turned to him and said, "Do you want to do something about it?" He said, "Yes."

Thus it came about that on opening night in 1948, we had a "curtain raiser" of "Pyramus and Thisby" from *A Midsummer Night's Dream* played by the boys. As a direct result of this amusing experiment, the next season Jim directed a full scale production of "Dream" as well as one of *Richard II*. Allen Fletcher directed "Shrew" and *Othello* and Richard Graham, who had joined the company in 1948 directed *Romeo and Juliet*. This was the first and the last time we attempted to produce five plays in the regular season.

I will never forget the night I first met Dick Graham. He arrived unannounced just before casting time, having read our ad in *Theatre Arts Magazine*. He had driven from New York as much to audition us as to be auditioned. He had made his professional debut on Broadway in *The Pursuit of Happiness* and had played bit parts in New York and on the road with Katherine Cornell in her productions of *Romeo and Juliet* and Shaw's *Saint Joan*. His only other Shakespearean experience had been in summer stock productions of *Twelfth Night* and *Macbeth*. He liked to play in Shakespeare, but was eager to get as much experience as possible in as short a time as possible. Ashland seemed to be the perfect answer for in 1948 the Oregon Shakespearean Festival was the only theatre on the North American Continent organized for the sole purpose of producing Shakespearean repertoire.

He auditioned for me in the living room of our tiny cottage on Mountain Avenue. I remember Gertrude was ill with the flu, but when he finished his audition, she applauded from the bedroom. I was very pleased and no doubt showed it, but I didn't dare show my full elation at this valuable addition to the depth of our company. He was a handsome six-footer with blond hair, resonant voice and easy movement.

His imposing stage presence, coupled with a personality influenced by a Prussian heritage, made it possible for him to play with gratifying success those roles which required authority or self confidence which was taken for granted. His logical mind and methodical technique made him easy to direct and also made it possible for him to work out readings of obscure lines in a way which made sense to a twentieth century audience.

His casting in his first Festival season was indicative of the kind of impact he was to make on our acting company for the 13 seasons he was with us. He played a powerful, satiric and amusing Berowne in *Love's Labour's Lost*, one of the "salad" boys (Salanio or Salarino) in *The Merchant of Venice*, a sprucely military and almost priggish Cassio in *Othello* and the heroic, golden Nordic Bastard in *King John*. His is the last speech in that play:

> This England never did, nor never shall,
> Lie at the proud foot of a conqueror,
> But when it first did help to wound itself.
> Now these her princes are come home again,
> Come the three corners of the world in arms,
> And we shall shock them. Nought shall make us rue,
> If England to itself do rest but true.

Before it rang in our ears, we were cheering the hero of that supposedly heroless play—not the Bastard, not King John, but the Crown, the Throne, the soul of England. He was justifiably proud of the fact that during those 13 years, he played in 35 of the 37 plays of Shakespeare's canon and directed the other two. He played everything from leads such as Benedick and Petruchio to little cameos such as Barnardine in *Measure for Measure* and a fisherman in *Pericles*. He portrayed Othello twice, Lear three times and Bolingbroke in *Richard II, 1 Henry IV,* and *2 Henry IV*.

He directed for us four seasons, but eventually became more valuable as an actor and in other capacities. Stage makeup was under his direction for all the seasons he was with us, and his privately printed book, *Stage Make-up Applied* makes several original and worthwhile contributions to the technique of that art. For eight years he was editor of our souvenir program and worked out formats and formulas which have been helpful to editors since. His assistance was also extremely valuable in helping me work out the format and wording of the recommendation questionnaire which served so well for us in those years before we were able to audition or interview prospective company members before accepting them.

You can see that Richard Graham made a unique and important impact on the Festival in those formative fifties and beyond.

In 1948 we had again toured *The Merchant of Venice* to Klamath Falls. In the audience was a young man by the name of Philip Hanson. He was employed in the fall harvest fields of Northern California but had wangled the afternoon off so he could make the trip to see our performance that evening. He came backstage after the show and we discussed the possibility of his joining the company the next season.

I was impressed with his enthusiasm and a kind of pent up vitality that was to be so effective in the roles he undertook for us in the next five seasons. These facets of his personality imbued his Hotspur in *1 Henry IV* with a kind of coiled spring intensity, his Angelo in *Measure for Measure* with banked up fires of passion, his Cassius in *Julius Caesar* with the tempestuous nature which made the famous quarrel scene memorable. His King John was spine chilling, especially in that scene where he entices Hubert into a promise to murder Arthur. Watching it was like watching a snake charm a bird.

These roles make obvious and exciting use of the kind of intensity that he brought to all his roles, but strangely enough that same quality he could use equally well in comedy. It gave his Dogberry in *Much Ado About Nothing* a kind of bumptious eagerness which was appealing as well as ridiculous. I still remember his Malvolio in *Twelfth Night* as one of the best portrayals of that role I have ever seen.

I also remember how he helped to achieve just the right impact in that extremely difficult and horrible scene in *King Lear* in which Cornwall gouges out the eyes of the helpless old Gloucester. That was the first time I directed Lear, back in 1951. I still remember vividly the revulsion that scene had aroused in me in the Komisarjevsky production which I had seen in Stratford in the spring of 1937. In an unsuccessful attempt to soften the horrors it had been played in very dim light and at a pace so agonizingly deliberate that I thought I would have to leave the theatre and be sick. I thought, "This is all wrong. The unimaginable horrors of the action are more horrible by being dimly lit and left to the imagination." And the pace was wrong. I decided that if I ever did the play it would be done in the frantic haste of hysteria.

Bill Patton, who was still our light designer in 1951, had been able to upgrade our equipment so he could light the scene effectively. There were heavy, forbidding shadows all around the edges of the action which was illuminated in bright pools that might have spilled from guttering torches. And as the action progressed, the lighted area shrank imperceptibly until it covered only that area immediately around the heavy chair in which Gloucester was bound. The pace is suggested in the first speech of the scene, as Cornwall speaks to Goneril:

> "Post speedily to my lord your husband; show him
> this letter: the army of France is landed. . . ."

Taking my cue from this talk of impending battle, I backed the scene with crisscrossing sounds of the approach and retreat of marching feet, the ruffle and beat of drums and the repeated peremptory challenge and frantic answer of bugles, near and far. This suggestion of the actual mobilizing of troops motivated the hysteric cruelty and racing ferocity with which the scene was done.

The first eye is gouged out with Cornwall's body hiding the actual act. Then in the upheaval of Gloucester's agony the chair gets turned around so that, while we see everything that takes place in the lighted area, we do not have to look at the bleeding eye socket during the ensuing fight in which a repentant servant wounds Cornwall and is in turn killed by him. Then the final mutilation takes place with Gloucester's face hidden but the ferocious expressions on Cornwall's plainly visible. When Gloucester is finally released and gropes his way out, he passes momentarily through a lighted area so the audience gets one brief glimpse of the bleeding, agonized face. Thus the audience's sensibilities were delivered one sharp, ferocious blow to the solar plexus rather than being slowly beaten to a pulp.

Much of the effectiveness of this scene was due to actor Hanson. The same vitality, which I have mentioned before, erupted in this scene with astonishing violence, and was articulated clearly in speech that was anachronistically machinegun-like in its rapidity.

In 1950 or '51 Phil married Suzanne LaMarre. She had developed tremendously as an actress since that first post war season. She played 13 roles for us in the seven years she was a member of the acting company. They ranged from Rosaline in *Love's Labour's Lost* to Emilia in *Othello*, Olivia in *Twelfth Night* and a particularly effective Countess of Auvergne in *1 Henry VI*.

After the 1953 season the Hansons left us to go to San Diego where Philip directed for the Old Globe Theatre and from there to go to Europe where he was Entertainment Director in Special Services for the United States Army in France and Germany for three years. In the five seasons he had acted for us, he had also directed three productions quite successfully. When he returned for the season of 1959 he did not direct but was one of a group of Equity actors as an experiment financed by the Ford Foundation. By this time Suzanne had given up acting and had become of great assistance to her husband as agent, secretary and consultant in the development of his one man shows which he later toured extensively in this country and abroad.

In 1951 William Oyler joined the company. He was a virile young man with a well muscled body and athletic coordination. He had come with Philip Hanson from Washington State College two years before but he left before casting. He returned the next season and was with us for six seasons spread over a 15 year period. He played roles as diverse as Orsino, Brutus and Iago. For some mysterious reason many fine actors seem to discount their work in comic roles, and I think Bill tended to do so. But he did a memorable Pistol in both 2 *Henry IV* and *Henry V*, and I will never forget the delicious drollery of his King Simonides in *Pericles*. Of his serious roles I remember most vividly his Edmund, perhaps because I directed him in that role in our first production of *King Lear*. As his doctoral dissertation at UCLA he wrote the first history of the Oregon Shakespearean Festival.

H. Paul Kliss, who also came to us in 1951, was small of stature but he had a rich, resonant voice, coupled with a clarity of articulation which made it possible for him to hold an audience in the most difficult expository scenes. He played a fine Prospero and, as the Archbishop of Canterbury, did wonders with those interminable speeches about the "law Salique" which make the early-on scenes of *Henry V* so difficult. He also had a flair for fantastic roles such as Lucio in *Measure for Measure* and Dr. Caius in *Merry Wives of Windsor*. He also directed for us, turning out a beautiful production of *Winter's Tale*.

Clara Daniels, a tall, statuesque actress did fine work for us from 1948 through 1953. I have frequently told a story about Clara on casting day at the Festival. In 1948 she played Emilia, but when *Othello* was repeated the next year, the director decided to use Suzanne LaMarre in that role. Clara played two bit parts: Lady Capulet in *Romeo and Juliet* and the Widow in "Shrew." However, the *next* year she played Cleopatra. She is now married to Paul Reinhardt who was with the Festival for three years: first, as an actor, then as assistant to Douglas Russell, in which capacity he designed the costumes for *The Tempest*. The next year Doug took a leave of absence and Paul was acting Costume Designer for that season. He later inherited Lucy Barton's place as the head of the Costume Department of the School of Theatre at the University of Texas. That fine school, developed under the aegis of Dr. Loren Winship, has, over the years, sent us many other fine theatre people. Among these are Patrick Hines, one of the most steadily employed character actors in the profession, and Robert Symonds who went directly from his season with us to the Actors' Workshop in San Francisco and with them to New York, where for many years now he has acted in productions at the Vivian Beaumont Theatre in Lincoln Center.

In 1950 Douglas Russell became a member of the faculty of the Carnegie Institute of Technology. In 1952 Allan Fletcher also went there to teach. As a result, for a number of years there were some fine Carnegie Tech people in our company. Perhaps the two most notable appeared in the summer of 1951. Their names may be familiar to you. Motion picture star George Peppard did his pre-professional internship with us, starting in 1951. Because of the death of his father he could not be with us the next summer. He operated his father's contracting firm for a year, but was back playing Shakespeare with us in the summers of '53 and '54. George was another one of those actors who discounted his ability as a comic. I will never forget his Slender in "Merry Wives" or his Biondello in "Shrew." He had a particularly keen feeling for the comic rhythms in the speeches, and his walk in the latter role was excruciatingly funny for his legs seemed to bend only at the knees. His long speech describing the approach of the fantastically equipped Petruchio, Grumio and steed still makes me laugh as I recall it, for George knew how to make the comic manner in which it was delivered appropriate to the comic matter of the content. However well he may have performed in the motion pictures in which you have seen him, I believe his success in those roles has deprived the theatre of a great comic actor. For us he was adequate in such roles as Bassanio and Horatio, but certainly more than adequate in others such as the Provost in *Measure for Measure* and Warwick in *2 Henry VI*.

George, in common with a good many actors, was a poor reader. As a result it was not surprising that his casting was not especially good that first year. However, I remember very well the mixture of delight and dismay the first time he was "off book" in the brief role of Morton. His description of Hotspur's death and the defeat of the rebels was literally hair-raising, and I suddenly realized that we had seriously underestimated the young actor's ability. Since that season, actors auditioning for roles at the Festival, are required to present two short previously prepared scenes. In this way we are able to judge an actor's ability to deliver previously memorized and rehearsed lines, as well as to get some idea of his ability to move and project.

I am afraid that George has never forgiven me for casting him as Horatio in my 1954 production of *Hamlet*. It is only recently that he has ever mentioned the Oregon Shakespearean Festival as a part of his early theatre experience.

William Ball, the General Director and guiding genius of the American Conservatory Theatre in San Francisco had his first experience in repertory with us while he was still an undergraduate at Carnegie Tech. He joined our acting company the same year as George Peppard and in the three seasons he was with us played an amazing 16 roles in 12 plays. Among his parts were Mark Antony in *Julius Caesar*, Claudio in "Much Ado," Ariel in *The Tempest* and Feste in *Twelfth Night*.

I sometimes played a recording of his performance as Antony for my students to demonstrate its superiority over the performance of Marlon Brando as recorded from the sound tape of the motion picture version of *Julius Caesar*. I like to think that Bill's experience with us may have had some influence in the shaping of his ACT repertory company, now one of the finest in America.

Space does not allow me to mention all those people who helped to shape the Festival in the fifties. There are some of them, however, whom, for one reason or another, I intend to introduce later.

I have spoken, so far, about the significant advances the Festival made in the fifties in terms of people. I would like to cover the same period again in terms of events. For during this time there were some revolutionary policies adopted, and several significant programs started which have determined the very nature and existence of the Oregon Shakespearean Festival.

XV

Crescendo

WILLIAM OYLER'S doctoral dissertation has one section in which he refers to a portion of the Festival's history as, "The Fabulous Fifties." This colorful title suggests the burgeoning that was taking place during that period. To be accurate, the period began in 1948 and extended to the late fifties. During that time the production machinery, though it squeaked and groaned because of necessary compromises and false starts, was constantly gaining momentum as we searched for a suitable artistic course and struggled to maintain theatrical integrity.

In exactly the same way, the Board of Directors was also groping desperately for its own place in the scheme of things. In my opinion it was during this period that, after much friction and fumbling, that body finally became a truly professional organization, having discovered its own identity, taking pride in its own unique function as an essential part of the complicated machinery of an eminently successful theatre organization. Without this sense of direction, function and purpose, it would not have been possible for the Board to harness the imagination, business acumen and courage which were necessary to carry us through the astonishing (and frightening) expansions of the sixties and seventies.

In the earliest seasons after the incorporation of the Oregon Shakespearean Festival Association, board members were chosen for either or both of two kinds of services they could render. Some were chosen because they could do publicity, for example, Roy Craft. Dorothy Pruitt, as another instance, besides acting could write articles, edit programs and make public appearances. Some because they could sell season tickets, either as Alice Egan because of her position in the community and her ability to organize and manage a team of community workers, or Etta Schilling, who had the energy, dedication and stamina to actually canvass Ashland from door to door. Then there were those who were selected for the Board because their names and positions were an important means of encouraging public approval for our organization and were helpful in giving us a "foot up" in our search for a dignified and permanent place in the community. Some of the "doers" were also in this latter class, but there were some whose names in association with the Festival were the only contribution expected. The first President of the Association was a well known and respected County Judge. Though he never attended a business meeting, he helped to lend us an aura of respectability which was an absolutely essential factor in those early years.

In our souvenir programs from 1937 through 1951 we published a list of "Honorary Board Members." Each member on the list had given us his permission to use his name. These names belonged to the important, near-important or would-be important from the local, state and national scene. Of the 20 or more on the list, I suppose the most famous were former President Hoover and Bing Crosby. Each year the Governor of Oregon was named "Honorary President." Even after we discontinued the list, the Governor's name as Honorary President was published each year until 1963.

This search on the part of theatre people for respectability by association was not a new idea. I have always thought it was the prime motive for the founding of Dulwich College by Shakespeare's contemporary rival, Edward Alleyn. But as the theatre grew throughout the frantic fifties we tried more and more to get men and women from the business and professional community to serve on the Board, for we desperately needed their guidance in financial and organizational matters.

The trouble was that some of the most successful businessmen, while they could manage the matter of profitably marketing such items as groceries, lumber, aircraft or real estate, could not bring themselves to look upon theatre as a legitimate saleable article. One Board member, whose business acumen and courageous tactics had earned him considerable wealth, told me that it was "mathematically impossible" for the Festival's gross income ever to exceed $17,000. With his warning in mind, you can imagine that it gives me a kind of gratification to contemplate the 1973 Tudor Guild gross income of $45,000 coming, as it does almost entirely, from the sale of souvenirs at the rear of the Elizabethan Theatre auditorium.

One of the disturbing and typical signs of the amateurishness in the relationship between the Board and the Producing Director in that early period was the assumption on the part of some of the Board members that every budget submitted to them had been automatically padded to take care of any reductions that the Board might make. This attitude revealed a humiliating lack of faith in me as well as a lack of experience on their part which might have provided them with criteria for judging the costs of operating a theatre. I repeatedly resisted the temptation to fall into the trap of padding the budgets to protect myself for fear of perpetuating this' unbusinesslike method of conducting our affairs. As a consequence, some of those early seasons were inexcusably underbudgeted.

During the early fifties however, my chief concern about the Board was to keep them on their side of the aesthetic fence. In order to do this it was necessary to lean over backward to make it plain that I expected to keep on my side. I made proposals concerning business and management affairs. I even argued at length to support such proposals, but always tried to make it clear that the final decision in those matters lay in their hands. Only in this way could I expect them to understand that all final decisions concerning aesthetic matters were to be my sole responsibility. The more possessive and jealous of their prerogatives they became, the more they were able to understand and to tolerate mine. I have always maintained that this separation of logistics and aesthetics in a theatre organization is as important as the separation of church and state in government.

When Louis B. Wright, past Director of the Folger Library in Washington, D.C., came to visit us in 1967 he was obviously surprised and delighted with our season. One day he drew me aside and asked,

"Do you have any ideas why the Stratford, Connecticut Festival has not been able to achieve an aesthetic identity and direction?"

I said that I had some very definite ideas on the subject and he expressed a desire to hear them. So I said,

"I think it is quite clearly the fault of their Board of Directors, who hire an artistic director and then interfere with his artistic judgment by dictating aesthetic policies."

I did not learn until afterward that Dr. Wright was a member of that Board! Fortunately, he did not disagree with my analysis.

You can imagine that this whole problem of demarcation became much easier when, in the fall of 1953, William Patton became our first fulltime employee as the Festival's General Manager. In that position he was responsible to the Board (and through them to our community and audience) for carrying out business and management policies. He is a creative and sensitive theatre person with the practical experience that soon made it possible for him to be taking the lead in management by presenting policies for the Board's approval.

We made a very good team, for in spite of the fact that our personalities and temperaments are very different, we worked together very closely. Bill, in those early days, was shy, self-effacing and always scrupulously punctilious—sometimes, I thought, agonizingly so. Yet he never seemed to resent that pragmatic part of my personality which sought the focus of spotlight, camera lens and reporters' eye. There were many areas in which our jurisdictions faded into one another, yet we always managed to work out our problems together so we invariably presented a united front to the Board.

The Festival owes a great deal to Mr. John Pletsch. He was a member of our Board during the years of 1957, '58 and '59. As manager of the Jackson County Federal Savings and Loan Association, he was respected by us all, not only because he was a successful businessman, but because he was a knowledgeable "organization" man as well. During those three seasons, whenever difficulties became personality clashes rather than problems to be solved; whenever operational policies developed out of whims rather than reason; whenever there was lack of respect for Board members as rational representatives of their community, or of Bill Patton or me as experts in our own profession, John's soft voice and calm reasonableness put us back on the right track. I think it was his influence that set the stage for the eventual professionalization of the Board and of the staff in their relationship with the Board.

My most difficult and prolonged conflict with the Board came in the years between 1948 when I returned from my first year at Stanford and 1951 when the Board finally authorized the issuing of scholarships to actors of the company.

The discussions started during the planning for the 1949 season. I felt a growing concern about the increasing difficulties in the future recruitment of experienced actors of talent. I was worried not only from a professional point of view, but from a personal one as well. For I discovered instances in which some members of the company were not getting enough to eat. In fact, in 1950 there was a group of the company who built a platform on the lawn outside the theatre and performed their own pre-show kind of entertainment. The girls made tarts at home, and other members passed through the audience with trays, selling their homemade merchandise to raise enough money to buy food for those who had run low on cash. Richard Hay, our scene designer, recalls carrying one of those trays.

Knowing the budget was a tight one, I first approached the Board with a request to offer scholarships, the money for which would not come from Festival funds. I was shocked by the firmness with which my suggestion was turned down. The opposition was not unanimous but was sufficient to keep the argument going for over two years.

Those opposed to the idea saw no parallel with the athletic scholarships at the College, to which several of them contributed. They did not object to paying directors, for the kind of supervision which they did somehow placed them in a different category. They approved of paying scene technicians for they "worked" and when they were through working they had produced an object that could be measured, felt and conceivably sold.

This was such a perfect illustration of the Lockean concept of the nature of things, that I should not have been taken by surprise. In my anger and frustration I'm afraid I called one Board member a Puritan, which merely confused him.

Then several things changed. There were some changes in the membership of the Board: there were by this time several other Shakespearean Festivals bidding for young actors and the Korean War had started. I finally convinced the Board in 1951 that we would not have a company unless we could meet the competition of other festivals, all of whom were giving scholarships or salaries and somehow overcame the danger of our company members being bled off by the military draft. Thus in 1951 we offered ten $100 scholarships to "actors exempt from the draft." How different it is now, when all non-staff members of the company in all departments receive scholarships which totaled in 1974 over $150,000.

I have not forgotten that I promised to deal in this chapter with events rather than people. But it is impossible to separate the two, short of getting involved with earthquakes, cyclones or other natural disasters. However, in 1948, that first season after I returned from

Stanford, a number of actions were set in motion which were especially important to the development of the Oregon Shakespearean Festival as we know it today.

For some time I had thought of including one of Shakespeare's English History plays in each season. If they were played in historical order, they would create a pageant covering a greater and more exciting span of history than ever attempted by another playwright. There are 10 of these chronicle plays. The first in the order of English history is *King John;* the last, *Henry VIII.* They are both separated in time from the middle eight plays by a number of years. But those central eight *(Richard II, Henry IV, part 1, Henry IV, part 2, Henry V,* the three parts of *Henry VI,* and *Richard III)* tell a continuous story covering the reign of five kings, the causes and results of the War of the Roses, the defeat of France and the establishment on the throne of England of Henry Tudor, the grandfather of Queen Elizabeth I.

It was impossible to consider more than one of them in each season, for many of them were among the less popular of Shakespeare's plays. Only four of them had been produced with even moderate frequency during my lifetime, and most scholars pointed out the obvious literary crudities of some of them which belonged to Shakespeare's "apprentice" period. I had not heard of a production of *King John* within the previous fifty years. And the unromantic, mathematical aura of a title like *Henry VI, part 2* could not be expected to draw great numbers of people to the box office.

That childish maxim, "If you're the only one you're automatically the best" still had a grain of truth. If we paid the price of having small houses for a time, it eventually became a matter of prestige to be the only theatre where one could see the least known of Shakespeare's plays. I know of several theatres in this country and in England who claim to have produced the entire canon, but not one of them has done all three parts of *Henry VI* in three separate productions. It is their practice to perform an adaptation of these plays, sometimes in combination wth *Richard III,* cut down so that they become, in effect, one or two plays. In fact, ours is the only theatre I know of which has done all 37 of the plays of Shakespeare's canon in 37 separate productions. In fact, at this writing we have only *Timon of Athens* to play again to have done them all at least twice—some of the more popular eight and nine times.

Audiences for the History plays were very small at first. I have played for as few as 75. But they grew steadily over the years, and enthusiasts became more dedicated as time went by. One night during the season of 1953 we were playing *Henry VI, part 1* when it started to rain. It was a warm, gentle rain that came in spasmodic showers. Realizing that this might be a once-in-a-lifetime experience, most everyone just hunkered down in his wraps and continued to watch the play. This situation continued without anyone being particularly disturbed by it. Then, toward the end of the play, the skies opened and the rain came in torrents. I was frightfully disappointed for I knew that there would be a mass exodus and we would perform the last scenes of the piece to an empty house. I was delightfully wrong. Not more than a half dozen people left the auditorium. The next day the Associated Press wires carried an item describing the scene at the last curtain call during which the entire company of actors stepped forward and spontaneously applauded the audience.

Enthusiasm for the Histories was not confined to the audience. The company approached each production, especially those of the earlier, lesser known plays with the kind of creative intensity that they would have felt had it been the world premiere. There were no precedents, no traditions—only the written words. Each production was a voyage of discovery. If I may generalize, let me say that the greatest discovery was that, though Shakespeare in his early plays imitated the artificial literary style and obvious theatricality affected by many of the successful hacks that preceded him, the crudity of his style frequently revealed a gut-gripping strength, and his theatrical gimmickry could create breath-taking excitement for a twentieth century audience.

Let me illustrate: In *Henry VI, part 1* there is a scene in which a sergeant enters on the inner above stage. He sets two sentinels to watch for signs of possible attack upon the walls of Orleans. Talbot's forces enter below and erect two scaling ladders upon each of which two soldiers mount to the "walls" of Orleans. The rhythmic movement of the four soldiers up the 12 foot ladders, to the accompaniment of rolling kettle drum, blaring bugle and the shouts of soldiers and clash of weapons, childishly simple in reality, became in imagination the exciting defeat of the French and the capture of Orleans.

Two more illustrations from the same play: The first is a piece of business that I was almost sure the director would cut. James Sandoe directed all three parts of *Henry VI* the first time around. I believe he is the first person, in modern times, to do so. The piece of business was simply this: a cannon was to be fired from one side of the stage and shoot half the face off a man standing only 55 feet away on the other side of the stage. Jim Sandoe firmly insisted on leaving it in. It worked like this. The cannon was fired out of sight through the window above the right stage entrance. Salisbury, the victim, stood in the window above the stage left entrance. For the sound of the cannon we used the old device of a blank cartridge fired into a barrel. For smoke we had to make do with a CO_2 fire extinguisher. Its puff of vapor was quite satisfactory, but the whooshing sound of the released pressure we thought might be identified and distracting. Rick Risso, as Salisbury, stood at the opposite window with his hand near a container of artificial blood. The sequence was, first, the boom of the cannon, then the puff of "smoke," the whooshing sound and Rick's scream as he put his hand to his face, staggered back revealing the whole side of his head as a bloody mess. Much to our surprise the "whoosh" was interpreted by the audience as the sound of the cannon ball going through the air. In fact, one member of the audience said he "saw" the projectile fly across the stage.

The heavy-handed rhetoric in the style of Seneca was very popular during Shakespeare's younger days. That pompous gentleman had been Nero's tutor until he had been poisoned by his pupil. However sympathetic you may be toward Nero's motives, his pupils writings, rediscovered by Shakespeare's predecessors, were the models for the popular blood-and-thunder drama during the period that ushered Shakespeare into the theatre. And Shakespeare, writing for a popular audience, did not hesitate to copy the master or copy the copiers.

One rhetorical device frequently used was called by the forbidding name of "stychomythia." The particular scene I have in mind to illustrate Shakespeare's use of stychomythia is the scene in which the brave warrior, Talbot, knowing that his army had been betrayed, surrounded and marked for complete destruction, tries to persuade his young son, John, to escape. John refuses to leave his father. The lines of the scene are typical of the method. Single line moralistic, antithetical speeches forming rhymed couplets. Some of them go this way:

TALBOT
Shall all thy mother's hopes lie in one tomb?

JOHN
Ay, rather than I'll shame my mother's womb.

TALBOT
Upon my blessing, I command thee go.

JOHN
To fight I will, but not to fly the foe.

TALBOT
Part of thy father may be saved in thee.

JOHN
No part of him but will be shame in me.

TALBOT
Thou never hadst renown, nor canst not lose it.

JOHN
Yes, your reowned name: shall flight abuse it?

You see from this sample of the method and the scene how flat the words lie on the page, how simple the rhythms and how obvious the rhyme scheme. Yet in the hands of Philip Hanson as Talbot and the youthful William Ball as John these became unforgettable, thrilling moments in the play. The two contrasting voices used the rhythms and the repetitive rhymes as two primitive drummers might use tom toms to beat at your ears and stir your pulse.

Shakespeare has been so frequently discussed as a man of ideas that we tend to overlook his mastery over us by kinaesthesia so that we are moved by his stirring of our muscles, tendons and joints.

So the project of producing all the history plays in their historical sequence had two important consequences for the Festival. First, it helped to solidify and promulgate the already existing feelings of ownership and dedication on the part of a large nucleus of our audience. Second, and perhaps more important, it gave us a kind of zealous faith in Shakespeare as an effective man of the theatre whose scripts could be taken literally. We became confident that, when problems of production or interpretation arose, the answers could be found within those scripts. Thus, because each play was approached with the question: "How can we make this production more like the one Shakespeare saw?" instead of "How can we invent some ingenious way of making it different for the sake of variety?" we developed among our audience a reputation for integrity which has been in part responsible for our steady rate of growth at the box office, as well as a steady growth in theatrical quality.

Another facet of the Festival's development started one afternoon during the season of 1951. On the grassy knoll outside the Elizabethan Theatre stage door, I encountered a modest-appearing, quiet-spoken man who introduced himself as Tom Cooke. He said he belonged to a recorder group in Los Angeles, and that he was interested in our music program. Fortunately, I am of a loquacious nature and have always been willing to talk endlessly about the Festival to anyone who shows the slightest interest.

I told him of my disappointment in not finding the same kind of purposeful direction in our music program that we had been able to see developing in the presentation of the plays. With no precedent and a colossal ignorance, we had bumbled through a number of experiments. We even went so far as to have a symphony orchestra on stage to play an overture. But the tedious interval required to clear the stage of instruments, musicians and music stands before the play could start made the error obvious. We used phonograph records for a season or two, but that proved unsatisfactory for a number of reasons. Our principal problem, I confided to Mr. Cooke, was that there was no continuity. Thus we were not able to profit from what had been learned the previous season. What we needed, I told him, was a director of music who would take the same interest in developing an Elizabethan style of music as we had done in the presentation of the scripts.

After talking for several hours, Mr. Cooke bid me goodbye and I thought no more about the matter—till the next afternoon when he sought me out again. You can imagine my amazed delight when he asked if the Festival would accept $1,000 a year for five years to pay the salary of a music director. When I assured him the gift would be gratefully received, he asked me if I had a candidate in mind for the job. When I said that I had not, he suggested the name of Hans Lampl, making clear that Lampl's appointment was not a necessary condition of the gift. He did suggest, however, that whomever was appointed to the position, should be given a minimum of two seasons in order to have time to properly find his place. I agreed with both suggestions and succeeded in obtaining the services of Mr. Lampl.

He was a talented, experienced, European-trained musician. He arranged music for three of the plays based on Elizabethan-Jacobean models. He persuaded us to use the music composed by a young San Francisco musician, Ellis B. Kohs, for *Julius Caesar*. As Mr. Kohs had studied under Igor Stravinsky you may imagine that the music was brilliant, but hardly suitable for a production on an Elizabethan stage. Mr. Lampl organized a symphony orchestra and directed a concert as the climax of the musical season. We also found ourselves again waiting for the stage to be cleared of music stands after the pre-play musical program each night. It was with more than a little relief that I accepted Mr. Lampl's resignation for the next season because we could not agree upon budgetary matters.

Completely at a loss as to what to do about the 1953 season, I invited to my home a number of the important musicians of the Valley. When I asked them what to do about a director of music, they turned almost as one to indicate a portly man whom I had known for some time. He was head of the music department of the Ashland High School and he had played the cello for several Festival music groups. What I didn't know was that his special interest was Renaissance music and that he had for some time been developing an ancient instruments group, had an active recorder group in his own family, and owned an impressive library of Baroque music. W. Bernard Windt became the Festival's music director that season, a position he held for 20 years.

Something of the nature of problems of providing music for the production of Shakespeare on an Elizabethan stage, and a very fine expression of Bernie Windt's point of view in solving them are expressed in an article in our souvenir program for 1956. The article is unsigned, but it is undoubtedly in the style of Dr. Bailey. A part of that article follows:

> When the actual songs in a Shakespeare play are considered, problems for the Elizabethan producer pile one upon the other. Shakespeare often wrote his own lyrics to fit the mood or situation in a scene and set them to a currently popular tune. Unfortunately, however, the name of the tune was not included in his script. Some of these songs have been preserved by historians or musicologists with the correct melody, but of the vast majority only the words remain with no inkling of what the music might have been.
>
> With the Festival's extensive library of Shakespeareana, it is sometimes possible for us to find the proper tune, or at least one that fits the words and is of the right spirit, but occasionally there seems to be just nothing that is appropriate. In such cases music must be composed in one of the popular forms of the day and conforming with Elizabethan mode and tonality.
>
> It may be argued that many of the fine poems found in the plays have been set to music by the 18th and 19th century masters; they are familiar to all and melodic: why not use them? These composers, however, wrote as it were, out of context and the music generally will not fit the production scheme of the play. As a case in point, it is with trepidation and humility that one undertakes to discard Franz Schubert in favor of resetting *Hark, Hark the Lark*, but, unfortunately for us, he walked the earth a little late to even think of writing in the Elizabethan style. The harmonic forms, of which he was master, far better served his purpose than the polyphonic Madrigal or Ayre.

The music in the plays, other than the songs, posed equally difficult problems. There were the funeral dirges, military marches, various kinds of trumpet calls. Even drum rhythms were different from modern beats. The dance music was also a problem for research or original composition. A constant concern for Bernie was the matter of trying to satisfy directors' demands for impressively heavy music for royal entries or military marches. Many times what the director really wanted was an anachronistic symphonic sound, which led usually to a compromise of brasses and kettle drum.

I suppose Bernard Windt is the only man who has composed or arranged all the music for the entire Shakespearean canon. He is at present preparing this material for publication. Most of the music was pre-recorded and when we improved our sound system, it was difficult to tell the taped music from live. It was possible for Bernie to get some very fine musicians to do this prerecording. It was much more difficult to assemble singers and instrumentalists who would play "live" for each performance for a whole season. Increasingly, directors wanted musicians in costume on stage. We experimented a time or two with a recorded accompaniment for singers on stage, but that never seemed to work out satisfactortily. Instrumentalists and singers on stage helped the impression of pageantry so necessary in many scenes. After 1960 when we played in our new house with a third story musicians' gallery, directors asked for musicians to perform from that location through all or part of a production.

It was obvious that we could not expect talented young musicians to come and spend a summer with us as long as they merely furnished musical support for the actors who got all the applause. Two different types of musical programs stemmed from this analysis. One was a continuation of and an increase in the number of Renaissance concerts. In this we were assisted by a number of Valley musicians. But as time went on we discovered that the attention span of the average Festival patron was limited where Baroque music was concerned. Then we added dance to the concerts and found that attendance picked up. However, in 1951 when we expanded the Festival schedule from 20 to 25 days we included Sundays. The concerts were forced to play in the afternoon and this never proved popular with our audiences.

The most successful of all the experiments designed to provide musicians with performance opportunities outside the plays also involved dancers. This has developed into our very popular "pre-show" entertainment that has not only an artistic purpose but also a very materialistic one. It is now a very important part of what we used to call the Tudor Fair. The other part of that nightly celebration before each performance was first made possible in 1952 by the incorporation of the Tudor Guild, an auxiliary organization for the purpose of assuming a number of duties in support of the Festival company members, duties which the Festival Board could not easily perform. The Guild was established on the suggestion of Dr. Bailey, who did much to set its course, and it was originally formed largely through the interest of Mrs. Margaret Schuler.

Aside from contributing considerable help in financing the Festival's scholarship program, the Guild established a non-interest loan fund for members of the company. To this end they are annually involved in several money-raising projects, chief among which is the souvenir booth at the rear of the auditorium. More recently this booth has been joined by a refreshment booth operated for similar ends by Beta Sigma Phi, and a pillow and blanket concession operated by Soroptimist International. Both of these organizations furnish several scholarships each year.

It was soon discovered that Festival audience members would not tarry after the performance to patronize these booths and as there are no intermissions in the Elizabethan Theatre productions, the only thing left was to entice them to come early and do their shopping before the productions. It was to this end that our pre-show entertainments were first planned. They have now become very popular and musicians and dancers have enthusiastic audiences to motivate a continued increase in excellence.

Perhaps one of the most valuable parts of Bernard Windt's contribution to the Festival was to provide 20 years of solid continuity and a firm direction to a unique music program which provides precedence and inspiration to those who follow.

One of the "trends" among modern young directors is to ask the musical director to score a Shakespearean play in the manner made familiar by motion pictures. Bernie was not in sympathy with such a technique because he believed it to be anachronistic when producing a play on an Elizabethan stage. I agree with him and object to the method specifically because it tends to create little musical introductions or transitions which separate rather than overlap the scenes, and because it tends to distract from or substitute for, the music of the language. It also in many cases makes the words unintelligible. In a motion picture theatre, the sounds come from a single source, or conceivably from a series of controlled sources. The mixture of sounds is expertly balanced in the laboratory so music and speech blend instead of combat each other. This is not possible on the stage. I have earlier made fun of the nineteenth century "fiddle in the wings." It seems to be returning in modern dress.

I will have more to say about Bernie Windt's work later, but first I would like to report a conversation which took place the same summer as the epochal conversation with Tom Cooke about our music program. This other conversation presented a revolutionary idea which resulted in a project which coupled exhilarating success with heartbreaking disaster—a project so important that, without it I sincerely believe we would not have the Angus Bowmer Theatre today.

XVI

New Theme

I HAD LONG BEEN ACQUAINTED with Jim Selleck, the manager of the local motion picture theatre called The Varsity. This theatre was owned by the Lippert Motion Picture chain which also owned another in town which they kept dark. In those days, the companies who owned chains of cinema houses made it a practice to acquire an extra theatre in each town where they operated. This theatre was not operated regularly unless a competitor threatened to move into town. Then they would open the extra house until the interloper was convinced there was not business enough to support the chain's regular theatre, their extra theatre *and* his own proposed picture house. When he had given up, the chain would close their extra house and all would go on as before.

Many of my theatre acquaintances across the country had tried to rent such empty houses to accommodate proposed live theatre enterprises. But the chains refused to make them available for either love or money. The obvious reason was that they thought it foolish to nurture any form of competitive entertainment enterprises.

I give you this background so you may appreciate just how startling Jim Selleck's proposal was. He stopped me on the knoll one afternoon toward the end of the season, just as Tom Cooke had done. He said something to this effect:

"I have noticed for the past several seasons that my box office income has increased each August over the take for the previous August. It occurred to me that there might be some correlation with the Festival expansion during this same time. In fact, the connection seemed so much more than a coincidence that this season I kept a chart, and with the cooperation of your box office I found that there was almost 100% correlation. That is, when you had a good house, I had a good house. When your attendance was low, so was mine. As a matter of fact, these figures were so persuasive that the Lippert people have authorized me to make you an offer. If you will produce a winter festival they will give you the use of the Lithia Theatre free of charge!''

You can imagine my surprise and delight. There were a number of reasons why a winter festival should be attempted. The first, naturally, was my own lifelong urge to be involved in theatre. This would be an opportunity to produce some modern plays with theatre personnel more mature and more experienced than my college undergraduates. There were a number of the Festival company who were not going, or need not go, back to college that fall. Some of them had been with us for four or five seasons. There was Suzanne LaMarre Hanson, Richard Graham, Philip Hanson, Clara Daniels, William Oyler, William Patton, Brad Curtis, Paul Kliss, Barbara Huggins and several others.

I had another reason for desiring the project. There were still far too many people in Ashland, and within commuting distance of Ashland, who thought Shakespeare too ''highbrow'' or too dull to warrant their attendance at the summer Festival. I had a theory that, if they could be enticed to see our young, talented actors in some non-Shakespearean plays that these people had not been conditioned to label ''highbrow'' or ''dull,'' they might turn up the next summer to see these same exciting artists—even in Shakespeare.

There was another strong motivation for taking advantage of the Lipperts' offer of the Lithia Theatre. That was the warm personality emanating from the rows of red plush seats, U-shaped balcony, snug theatre boxes and central chandelier—all reminding nostalgically of the houses at the turn of the century when theatre was a part of everyday life. It was an intimate house, seating 570 people.

There was a full loft over the stage, making it possible to fly scenery, a necessary adjunct to playing four plays in repertory, as there was little or no storage space backstage. There was ridiculously little space for a shop which turned out to be merely a closed-in loading platform. The offstage space on either side was very cramped, but not impossible. As for dressing rooms—they were typical of most commercial theatres, too few, too small, and, being under the stage, were dank and had no ventilation. But like the ladies of her day whose corseted waists, ruffled busts and ratted hair, if inconvenient and highly personal, gave the observer an impression of luxuriant charm, the Lithia, in spite of inconvenient backstage amenities, presented to the public a gracious theatricality that mellowed the most cynical heart.

One of the unpleasant facts of life I learned very early was that there is a vast difference between wanting a thing and having it. No matter how convincing the arguments or noble the reasons why we should have a winter repertory company in Ashland, there were a number of fairly convincing reasons why we *couldn't*.

The first and most vital question to be settled was whether or not there was an audience, within commuting distance, big enough to support a season of rep. I believed there was. But all my reading on the subject and all the experiences related to me by my theatre friends indicated that even under the most favorable conditions it would take two or three years for the receipts to begin to cover expenses. This meant the operation would have to be subsidized for at least two years.

The Festival was the most obviously appropriate patron, for it had the most to gain. But I could not in good conscience argue with the Board's decision that they could not gamble inadequate reserves on a winter rep without endangering the operation of the Festival. The College said they had no funds that could be used in such a venture. I gathered that the administrations of both institutions thought the idea more than a little foolhardy.

To make it even more foolhardy, Richard Graham and I put up the money to subsidize the capital expenditures and expected operating deficits for that first season. Richard was able to contribute $1500 and I was able to scrape up $500. This $2,000 had to cover the purchase of a sky drop, scene paint, lumber, nails, screws and other hardware; pay the salaries of the company for several weeks until box office receipts started to come in in sufficient quantity; utilities, royalties, scripts, printing of tickets, advertising, programs and many other necessities.

I remember that Bill Patton designed a lighting control board which was wired into our temporary light system by a licensed electrician so it could pass the fire marshal's inspection. The board incorporated portable dimmer units from the College and the Festival. In fact, both institutions were generous in lending us spotlights, flats, platforms and other equipment without which we never would have made it.

Each member of the company did any theatre task for which he had the capability and/or the time. Actors did technical work, technicians acted, actors directed. My fulltime schedule at the college, teaching 15 credit hours, directing plays and the many routine academic chores unhappily prevented me from directing or playing anything but bit parts which could be rehearsed at night.

William Oyler was a very efficient and skillful technical director. We had no designer, but each director with the help of the rest of the company decided what units of scenery were available for his production and in what arrangement they should be placed. Thus the flats, curtains, platforms and properties borrowed from the College and the Festival, plus the properties and furniture which we were able to scrounge from the Bowmer household and from other sympathetic ménages, were arranged in convenient and appropriate combinations and placements. Bill Oyler built other pieces we needed and supervised the more or less unskilled company in practically every offstage moment in driving nails, sawing lumber and painting. His biggest project was a ceiling piece which we used in the two box sets of the first season and in several of the other productions of later seasons.

Bill lived in the theatre that first season and still talks occasionally of the theatre ghost which he sensed and heard almost every night. Every theatre seems to be haunted, as any actor can tell you. I accept that fact, but do not agree that these manifestations are the spirits of dead persons. I believe that every theatre is haunted by the ghosts of all the productions that were once excitingly, vibratingly alive, and are now melted away into air—into thin air—and the emanations of the spirit they once inspired. Where else do old productions go?

Bill Patton, aside from being our lighting crew, handled all our publicity and public relations and played some bit parts. Bill had had two years of public relations experience promoting floor shows and dinner dancing for the Mark Hopkins Hotel in San Francisco. This experience plus his personal knowledge of and affection for the people of the Rogue River Valley made his work for us particularly effective. He also had an opportunity to show a flair for organizational detail which was to be very important in his later career with the Festival. I had an opportunity over the years to watch Bill mature into a knowledgeable and dedicated theatre person. All these factors put together led to my suggesting to the Board in the fall of 1953 that he become General Manager, the Festival's first fulltime employee.

Our beautiful little theatre had been built soon after the turn of the century by two brothers, one of whom was Professor Vining of the "old Normal School," a long defunct ancestor of Southern Oregon College. He taught Shakespeare and acted in and directed some

Shakespearean productions for that older institution. I have mentioned before that he had developed a national reputation as an orator of the declamatory school. He and his brother were both dead by 1951 so we decided to name our aspiring young troupe "The Vining Repertory Company."

Our audience was accustomed to the Festival's four play repertoire, so we decided to use that format. The first season's fare was frankly aimed at the popular audience. The formula was one for the discriminating to three for the whole spectrum of prospective theatre patrons: Anouilh's *Antigone*; Agatha Christie's *Ten Little Indians*; *On Monday Next*, a farce by Philip King and *The Late Christopher Bean* by Sydney Howard.

The formula proved to be faulty, for *Antigone*, which we had assumed might be "caviar to the general," proved to be one of the more popular plays of the season. Bill Oyler was a strong, if overly temperamental director. The production was sensitive and meaningful. Especially effective performances were presented by Sally Cassell as Antigone, Paul Kliss as The Chorus and the best Creon that I have ever seen was done by Richard Graham. His logical arguments for the reasonableness and efficiency of the ruthless practices of dictatorship were so clear and convincing that one could see why the Germans allowed the French to produce the play during the Occupation. Their willingness to be persuaded by that logic must have blinded them to the total meaning of the play which proclaims the ultimate triumph of the human spirit.

Dick Graham directed *On Monday Next*, a ridiculous piece about a second-rate English rep company in rehearsal of a worse than second-rate script. We all thought it so funny that we couldn't get through a rehearsal without breaking into uncontrolled laughter. We all had fun doing it. I especially enjoyed playing the stupid author who could have been played by Stan Laurel. The audience didn't think it nearly as funny as we did. It was only moderately successful. "Chris Bean," directed by Barbara Huggins was also only so so at the box office.

As I remember it, *Ten Little Indians* was the most popular show of the season. This was not only because of the mystery story appeal, and more than adequate performances, but because of the astute direction of Philip Hanson. He used the usual devices available to a director whose job is, in part, to center attention on the key character, idea, facial expression, gesture or speech during each moment of the play. But he used the same techniques for an opposite reason. If you remember the play, it concerns 10 people isolated on an island, and one by one they are murdered until apparently only two are left. Featured in the decor is a group of 10 little Indian figurines. Just before each murder is discovered, another of the little Indian figures disappears. The usual method of handling this melodramatic portent is to have threads or springs operated from off stage so that the disappearance in that way goes unnoticed. Philip managed these vanishing Indians by having the murderer take them from their bases in full view of the audience. However, he managed to misdirect the audience's attention by a big movement or other business so that no one saw the figure taken. Moreover, some of the murders took place on stage, and in the two cases that I remember, one a stabbing, the murderer left a knife in the victim's top jacket pocket; in the other, a hypodermic needle was left in the victim's lap—again in full view of the misdirected audience. We had people coming back several times for a chance to spot the murderer in the act. Even though they knew who the villain was by the end of the first performance they saw, they could not keep their eyes on him during the calculated distraction of the stage business. Moral for beginners: learn how to stand still on stage.

As we had expected, though our audiences had been as good as predicted, our original investment was still invested at the end of the season. Not only that, more operational money was needed to start a second season. Fortunately, Dick Graham was able to ante another thousand dollars. Because we thought the winter weather would not be conducive for that goodly part of our audience coming from Klamath Falls, Yreka and Grants Pass, we scheduled our second season for the next spring.

For this round there were a few new faces, but many of our former company were still with us. One of the newcomers was Elmarie Wende from the University of Oregon. She showed surprising versatility in playing the title role in *Claudia* and a heartbraking Linda, Willie Loman's wife, in *The Death of a Salesman*. Dick Graham's Willie was a superb presentation of that exhausted man, old before his time, destroyed by all the wrong values of middle class America.

Claudia was a good performance of a script which is not particularly memorable. *The Importance of Being Earnest* was the least successfully realized of all our productions. Clara Daniels and Suzie Hanson were delightful as the two precious loonies in *Arsenic and Old Lace* and they had for the most part an unusually fine supporting cast. Brad

Curtis was a startlingly convincing ersatz Boris Karloff. The ebullient Eddy Barron, who played Biff in "Salesman," charged up San Juan Hill with zany enthusiasm accoutered with teeth, mustache and glasses which were amazingly Rooseveltian. Paul Kliss as Dr. Einstein recalled the performance of Peter Lorre in an entirely chilling and satisfactory way. The production was a success—due in no part whatsoever to the efforts of Bill Dawkins or me as policemen!

The box office receipts for the second season exceeded those of the first by a considerable margin, and we could look forward to the next fall season, without the necessity of digging further into our pockets. Though, of course, the operation still owed Dick $2500 and me $500.

We opened the 1952 fall season with a midnight matinee of *Dracula* on Hallowe'en. That old war horse was terribly dated and should have been rewritten or skipped, but the theatre was crowded that opening night and started the season off with its own kind of theatrical flourish. *Vinegar Tree* was another adequate though not memorable production, but *The Glass Menagerie* and my old friend, *The Show-Off* are both fine pieces and our productions did credit to them.

Again there was an increase in attendance and, by half way through the run, we anticipated our first season in which all current operational expenditures would be covered by current receipts. Gertrude and I were present at almost every performance and on the night of November 19, we had enjoyed a fine performance of *Vinegar Tree*. As usual we enjoyed greeting our friends and acquaintances on the way in and out of our beautiful little miniature opera house. We were home and fast asleep by midnight, but at 2:00 A.M. the raucous ringing of the telephone woke me and I stumbled into the other room, still not fully awake, to answer it.

I picked up the phone impatiently, fully expecting a wrong number call. Answering my gruff "Hello" was a voice so strained with emotion that it was not until after he had hung up that I realized it was Phil Hanson saying what must have been, "The theatre is burning! Come down! Come down!"

I threw on some clothes and drove at an unlawful speed toward the catastrophe. As I could see the flames shooting high in the air long before I arrived at the scene, I drove the car around a block to park it up the hill from the burning structure, for fire hoses blocked a direct approach. I joined the huddled little group of our company in front of the Lithia (Mark Antony) Hotel. The silent company members stood in the intense heat with drawn faces, reflecting variously grief, suffering and anger.

When the firemen had arrived from only two blocks away the flames were already shooting above the roof, and now the fire was gutting the entire structure: the beautiful red plush seats, the elegant boxes, our brave central lighting bowl that had tried so hard to be a chandelier—all gone! Toppled by the weight of the cantilevered balcony, the front wall was the first to crash with a loud noise, a geyser of sparks and flame, and a wave of heat that drove us back to the hotel entryway. Thus exposed, the proscenium arch could be seen still standing, shooting flames around its stage opening in what could only be its last and most spectacular theatrical display. When that whole stage wall collapsed into what had been the auditorium, I turned away.

Strangely enough my thoughts at that moment were not on the lost investment, the crippled season, nor even the ending of the Vining Repertory Company, but rather filled with horror and grief at the agonizing death of the gracious little old lady of a theatre across the street.

Through the generosity of the College we were able to finish the season in Churchill Auditorium. Attendance was not disappointing, but the company members were in trouble. The first season we had paid each of them $25 a week—not a munificent sum even in those pre-inflation days. But when state and federal taxes were deducted there was too little left on which to survive. After that, we paid them enough so they had approximately $25 per week after taxes. You can imagine that this income was much too small to insure against the necessity of belt tightening. After the fire, however, they were in much deeper financial difficulties. In those days each actor was required to furnish his own wardrobe, so every member of the company had lost practically every article of clothing he possessed. Only one member had been able to afford insurance. As a result there were several benefit programs arranged in the Valley to help them replace these losses.

That was the end of The Vining Repertory Company, for there was no theatre in which to play. The College could not give over the use of Churchill Auditorium indefinitely, for their own schedule made more use of that facility than was comfortable. Besides, school auditoriums with their inadequate stages, creaky flat floors, their institutional smells, could not substitute for our late, little old lady downtown, with her elderly charm.

Ironically, there were negotiations for the purchase of the theatre for our use at the time it burned. Only a week or two before the fire, Julie Carpenter, a member of the Vining Board, told me that she had persuaded her father to investigate the possible purchase of the building as a gift to the Vining Repertory Company.

I shall have more to say later about members of the Carpenter family, for they have been essential friends of the Festival for a long time. For many years the entire Festival company was entertained each season at the Alfred Carpenter estate, "Topsides," for a full day of luxurious eating, swimming, games and relaxation. Without the help of that truly gentle man, Alfred Carpenter, the financing of the rebuilt Elizabethan Theatre in 1959 and the construction of the Bowmer Theatre in 1970 would have been impossible. Alfred's nephew, Dunbar Carpenter, was a long time member of the Festival Board, serving during that time as a very effective president. Dunbar's wife, Jane, was an active member of Tudor Guild and one of his daughters became a valued member of our dance company. Julie's relationship with the Festival has a personal touch which I will relate in a later chapter.

You can imagine my excitement as Julie related the plan to purchase the Vining Theatre for us. But after a moment my excitement turned to disappointment, for the Vining Repertory Company had no prospects for the necessary funds to keep such a theatre going: pay the insurance, taxes and so on. I suggested that the theatre be offered to the College, for the Festival had no reserves to pay these additional expenses. If the college would guarantee us the use of the theatre for a part of the year, the purchase would still be of great benefit to us. The State System of Higher Education agreed to accept the gift if certain improvements were made, such as bringing the ancient wiring up to code. This is where negotiations stood when the fire occurred.

Vining was dead, but we had proved a point: there was potential audience for the presentation of a repertoire of non-summer, non-Shakespearean plays. For many years we were frequently asked, "When are you going to revive Vining?" We always answered, "When we get a theatre." This attitude on the part of the public was one of several factors which gave the Shakespearean Festival Board the courage to start a fund-raising drive in 1968 to build a modern indoor theatre which became known as The Angus Bowmer Theatre.

XVII

Love Song

S TRANGE CIRCUMSTANCES, coincidences, even misfortunes
have more than once led to happy developments at the Festival.
One such misfortune was the fatal accident which precipitated an
airplane into the streets of downtown Los Angeles. One of the seriously injured survivors of that wreck was a famous NBC radio broad-
caster by the name of Jennings Pierce. When he recovered, after nearly
two years in the hospital, he chose not to face again the extreme
pressures which he knew awaited him if he again became a part of the
upper echelons of the NBC staff. As a result of this decision he shortly
found himself the manager of Radio Station KMED, an NBC affiliate,
in Medford, Oregon—12 miles from Ashland.

In 1951 Jennings arranged with the NBC network to broadcast a
live coast to coast half hour arrangement of *King Lear* from our stage,
before a daytime audience. As his former confrere, NBC producer
Andrew C. Love was conveniently scheduled to pass through the area
that summer it was only natural that Jennings should ask Mr. Love to
produce the show. It was a case of love at first sight: Andrew for the
Festival and the Festival for Andrew. He not only produced that first
NBC coast to coast broadcast, but has continued to do that and more for
the Festival each year for over 25 years.

We consider ourselves very fortunate to have on our staff a man
who, before his retirement from NBC was known over the radio world
for his production of such radio classics as The Standard Symphony
Hour, the University Hour, The Eternal Light and many others.

Through the facilities of their affiliate station KMED in Medford,

237

NBC continued to carry this program until 1974, long after they had ceased to produce other programs of this sort. In later days the show was taped, but was made available to their stations across the United States. But each season Andy also produced an hour-long tape of another play which was distributed to stations who requested it. Through these two programs, which were also broadcast by Armed Forces Radio and Radio Free Europe, literally hundreds of thousands of listeners throughout the world got a taste of our quality and a chance to hear of our progress.

The unmistakable Love touch is easily detected in his productions of the full length performances taped of every one of each season's plays especially for our own library and is also heard in our minute long radio spot advertisements during those Love years, run as a public service by many stations throughout the West. For many years the music of Bernie Windt's musicians, recorded for our productions, was produced by Andy.

Andrew Love is of Danish extraction with the Dane's natural flair for practicality in his art. During dress rehearsals and in early performances one would see him with a script, stopwatch and pencil, making notes on the actual elapsed time of lines, speeches and scenes. Lest I have made him sound cold or distant, I must mention the quizzical lights that dance in his eyes as he speaks of the most prosaic subjects with a straightfaced humor which is uniquely his own. In rehearsal or performance of one of his productions, one could identify him by his earphones and stopwatch. Otherwise he is the unidentifiable source of the unmistakable "Love" hallmark. The only other artist I have seen at work who could so distinguish himself as unobtrusively was the motion picture director Frank Capra. It has been one of the many personal rewards the Festival has bestowed upon Gertrude and me that over the years we have come to count Andrew Love and his sprightly little wife, Hazel, as our very close friends.

I must relate an interesting incident that happened when Gertrude and I were visiting Hollywood during the time when Andrew was still one of NBC's top producers. When I called him to let him know we were in town, he said, "Why don't you come over to the studio this evening. We're taping Frankie Sinatra's weekly show." Then added in his typically droll fashion, "It might even be interesting."

When I parked my car in the lot behind the huge NBC studio building at the corner of Sunset and Vine, Frankie had already arrived, for there was his shiny black Cadillac which seemed to my small town eyes to occupy a disproportionate length of the block-long parking lot. I sighed with envy of one who could afford such elegance.

Following Andrew's directions, I found my way to his broadcast booth. As I opened the door, I was confronted by a swarm (I would say "mob" but the word is overworn) of people. I learned later they were Frankie's bodyguards, agents, lawyers, writers and God knows what else—all part of his unescapable entourage. Frankie was out in the studio with the small combo which was to accompany him. Through the glass I could see him going over the music with his assistant. Several numbers were taped. I have never been an incurable Sinatra fan, but he and the boys were in fine form that night, and I enjoyed the songs. Andrew told me later the orchestra was not a regular group, that is, they did not habitually play together. This was a surprise to me because they seemed to be wonderfully coordinated.

Finally there came a hitch because Frankie was not happy with one of the songs which had been selected. Because the show was being taped and it was possible to stop between numbers, the assistant was sent down to the NBC library to find an alternate song. While they were waiting for his return, one of the musicians—I think it was the pianist—said, "Frankie, how about *Night and Day*?" He began to play, then the flutist said, "How about a little flutter tonguing?" and began to demonstrate by joining the pianist. The string base and bongo drums had already joined the party as the strings and brass began to do their own harmonious thing. Frankie sang a chorus and then said, with obvious excitement, "Okay, let's record it." And they did. Immediately, without music, without rehearsal, even without the experience of having performed together before. The creative excitement was electric and contagious. I even caught it in the booth. I still remember that spontaneous rendition of Cole Porter's *Night and Day* as the best thing I've ever heard Sinatra do.

After the taping was over, Frankie came into the booth and Andy introduced us. After the initial perfunctory greetings, Andy said in his usual droll manner, "Frankie, Angus produces the Oregon Shakespearean Festival. He might have a job for you." Seeing the humorous gleam in Andy's eye, I took my cue and went along with the joke.

"Sure, Frankie," I said, "We're doing *Winter's Tale* next season. You'd make an ideal Autolycus." But Frankie didn't laugh. He didn't crack a smile. It was almost as if he were afraid he might say something that might be used against him. Every nerve was as tight as a string on the guitar which had just played an obligato to his definitive *Night and*

Day. He said quickly, "Nah, Nah, that stuff's not for me. Ya know, Ferrer called me from New York and wanted me to be in his *Richard III*, and ya know, I hung up on him." With that, he turned and disappeared into the great mass of his equally high strung followers.

When I went to get into my car on the way home, I was no longer envious of the owner of the long black Cad. It is quite evident that, to Frank Sinatra, playing in Shakespeare is no joke. I'm not sure that my admiration of Sinatra as an artist was not increased by the incident, but I am appalled when I think what it must be like to live the life of a star. Andrew Love and I have frequently recalled the time Frankie turned down his golden opportunity to play at Ashland!

You can see why Andy has become a valued member of our production and public relations operations, producing, as he does, much of our production music, and the radio programs that have carried the name and nature of the Oregon Shakespearean Festival literally around the world.

It is perhaps not a coincidence that radio gave us another man who, for a period of 11 years was a key figure in developing the unique relationship that exists between the Festival and the public through the media people of the Western states. These people who create or control, especially in Oregon, the contents of newspapers, magazines, radio and television programs, have, to an amazing extent, literally adopted us as one of their public service responsibilities, in part because of Carl Ritchie's remarkable ability as a writer, and also because of his sensitivity to, and knowledge of, the relationships between the needs of the media and the Festival.

Carl first came to us as an actor in 1950, leaving his job as Traffic Director at radio station KOCO in Salem to do so. The circumstances of his first introduction to our household were so unusual and so truly hilarious in retrospect that instant laughter is evoked when, in each other's presence, Gertrude, Carl or I mention, "Gin and Roses." Jay Gordon Thornton was a promoter, and he had decided to "promote" Carl. The young Ritchie was his discovery and Thornton was determined to launch Carl's career with the Oregon Shakespearean Festival. The knock at our door came at a most inopportune time. We were entertaining at dinner that evening Bob and Audrey Stedman, those graduates of the "Teensy Weensy Theatre" who had been so essential in the initial days of the Festival—15 years before.

Anticipating such a complication Jay Gordon Thornton came bearing gifts: a bottle of imported gin and a huge florist's box of beautiful, long stemmed red roses. He introduced himself and Carl and then proceeded to "promote." If you combine the psychology of a carnival barker, the vocabulary of a knowledgeable theatre person, with the charisma of a Hyannis Port candidate, you have Jay Gordon. It is not in Carl's nature to "push" himself, and it was as much because I sympathized with his embarrassment as it was because I was moved by Jay Gordon Thornton's entertaining sales pitch that I agreed to an audition the next day. I was pleased with his reading, and very much impressed with the recording of his radio production of *Cyrano de Bergerac.*

I agreed to take him into the company, but there were complications. He had very little money, and as this was before scholarships were offered, it was decided that he would have to get a job. He obtained one immediately in one of the lumber mills which then existed in Ashland. A few days of this work proved the plan impractical. It not only kept him out of the two plays which rehearsed in the afternoon, but the unaccustomed physical labor left him so exhausted and crippled at night that he couldn't rehearse then, either. He was terribly discouraged and decided he would have to go back to his home in Salem. I couldn't bear the thought of his being cast adrift in this manner. After talking it over with Gertrude, I persuaded him to make use of the new guest room in our garage, and to live with us that summer. Thus it came about that Carl became part of our personal as well as our professional family.

However, personal and financial circumstances kept him from returning to the Festival company for seven years. By that time he had become program director for radio station KSLM and was Acting Instructor in Speech and Drama at Willamette University. He has a great potential as a teacher, but has not been able to pursue a career in education to its ultimate stages of development for he does not have a master's degree. I suspect another reason was that he never would have been able to live long within the confines of academic regimentation.

In 1957 we were in desperate need of a public relations director. Because William Dawkins, a professor at Southern Oregon College, who had served as part-time public relations man for six years, had left his teaching position to go into the advertising business, it became necessary to find a replacement. There were special circumstances which demanded urgency.

I must explain that we were living through rather troublesome times within our Festival organization. We had gradually expanded the season until, by 1956, we were playing the entire month of August, seven days a week. Without being able to put a finger on causes, we were already beginning to feel the pressures which were to become so crucial during the sixties. In groping for methods of expanding our sphere of influence as well as our income I was attracted by the opportunities offered by several invitations to tour our repertoire. There was a faction of the Festival Board which was violently opposed to such expansion. I was not by any means certain of the advisability of such a method of expansion, but insisted that all such offers should be investigated. This question became expanded out of all proportion during the middle fifties. We were invited for a post season run at Santa Barbara; the University of California asked for us, several seasons in a row, to play in their Greek Theatre. We even had an invitation from a group in Alaska. At one point the relations between the Board and me became so strained that I was ordered to refrain from discussing touring with anyone. Of course I ignored this silly order. No one knew better than I that the final decision to tour or not to tour rested exclusively with the Board, but how were they to make an intelligent decision if they deliberately chose to remain ignorant as to what a tour invitation involved.

By 1957 the climate had changed. Perhaps because there had been changes in Board membership, or perhaps because the storm had just run its course. At any rate, I was authorized to investigate an offer from the San Francisco Fine Arts Commission to bring our company to the city and stage our season's repertoire of Shakespeare at the old Alcazar Theatre.

I was in San Francisco to discuss details of the offer with the head of the Arts Commission. By coincidence, Carl Ritchie was there also. I knew that, if ever we needed the talents I now was sure he possessed, we needed them now. I remember that after dinner we went for a walk that ended in Union Square. There we sat on a bench with the muffled late-night sounds of the City all around us. I was unashamedly relying on the romantic atmosphere to do part of my persuasion. I told him of the proposed tour and spoke of the important part he could play in its success. My glowing description was enhanced by the brilliance of the giant Old Crow and TWA signs flashing high over our heads. In the end, he promised to apply for the position of Public Relations Director with the understanding that he could live and work in Salem during the winter months, driving regularly to Ashland for necessary business and be in residence there only during the summer.

He was hired that season as public relations director and maintained that impossible commuting schedule for 11 seasons. But ironically the tour to San Francisco never materialized. When the Royal Shakespeare Company of Stratford, England, announced that they would play in San Francisco that year, our decision to withdraw was not unhappily accepted by the Arts Commission. Looking back on it now, I think it was most fortunate that we did not tour at that stage of our development. We simply were not ready.

One of the many strings Carl Ritchie had to his bow was his practical knowledge of theatre. He was an ideal person to form a liaison between the media people and the theatre for he was intimately familiar with both mystiques. His theatre experience went back to a time even before he was acting and directing for the Pentacle Theatre in Salem and extended through the time when he was on the faculties of Mt. Angel College as well as Willamette University, sometimes combining students from both institutions in theatrical productions. He tried to keep in touch with the performance end of the Festival by playing messengers and banner-bearers which he always did with a flair.

When in 1959 Oregon was celebrating the hundredth anniversary of its becoming a state, we asked Carl to write a special production as the Festival's salute to that event. Carl's *Maske of the New World* portrayed a vision of America as seen through the eyes of Elizabeth's court. It presented such romantic characters as Frobisher, Drake, Raleigh, Inigo Jones Indians, and, of course, Elizabeth herself. It gave opportunity to display the cloud machine and other features of our brand new Elizabethan stage house in a double celebration of its initiation and the Oregon Centennial. It was directed by a young actor, Jerry Turner, who, after directing many other productions for us is now our Producing Director.

Three seasons later, Carl wrote, in collaboration with Leslie Carlson, another music-dance production called *A Thieves Ballad*. This was in response to Bernie Windt's long held desire to make use of Orlando Gibbon's sixteenth centurey concert piece, *Street Cries of London*. This production, for which Bernie created a complete score, was directed by Carl, choreographed by Amanda Taylor, and appeared as an after-piece to fill out the evening after Shakespeare's shortest play, *The Comedy of Errors*.

Our movement into dance-drama was given impetus by the advent of Shirlee Dodge, who became our choreographer in 1963. She had an impressive background of study and performance in this country and abroad, and came to us from the University of Texas where she was Associate Professor of Dance Drama. She and Carl and Bernie found themselves drawn together by an unusually sensitive compatibility in their individual approaches to creativity.

Their first collaboration was a version of Ben Jonson's masque, *Lovers Made Men*. As it was impossible to consistently produce Shakespearean plays to which fore-pieces or after-pieces could be fitted, the masque was produced in eight matinee performances at the Varsity motion picture theatre. A production on this agonizingly small stage, with no backstage space whatsoever, was made possible because a revival of the old Vining Rep had been sponsored by the college in 1961. The expense of remodeling the wide screen to make it portable, as well as the prohibitive rental made a continuation of that plan impossible.

The success of the masque encouraged the attempt of a more ambitious production in the summer of 1966. This was a revival of John Gay's famous musical satire, *The Beggar's Opera*. Bernie arranged the score in a compelling jazz beat which I thought was immediately appealing. I was cast as Peachum opposite Claudia Wilkens who was at least four or five inches taller than I. I had never worked with a choreographer like Shirlee. In our first dance session, she had us listen to the music and then as it was repeated, encouraged us to make "character movements" in rhythm with it. The youngsters who had done this kind of thing before had a kind of "dance vocabulary" from which they could draw, but I bumbled along in what I considered a very unproductive way. But as awkward and "un-dance-like" as those first movements were, I was amazed to find some of them turning up in the dance that gradually evolved from those first gropings.

There was no dressing room space at the Varsity, so we made a virtue out of necessity and formed a parade from our own theatre through the town, in full costume and makeup, singing one of the songs from the Opera, accompanied by the rhythmic banging of bass drum and tamborines. As there was no room back stage, we waited for our entrances in the stifling heat of the alley outside the stage door.

Carl made imaginative use of minimum scenery and entrances down the aisles of the theatre. I will always remember the curtain calls which were made by bringing the entire company singing the finale and swinging down the aisles through the audience who usually stood and clapped in time with Bernie's rousing rhythm. The cast exited onto the stage and out into the alley and around to the front of the house. The first to exit joining the last to enter so that the parade seemed to swell the company miraculously to the delight of the cheering patrons.

This rowdy success was followed by a ballad opera each season for the next three years: The Isaac Bickerstaffe-Mathew Arnold *Maid of the Mill,* then *Lock Up Your Daughters,* adapted by Bernard Miles from Henry Fielding's *Rape Upon Rape* and finally, *Virtue in Danger,* adapted by Paul Dehn and James Bernard from John Van Brugh's *The Relapse.* The three directors worked beautifully together: production, music and dance moving in such close harmony that Carl, Bernie and Shirlee seemed to operate by some kind of telepathy. Then several things happened. During the production of *Virtue in Danger* something happened to the triumvirate, something which mystified and saddened all concerned, but which broke up, for all practical purposes, the formerly close knit team of collaborators.

Ironically, the cessation of the Ballad Opera series occurred long after Carl had become a Fellow of the Folger Shakespeare Library where he launched a continuing study of the form and followed up that experience the next year by a return to Folger and a session of research at the British Museum. His interest and experience with Ballad Opera should make for an interesting and useful book on the subject which I hope will be forthcoming. Carl had already left the position of Public Relations Director when, in 1968 it was decided that we must have a resident director and Carl was working part-time on what shortly became a full time position on the staff of Governor Tom McCall. Robert Knoll, who had been Carl's assistant in 1962 was hired to head our P. R. department. The Festival was facing some crucial problems of which I will write in a future chapter. But let me say now that the appeal of the Ballad Opera performances was another important piece of evidence added to the memory of Vining, pointing to the practicality of non-Shakespearean matinee performances as well as to the dire need of an indoor theatre in which to perform them. But again I'm getting ahead of my story. Let me return 10 years to an earlier crisis.

You will recall that when the post-war Elizabethan Theatre facade was built, it was of necessity embarrassingly incomplete. No paint, no roof, no dressing rooms, shop, costume shop, wardrobe or any of those amenities which any sane theatre person would label necessities. You will also remember that, because of President Elmo Stevenson's promise to hire me each and every summer, the city built us a roof.

That was a year after our post-war opening. Each year after that, the Festival managed to make some kind of improvement in the structure. A miniature make-do shop was installed in the basement where the old Chatauqua restrooms had been. One year a costume room was built. I remember we moved makeup tables several times. One year when our company was larger than usual, I recall some of us put on our makeup at a long table set up outside on a grassy knoll. It was usual for passers-by to stop and watch. Finally, the men's makeup room was constructed in the space behind the inner-above stage. You can imagine the tremendous racket a dropped wire coat hanger could bounce around into a quiet scene a few feet away on stage. But inconvenience and disturbed scenes were not to prove as disrupting or as hard to cope with as the edict of the Fire Marshal.

The theatre plant which had gradually evolved over a period of 11 years was jerry-built bit by bit as the necessities of each season demanded. The work was done by our already overworked staff, as hastily and as cheaply as possible because of our cramped schedule and budget. As a result, the Fire Marshal had for a number of years been disturbed by such things as the difficulty of quick and safe exits from dressing rooms, the weakness of a structure in which supporting walls on one story were located between supporting walls on the story below. Each year he would rule that we could operate another year if such and such a fault were corrected.

Eventually we realized that we were spending each year monies which were desperately needed for production and company improvement on a building which could never be anything but a temporary structure. By the middle of the decade we had decided that eventually funds outside regular Festival income must be found to finance a permanent remodeling of our haphazard plant. It was thus that Richard Hay was already gathering ideas about a new Elizabethan theatre plant when he went to England on a Fulbright scholarship. While there, he became visiting Technical Director at the University of Bristol.

It was the Fire Marshal, however, who eventually made up our minds. In 1958 he said, in effect, "Not another performance in this building." Therefore at the end of the 1958 season, we tore down the old structure and started a fund-raising drive for a quarter of a million dollars to build our new Elizabethan Theatre.

We hired a professional fund-raiser who did a fine job of organizing the drive. The real keystone figure in the financing of the new theatre was our very good friend, Alfred Carpenter. Being the kind of

person who knows a hand up from a hand out, he offered (anony-
mously) to match every dollar that was raised in Ashland. As a result,
every one in Ashland who donated to the building fund, felt that he
was giving two dollars for every dollar he withdrew from the bank.
This gesture was coupled with a good-natured competition between the
towns of Ashland and Medford. But largely due to Alfred Carpenter's
generosity, Ashland, on its own, exceeded its quota by about 40 percent.

Rather than give you a blow by blow description of the drive, let
me quote my thank you letter from the 1959 souvenir program:

> This is a letter of appreciation from the Shakespearean Festival
> producing company to all of you who built our amazing new stage.
> We know who you are. You are the little boy who contributed a
> dime saved from your weekly allowance. You are the couple from
> Pennsylvania who sent a cheque because you were "too far away to
> come, but not too far away to care." You are the logger from
> Eureka, California, who had no business contributing to anything.
> You are the anonymous donor who matched dollars and pride when
> the proud citizens of Ashland oversubscribed their quota by more
> than forty percent. You are the theatre groups in two states who
> made us proud to be show people when you gave us benefit perfor-
> mances. You are the Oregon Shakespearean Board of Directors and
> their building committee and fund-raisers, who took the enormous
> responsibility of launching the building program. You are the busi-
> ness men who donated much of the raw material which has gone
> into our building. All of you wonderful men and women who gave
> of your time, money and energy, more than you could afford. We
> know where you are. You are here in the Rogue River Valley, in
> Ashland, Medford and Grants Pass; you are in the towns and cities
> of Oregon: in Portland, Eugene, Salem, Pendleton, more than we
> can name. But we know where you are. You are in Seattle, Tacoma,
> San Francisco, Los Angeles. You are scattered throughout this con-
> tinent in twenty-five states and in British Columbia. We thank you
> for making our stage possible.
>   And the fortunate triumvirate who dreamed, planned and wil-
> led the building into shape, we know who you are. We have met
> you; we have shaken your hands; we have known you for years.
> But we know you better now. All you who behold our stage, you
> know them too, though you may never have shaken their hands.
> Richard Hay, the designer; Jack Edson, the architect; "Scotty"
> Fairweather, the builder—you know them better than if you had
> met them face to face, for there is a vital part of each in our
> building. Knowledge? Yes. Skill? Yes. But there is something more
> personal. Dedication. Devotion, if you will. Whatever it is, it ema-
> nates from the stance of every sturdy timber, from every compli-

cated angle of gable and every carved cornice. Whatever it is, without it our stage would lose its identity. But it is there, we see it and we know who you are.

George Wickham, we know who you are. You are the foreman who wheedled, coaxed, cajoled, yes, even bullied the men into doing their work skillfully, accurately, and rapidly enough to meet the deadline. You did more than was expected of you because this is your building too, and you take pride in your work. All of you who worked with hands, skill and heart, we know who you are. You are the electricians, the plumbers, the carpenters, the specialists, the laborers who put our building together. You erected the forms and poured four hundred yards of cement, you nailed together 77,000 board feet of lumber, and placed thirty-five tons of steel. You ran twenty-eight miles of pipe. You painted and plastered on scaffolding at dizzy heights. You built our stage and we know who you are, and in a way, we envy you. We envy you the memory, in your muscles and sinews and bones, of the feel of the timbers going into place, the nails biting into wood, the shaping of the wood, steel and cement into our stage. We envy you, but we shall be forever grateful.

We thank you all. All who built this monument of a hundred years. And generations of players, and audiences yet unborn will be grateful that you were the builders.

Angus L. Bowmer, Producing Director

The erection of this third Elizabethan stage was a giant step toward our present level of development. I say "Elizabethan stage" for the stage was the only part of the building that was Elizabethan. But the term is misleading, because for the first time we had a professionally planned theater PLANT. The facade itself projected the firm solidity of sixteenth century architecture, and in addition to the features of our former theatre, contained the third-story musicians' gallery as well as the "hut" which housed the hoisting "machine."

Behind this facade were costume and stage shops, dressing rooms, musicians' room, even a night watchman's sleeping quarters. In front, two huge steel towers outside the seating area with cantilevered catwalks over the audience gave correct positions for spotlights. These monsters, with their firm bracing ties to the old Chautauqua walls are ugly in themselves but disappear when action starts on the stage, made vivid and magical in the lights held aloft by these ugly twins. By dint of much excavating and filling, the rows of seats rose at a much steeper angle than formerly and the cement risers curved so that all seats faced the center of the stage.

Richard Hay's designs for this plant came from a thorough knowledge of our theatre objectives, our logistical problems and also acquaintance with fifteenth and sixteenth century architecture. Dick had joined the company as a technical assistant and, since that time, had spent five summers as our technical director and stage designer. In 1955 he had gone to England on a Fulbright scholarship where he was visiting Technical Director and Designer for the University of Bristol. When he returned to us the next year he continued preliminary studies which were a necessary prelude to the realization of the designs for the Ashland Elizabethan theatre.

When we occupied the plant in 1959, many of us were in temporary quarters, for it was the central unit of a much larger complex, the rest of which was still in early conceptual stages on Dick Hay's drawing board. Dr. Bailey held the Institute classes and lectures in the Episcopal parish house and in the basement of the Ashland Public Library. Bill Patton, after many years of sharing the Chamber of Commerce office had moved to a room on the mezzanine of the Mark Antony (Lithia) Hotel. The costume shop was located in the storage area back of the inner below stage; dressing rooms in what is now the costume storage area in the basement.

We were out of debt and could start immediately to explore the possibilities of starting to expand the plant. There were a couple of ways in which we needed to improve and to add to the theatre as soon as possible in order to satisfy the constant urge to improve the quality of the productions and promote essential efficiency. One thing we needed badly was the addition of the basement wing to house our costume shop. The backstage area it currently occupied was cramped, and besides, was much needed for the storage of furniture and properties which were used in current productions. The second much-needed improvement was the addition of a new switchboard. The old one that Bill Patton had wheedled out of The Otto K. Oleson Company in Hollywood had, over the years, been added to and modified until it had become as jerry-built as the theatre structure we had just torn down.

The effectiveness of actors and setting during any moment in a play is enhanced, impaired, or even destroyed by the lighting. It is not surprising that Dick Hay, being a designer, was most anxious to replace our outmoded and inadequate board. The rest of the staff agreed most heartily, but we were staggered at the cost of the kind of board that would work best for us. A new kind of switchboard had just come out that seemed for many reasons to be exactly right for our needs. This was a Silicon Rectifier board which had what in effect was a memory system so that a number of scenes could be pre-set. This allowed each complicated combination of colors and intensities of light falling on different areas to be faded into the next combination by the moving of two levers. You can see how these smooth transitions in scene after scene would greatly enhance the storytelling tempo of the plays—a continuity which is so essential to the presentation of Shakespearean plays on an Elizabethan stage.

The $50,000 price tag the Kliegl people put on the board they could design to our individual and unique specifications, almost literally set us back on our heels. Where could we get this kind of money? Going to the public again so soon after our quarter of a million dollar fund-raising drive was impossible. The foundations were certainly not interested in subsidizing the purchase of theatrical equipment. I was frankly discouraged concerning our chances of making such a purchase in the foreseeable future.

It was Bill Patton who pointed us in the right direction. He had gained a half dozen years of Festival management experience; the maturing trauma of the first major fund-raising drive was behind him, and from this time on he demonstrated more and more frequently the innate managerial leadership which has kept us on even keel among the mountainous financial and political waves as they became more and more exhilarating and at the same time potentially more dangerous during the next decade.

It was he who made an appointment for a small group of the staff to meet with our old friend Alfred Carpenter. I remember how disappointed I was when, in spite of Dick Hay's detailed explanation of our need for the switchboard, Mr. Carpenter seemed to be more interested in the building of the basement extension for the costume shop than in the purchase of the board. In fact, the switchboard seemed to interest him not at all. Mrs. Carpenter's illness had kept her from attending the conference, but when she heard the old switchboard might actually endanger the life of its student operators, she was much concerned. As a result, a few days later the Carpenters made us an offer: if the Festival would go in debt for the $50,000 board, they promised to finance the building of the costume shop.

It took courage on the part of Bill Patton to take the responsibility of making a very strong recommendation to the Festival Board that we accept the Carpenter's generous and stimulating offer. I must say, also, that it took a good deal of faith and courage on the part of those Board members to accept the offer, and to agree to go in debt for an unprecedented $50,000.

The success in paying off that obligation gave us courage to buy the Stiles property in 1964. That parcel of land which might now be occupied by a high rise apartment building or something much less desirable, actually is graced by a portion of the Bowmer Theatre and those beautiful grounds which form a courtyard and impressive entryway to our theatre complex. Another step in the growth of financial self-confidence was the purchase and remodeling of the building which now houses our business offices, design room, box office, the Institute of Renaissance Studies offices and the commodious Margery Bailey room.

Because of the satisfactory completion of all these contracts, our credit rating is better than that of any other theatre I know. The Alfred Carpenters have given many thousands of dollars to the Festival, but they have always given us more than money, and it was they who first showed us the way to financial independence.

XVIII

Reprise

FOLLOWING BILL OYLER's method of alliteration in naming a chapter of our history "The Fabulous Fifties," we should call this one "The Soaring Sixties." For in the decade following the building of the new Elizabethan Theatre, the Festival literally "flew" to unprecedented heights in a number of ways: the gradual lengthening of our season and the steady increase in the number of "standing room only" nights, the frightening but continual increase in the cost of operation (fortunately always covered by a comparable increase in income), the broadening of our sphere of influence to a national scope, the rapid jump in the number of applicants for company membership (with the natural corollary of an improvement in the quality of the company).

Let me say here that the improvement in the company was most noticeable in the lower echelons. Almost every season we have had adequate or superior actors and technicians to fill the most responsible positions, but in the earliest days, the drop-off from these positions to the middle and lower ones was precipitous, sometimes embarrassingly so. Later, the middle of the company improved and finally, in the sixties the reputation of the Festival as a stepping stone to professional theatre became so widespread that talented young theatre people were willing to spend a season or two doing walk-on or bit parts or assisting in one or another of the technical departments in the hope of improving their positions the next season while learning from their co-workers.

The 1965 edition of the *Biographical Encyclopedia and Who's*

Who in American Theatre contains some objective evidence of the Festival's success as an intern theatre. That volume contains the playbills of 12 resident U.S. theatres outside New York for the years of 1959 through 1964. We are among those 12, although we are not a "professional" theatre. But more significant is the fact that the playbills of 10 of the other 11 theatres contain one or more credits for people who received their early post-collegiate experience with us. During the same time there were 69 productions in New York with one or more credits for former Oregon Shakespearean Festival company members.

During these years the Festival, with the cooperation of the College, sent Gertrude and me on numerous extensive trips to survey the university and college theatre departments throughout the United States. We not only auditioned and interviewed candidates for the next Festival season, but we also were able to become acquainted with the faculty people who were going to be writing recommendations for them. We also found it invaluable to be able to acquaint ourselves with training methods and philosophies as well as the artistic standards of those institutions which were furnishing our applicants. Of course this was a two-way street, and those institutions became more fully conscious of our existence, our artistic attitudes and theatre practices.

The success of some of our "graduates" encouraged more and more educational theatre faculty people to send their best students to us. There are people like Pat Hines, an extremely talented character actor, who, because he does not have to wait for a starring role, has played more constantly over a longer period of time than any other actor I know. Ann Guilbert, well-known to many television watchers, especially for the funny neighbor she played for such a long time on the Dick Van Dyke show, Joan Darling (Joanie Kugell) of motion pictures and T.V., Richard Graham on Broadway (*Saratoga*) and "out of town" with Ethel Merman in *Call Me Madam*, T.V. specials and more recently the musical *1776*; the list is too long to include. But aside from these people who have done well in theatre, there are the well-known stars: George Peppard, Stacy Keach, Monte Markham, Michael O'Sullivan and Dick Cavett.

It was during this decade that our public relations coverage became nationwide, articles appearing repeatedly in several national magazines and Eastern newspapers. We had long been happily represented in the Western press, but there, too, the coverage began to be more intense and widespread. We began to get critical reviews from such worthies as Henry Hewes in *The Saturday Review*, William Glover, Associated Press drama critic, as well as Richard Coe of the Washington Post. One of the signs of our maturity was that the reviews (from both East and West) were written without the condescension that had marked some of the earlier articles about our productions. Richard Newberger's article for the New York Times, for instance, written many years before, was reprinted in the Paris Edition of that publication with the headline: SHAKESPEARE IN THE WOODS.

There was a certain kind of satisfaction to be felt when occasionally well-known people from stage, television or screen revealed that they were aware of our existence. It was even more pleasing when, less frequently, they spoke of our work with knowledge and respect.

My encounters with the great and near-great have not always ended with complete satisfaction, and I would like to relate the stories of three such incidents, each of which has its own thrust of interest.

The first is the funniest. It occurred when Gertrude and I were auditioning at New York University. Fred Blanchard, who headed the department for years, had been in that production at the University of Washington where I first met Iden Payne. We were waiting in the outer office of the department for a faculty meeting to dismiss so we might have the use of the auditorium for our auditions. When five o'clock came the place was inundated with homeward bound teachers. We greeted several of our friends and then were approached by a middle-aged gal who looked like a typical college professor after a hard day of teaching. Her grayish hair was a bit rumpled and her clothes looked like those of most teachers at five o'clock. Her eyes sparkled as she smiled a greeting and told us that she was happy to have representatives of the Oregon Shakespearean Festival at NYU.

"We have met, of course," she said.

As I had no recollection of ever seeing her before, I resorted to an "easy out" fib.

"Oh, of course!"

"At Stratford in 1945," she continued, sawing off the limb behind me.

As I had not been out of the United States from 1937 to 1960, I sought for a way to save face for us both:

"Perhaps it was in 1960."

"Oh no," she said firmly, "it was in 1945 when I was acting there."

"B-but I wasn't there in 1945."

She cut me off short: "Oh yes, I remember it well. It was there in Stratford in 1945."

"B-but," I was floundering, and the argument had grown ridiculous. She knew it, too, walked to the door, opened it, and turned with the expertise of an actress who knew how to make the most of an exit.

"I'm Claire Luce, you know."

It was an exit line worthy of a great actress.

The ironically educational experience with Sir John Gielgud occurred three years before the turn of the decade. It started when, during his West Coast tour of his one man show, *Seven Ages of Man*, he was heard to say as he deplaned at Portland, "I'm surprised that there is no one here from the Oregon Shakespearean Festival." The media people immediately siezed upon this quotation, and when the news was received in Ashland it was decided that Sir John and I must meet in San Francisco where Gertrude and I were spending some time on Festival business and where Sir John's show was to open the following week.

A lunch date was set up through Sir John's secretary for the following Thursday. I immediately began to have qualms, for two reasons. I began to feel uneasy about the whole thing when I heard from the Festival contingent that they wanted me to get a photographer to take P. R. shots. I felt this was in poor taste. We should have set up either a lunch engagement or a public relations meeting, but not both. Then I realized that the date they had chosen was Thanksgiving Day. That was my out. So I called the Fairmont Hotel and asked for Sir John Gielgud. Someone said, "Who?" I repeated, "Sir John Gielgud." The rough voice at the other end said "Just a minute." There was a long pause, then the voice came back on the line: "There ain't nobody works here by dat name."

When I finally got through to Sir John's secretary, she agreed about the lunch but invited me to their press conference on Friday. I accepted with thanks.

I went to see an old friend of the Festival, Terence O'Flaherty of the San Francisco *Chronicle*. I needed to know how to get a photographer, and he was very helpful. Then he said,

"Of course you know that Sir John will not be interested in Oregon at this point, his only concern will be in promoting his show in San Francisco." I said that I was painfully aware of that fact, but that his secretary had said that he would pose with me for a picture.

The press conference went well. I arrived early enough to meet the star performer and to tell him how much I had admired his Hamlet in 1936. This may have been the start of my downfall. Now, I realize that the vanity concerning age prevalent among actors kept him from enjoying the reminder that his greatest work on the American stage had been done 20 years before.

His handling of the press conference was superb, and he soon had the reporters eating out of his hand. He was just "folksy" enough, just modest enough, just relaxed enough so everyone was put at ease. I enjoyed the hour very much. I had slipped five dollars to one of the press photographers to take the picture of Sir John and me, so when the others started to leave we set up the shot. Sir John was to be looking over my shoulder as I showed him the plans for our new Elizabethan Theatre in the souvenir program. All went well, the picture was taken and I thanked the worthy knight and left feeling quite satisfied. Then, a few days later the picture arrived! It showed a surprisingly innocent-looking, wide-eyed, little college professor pointing proudly to the program, and, towering over him (I'm sure he was standing on his tip toes) was the impressive figure of the famous actor, looking down, not at the program, but at me, with such a superior, condescending smile that the picture was not usable in any sort of public relations way.

It was thus that I learned never to try to do my own public relations chores. Thank you, Sir John.

The Charles Laughton story is much the most exciting though it ended in sadness. It started inauspiciously many years before in Hollywood. Just a few days before I met Mr. Laughton, I had been treated handsomely by Bing Crosby on the set for *Here Comes The Groom*. He had even called over a photographer to take a picture of us, for he knew it would be helpful publicity for the Festival.

I suppose the contrast of this treatment with the Laughton episode was one of the reasons I was so upset with the latter experience. I had expected a certain amount of interest on the part of Mr. Laughton, for I knew that he was aware of the Festival. Bill Cottrell, of the Teensy Weensy Theatre gang, who had been my assistant director, and later director, at the Festival was acquainted with Laughton.

After the war, Bill had spent considerable time in Hollywood. He had put a small ad in the L. A. Times asking for those who were interested in forming a Shakespeare performing group to get in touch with him. He expected perhaps a dozen answers. Instead, he tells me that he received 1200! He had been in *Naked City* and *Man On The Eiffel Tower*, two of Laughton's pictures. Not knowing what on earth to do with that many applicants, he took the whole project to Mr. Laughton. This was the start of the Laughton Shakespeare Group. Bill worked with the group for a long time, but they never did get to the point of actually producing a play.

Nor was this his only source of probable knowledge of the Festival. Just the night before the "incident" took place, a friend of mine had given Mr. Laughton one of our souvenir programs. This same friend took me back-stage to meet the great man. I was introduced as Angus Bowmer, Producing Director of the Oregon Shakespearean Festival. Mr. Laughton, who had been laughing and joking a moment before, drew himself up pompously and said, "What was the name?"

I said, "I'm Angus Bowmer" and then to fill the ghastly silence that followed, I said, "Give Bill Cottrell my best regards."

"I'll see him tomorrow" he intoned, turned on his heel and left the vicinity.

I was hurt and humiliated. I would have expected such treatment if I had asked him for a dime to buy a cup of coffee. I thought I never would forgive him.

Carl Ritchie knew this story and of my feeling toward the man. Thus it was that no one told me of his arrival to see one of our productions in the season of 1961. I learned afterward that he had said he could only see the one production because he had to be in Hollywood the next day. However, he stayed the second day (which again he said must be his last) and the third. That *must* be his last, he said, for he had a costume fitting appointment in Hollywood for his forthcoming movie, *Advise and Consent*. However, he telephoned to the studio that he was unavoidably detained—and saw the fourth production. After the show there was a party for him at Bill and Shirley Patton's house. During the evening he drew me aside and said,

"I have just seen the four best productions of Shakespeare that I have ever seen in my life. How I wish Peter (Brook) could be here to see how Shakespeare should really be done."

These were very pleasing words, but I have always tried to take such extravagant compliments with a grain of salt, realizing that people, especially artistic people, get carried away with the emotion of the moment.

However, two weeks later I received a telephone call from Hollywood. Mr. Laughton apologized for calling me and said,

"I want to talk with you about something that should not be discussed over the phone. But I want to present you with a problem which I am sure you will want to discuss with your staff. You may very well want to say no. If you do, I will understand. I am coming back to see two of the productions again. To put the matter bluntly, I am throwing myself at you. I want to play with that wonderful company of yours, and it won't cost you a cent. I would like to play Lear. I would also like to have Dr. Loper direct, as I admired his production of *Ham-*

let so much. However, these are not requirements. I want to come with no strings. I can't come next year (1962) for I will be in Paris filming *Irma La Douce.* Can we make it 1963?"

After discussing the matter with the Board and the Staff, it was decided that, in spite of the departure from precedent, we would accept his offer. He came to Ashland the next week and spent one memorable afternoon with Gertrude and me in our home. I told him there was something that I must get off my chest if we were to work together. I then related the story of my first meeting with him and of my reaction. I still did not understand his actions but I felt that I had misjudged him all these years. He really didn't explain or apologize, I suppose that he did not recall the incident. All he said was,

"You have no idea the agony it is to be a star."

The most moving moment of his visit took place after he said that he would like to make a gesture toward playing in repertory just like the rest of the company. He knew that he couldn't play another strenuous role along with Lear, but wondered what other plays would be on the bill in 1963.

Gertrude said *"Henry V."*

In an instant he was across the room giving the stirring opening speech of the Chorus in that play, and tears came to my eyes when I realized that I was auditioning Mr. Charles Laughton.

You will remember that he died before he could film *Irma La Douce* in Paris and before he could come to Ashland to be a part of our company which he admired so much. Mr. Laughton wanted desperately to achieve a creativity in Shakespearean performance that he had never experienced. Those attempts he had made had never been entirely successful. I am sure that he had looked forward to becoming one of the company at Ashland so that with these bright-eyed young artists he could accomplish his lifelong desire.

This story is passed on from generation to generation of Festival companies each year, so each year the familiar ghost that nightly sighs through our theatre is identified by them as that of Mr. Charles Laughton.

The growing awareness of the Festival across the country among professional people in both commercial and educational theatre, motion pictures and television, as well as those who controlled public relations and critical media, had an understandable effect on the quality of our company and, in turn, on the public who were customers for our tickets. Such notice increased our audience, of course.

We began to have standing-room-only performances night after night. During the decade we increased the number of seats in the auditorium from about 1100 to close to 1200. We had increased the number of performances so in 1960 we played 41 nights with 19 sold out. We continued to increase the number of performances as much as the summer months would allow and still give us adequate rehearsal time. Remember, our company members were almost all either college students or teachers. By 1963 we had squeezed out 46 nights but we still sold out 38 of them so we played to an amazing 98.2 percent of capacity.

Shakespeare's 400th anniversary in 1964 was an important turning point in our thinking. Stanford was staging the first of its series of Summer Arts Festivals under the direction of Dr. Virgil Whitaker. We were invited to open their Festival with a twelve night run of three of our season's plays, on an Elizabethan-type stage designed by Richard Hay especially for Frost Amphitheatre. In order to meet their opening date of June 23, we had to assemble a large part of our company in April, and thus were able to play a total of 70 nights—12 of them at Stanford and 58 at Ashland. Of the 58 in Ashland, 38 were sold out. Besides this, we played to 25,519 people at the 12 Stanford performances, two of which were SRO.

There were several valuable fringe benefits stemming from this experiment. The national critical coverage brought us to the attention of a great many more people than had previously been aware of our existence. Then we learned there was a waiting audience much larger than we were prepared to handle under ordinary circumstances. We also found that it was possible to assemble an intern type company outside of the time limits of summer vacation.

After the increased exposure provided by this special 1964 season, attendance skyrocketed till in 1967 we played (counting standees) to over 100% of the number of seats we had for the season. *The Taming of the Shrew* was sold out for the entire season before opening night. This was all very exciting and sounds very encouraging, but nevertheless we were frightened. We were in the same kind of situation as that of a man who paints himself into a corner. Costs of production were increasing every year, but we obviously had reached a point close to the limit of our increase of income. We had asked our audience members to contribute to funds for major capital expenditures, but unlike any other important theatre, we had never asked them to contribute to our operating costs. We felt we were in no position to do so. We could not go to the major foundations, for there is not one which contributes to the regular expense of operating a theatre.

Aside from that problem, we were disappointing so many of our potential customers that we were afraid many would get discouraged and that income would start to fall off. In 1968 alone, over 11,000 would-be theatre goers were turned away from our Ashland box office without the tickets which they wished to purchase.

That same year, a panel of economists from the University of Oregon's Bureau of Business and Economic Research made a report which confirmed our fears. They made the need for additional box office very clear. "With operating expenditure increases of at least 10 percent annually, the Festival cannot stand still and hope to provide the annual repertory for very long."

Meanwhile, things had not been going so well at the College. We had at last been authorized to offer a degree in theatre, but we were understaffed and without a theatre in which to play. We had been temporarily appeased by being shunted to an old, semi-condemned hospital building in which we had managed to arrange for a tiny theatre in the round. Then the building was condemned and wrecked. Because the College auditorium was to be remodeled, we were in danger of being without any place to produce plays. I attended the annual luncheon meeting of a scholastic honorary society at which it was traditional for President Stevenson to give a speech on what he called "The State of the 'U'." This time he talked enthusiastically of several new buildings which he had requested from the State Board, waxed eloquent about several new academic programs to be offered, but not one word about a theatre plant or the development of our new theatre degree program. I was terribly discouraged and very angry. I left the meeting, went home and called my friend Asher Wilson, the head of the theatre department of Portland State.

Two different years I had been a guest artist in his department: once as Shylock, with his students under his direction in *The Merchant of Venice*, and once as Sir Toby Belch. I had been told by him and by some other administration people that any time I wanted a job with Portland State I could have one.

I told Asher, "I think I'm ready, unless I soon see the chances of a theatre plant in Ashland."

He called me back in a couple of days with an unbelievable offer in which it was proposed that I teach some of my courses by taped television so I could have part of the year to spend with Festival business and operation.

Would you believe *two* theatre plans for Ashland surfaced simultaneously? Well, not really two, for the College theatre never got beyond the embryo stage. It started when, through the influence of a friend of Ed Fitzpatrick's, Donald Higgins, and an organization of lumber men called the Hoo Hoos, offered to donate all the lumber for a college theatre building. We were very excited until we learned that the cost of all the lumber of a wooden structure would cover less then ten per cent of the total cost. Even so, there was some serious consideration given by the college to the project.

About the same time, stimulated by the University of Oregon report, the Board decided that in order to survive, the Festival would have to draw to a conclusion its two year old campaign to build a new indoor theatre. The campaign had started with a two day gala called "The Revels" celebrating the beginning of the Festival's second quarter century and launching a fund-raising drive to build the new theatre.

The celebration was produced by Andrew C. Love and featured Duke Ellington and his orchestra, a champagne supper and other attractions. Special bleachers were erected in the rear of the Elizabethan theatre to accommodate the expected crowd. It was particularly exciting to see and hear the Duke and his fine orchestra on an early June afternoon on our big stage in a concert, the most appropriate number of which was "Such Sweet Thunder." This was Mr. Ellington's own suite—a set of musical impressions he had drawn from the works of William Shakespeare.

By the fall of 1968 the fund-raising campaign had realized over one million dollars. Again we were deeply indebted to the General Chairman of that committee, Alfred Carpenter, for his devotion and support. Much of the organizational work had been done by Mrs. John Cotton, former Board Chairman and long actively interested in Festival affairs. Major Gifts Chairman was Frank Bash of Medford; General Gifts Chairman, Gary Boshears, Ashland; Coordinator, Suzanne LaMarre Hanson, Ashland.

When bids came in from contractors we discovered to our dismay that the one million dollars was scarcely more than half enough to complete the proposed project. For the plans for our expanded facilities were complex and necessarily extensive. They included not only the new 600 seat indoor theatre, but also the remodeling of the administration building, including the Institute of Renaissance Studies, a new box office, acquisition of a building on Pioneer Street which would house the Festival scene shop and a new exhibit hall.

Also included were conversion of nearly a full city block on adjacent Hargadine Street into landscaped parking for 175 cars; realignment of Pioneer Street for easier theatre pedestrian access; completion of landscaping and improved access from Lithia Park and a theatre courtyard.

This was a traumatic period for all of us. The need for so much more money came at a time of economic depression. Costs of materials were mounting at an astronomical rate, and at the same time the value of large gifts of stocks was plummeting. The overall cost of wood for the theatre increased by $85,000 in a matter of days.

I take this opportunity to pay special tribute to William Patton for his courage, stamina, faith and foresight during those trying times. There were times when I thought we would have to give up, but if Bill ever entertained such ideas, he didn't let any of us know about it. He was sustained in undertaking the tremendous responsibilities of that period by the Festival Board, especially by the Board President, Walter Crosby, who spent countless hours in Ashland helping and advising Bill during the roughest times.

As it turned out, the fact that our area was economically depressed was the factor that brought us the money we lacked. Word finally came from Washington that the Economic Development Administration had approved a matching grant of $896,000 for the project. In a strange kind of twist, they could not give the grant to the Festival because the theatre was to be built on city property. We therefore gave the entire building fund, plus our real estate holdings to the City of Ashland, and it was the City which received the grant. We then negotiated a long-term lease on all the property from the City.

The new theatre bears my name because of Julie Carpenter Daugherty. Julie and I had been friends for many years. She was on the Vining Board of Directors and had been interested in theatre as long as I had known her. She was a wonderful gal with a zany sense of humor. For instance, one dawn in New York, after a long gabfest about theatre she accompanied us in the cab back to our hotel and on the way took us *and* the cabby to breakfast.

Therefore, when she offered a major gift to the building fund, providing that she could name the theatre, I didn't know what to think. The decision on such a matter was up to the Board, but she sensed my hesitation and long afterward told me she thought I was afraid that she would name it the Carpenter Theatre. Though such an idea had never crossed my mind, I certainly would not have thought the name inappropriate. The Board did accept her gift of $50,000 with her stipulation, and it was she who told me the building was to be called the Angus Bowmer Theatre.

The architects, Kirk, Wallace and McKinley have designed a building which blends with its surroundings beautifully. It does not overpower the Elizabethan Theatre and, at the same time, does not appear in the least apologetic. The traffic patterns which make the plant efficient and tie the two theatres together into one workable plant were planned by Richard Hay, who also designed the stage and auditorium.

Early on in the planning stages several basic ideas were agreed upon. The new theatre must be an indoor theatre because it is too hot in the Elizabethan Theatre for summer matinees. The most logical increase in available seats would be to perform in the daytime as well as at night. It was not to be an indoor version of our Elizabethan stage. Rather it was to represent the most modern ideas in theatre architecture.

I asked Dick, one time, just what a "modern" theatre was, and he said,

"It is one in which the actors and the audience are in the same room."

This is why, in the Bowmer Theatre, the auditorium walls seem to continue right on up the stage. The two "splays" which appear to be extensions of the auditorium walls are hinged at the edge of the platform so they can be swung in or out, thus varying the shape and size of the playing area. There is also a part of the platform that thrusts into the auditorium, around which the rows of seats seemed to be wrapped.

Once, Dick also said that the difference between an old fashioned proscenium production and one in a modern theatre is much the same as that between a painting and a piece of sculpture. This is one of the chief reasons why the auditorium is sharply raked at an upward angle so the audience can see the depth as well as width of the designs of scenery and actors' movements. As a result of this elevation, the floor of the stage becomes as important as the walls of a scene design. Thus in each production, the stage floor had a different shape, color, texture and pattern.

I suppose the most immediately noticeable quality of the theatre is its intimacy. The seats encircling the thrust of stage, combined with the steep rise of the rows make actor and audience seem much closer than could be ordinarily expected in a six hundred seat house. The actors are aware of this and their performances are influenced by that closeness in a way which stimulates their excitement of communion with the audience.

I am very happy I had the opportunity to direct two productions in my favorite theatre before a bout with angina persuaded all of us that the strenuous job of producing the Festival should be turned over to someone else. We were extremely fortunate to be able to persuade a very good friend of mine, and of the Festival, to take over the task. It has been a pleasure for several years now to have Jerry Turner as our Producing Director. He had worked many seasons for us as actor and director, and is an experienced administrator, having spent a number of years as head of the theatre department at the University of California at Riverside. The Festival is prospering under his guidance.

Now that I am no longer Producing Director, but hold a position called Development Consultant, I can look on a good deal more objectively than before. What do I think? To my mind the most exciting thing that has happened is our success with the young. The Bowmer Theatre, aside from providing us with a place to do matinees, also made it possible to produce a second season each year. This we call Stage II. More than half of our Stage II audiences are students. Many of them bus in from as far away as southern California and northern Washington.

This influx of students has developed because of two factors. One is the timing of the Stage II season, coming as it does during the school year. The other is our School/Theatre Project started with the assistance of the Oregon Arts Commission and expanded with the aid of a matching grant to the Festival from the National Endowment for the Humanities, the National Endowment for the Arts and its joint project with the U.S. Office of Education, the Artist-in-the-Schools program.

This project was spearheaded by Forbes Rogers who saw it through from the grant application stages to the early years of its development. After serving for four years as the Festival Educational Coordinator and Administrative Assistant to the General Manager, William Patton, in 1973 he accepted a position as Executive Director of the Alliance for Arts Education at the John F. Kennedy Center for the Performing Arts in Washington, D.C.

In the fall of 1973, under the guidance of Peggy Rubin, 10 actors and actresses, traveling in teams of two, three or four, visited 97 schools, hundreds of teachers and thousands of junior and senior high school students in Oregon, Washington, California and Idaho. The actors concentrated on classroom presentations which augmented teachers' plans for English literature, social studies and drama. These included a session called "An Hour in a Renaissance Classroom" dealing with the belief systems and society of Elizabeth's day as illustrated by passages from Shakespeare; "For Love of Language," a study of poetry, poetic imagery, the use of words and sounds and "The Playwright Brotherhood," a discussion/participation program focusing on the way playwrights and plays work, as seen through actors' eyes.

Letters of appreciation and joy from both teachers and students poured in by the hundreds. I remember one particularly. A teacher wrote that a boy in her class who was so introverted that he had never said a word in class—on the day after the Festival team visitation—had spoken enthusiastically for several minutes to his classmates about the experience. His teacher was convinced that this was a turning point in the boy's life. To enrich, inspire, to change lives is a heady experience.

Until the fall of 1974, these visitations were coupled with a fall production in the Bowmer Theatre. Now the fall production is omitted because so many students can come for the Stage II season, and even for the mid-September performances of the summer season offerings in both theatres. Starting in the fall of 1974 the program of school visitations continues without benefit of foundation grants, the cost of the project being born by the schools themselves, with the cooperation of the Festival. The continued warm praise from students and teachers is immensely satisfying, but from a purely practical point of view the most firm assurance of a long life for our enterprise is the certainty that we have developed a young and increasingly aware audience.

Another factor in the development of this youthful audience is the imaginative and innovative administration of the Institute of Renaissance Studies by Homer D. Swander. On the faculty of the University of California at Santa Barbara, he had been a lively audience member of the Festival for many years, but it was not until 1972/73 that he became officially associated with the Festival as a consultant for our School/Theatre Project.

From the first season Dr. Swander assumed the direction of the Institute there has been an increase in interest reflected in a large increase in enrollment among college students and college and high school teachers. Aside from the traditional lecture series and many of the classes introduced by Dr. Bailey, and later carried on by her successor, Dr. Dolora Cunningham, Dr. Swander arranged for many new and different ones. "New Strategies for Total Teaching" was a course designed to stimulate high school and college teachers to consider and experiment with a wide variety of more dramatic ways to teach. A unique series of interdisciplinary courses called "Drama and the Humanities" was taught by one faculty member from each of the four universities of the Oregon System of Higher Education as each of the four teachers represented a different discipline (English, history, music, art). This course has since been given up by the State System and is now conducted by the Institute in cooperation with Southern Oregon College. "The Shakespeare Renaissance Academy" is a four week round-the-clock retreat for college students centered around Renaissance daily life and values, the activities at the Institute and the Festival plays.

In 1974 for the first time the Institute conducted educational and entertainment activities outside the summer season. A class called "Ski and See" brought around 60 college students to Ashland during spring vacation to have classes in the morning, ski in the afternoon and to see the Stage II plays at night. All this creative educational activity has increased the number of young theatre goers many fold, but our maturer audience members have also increased in number and awareness.

Those dreams that Bob Stedman and I conjured up that rainy March afternoon so many years ago, those dreams that were nurtured in the Teensy Weensy Theatre, those dreams have materialized not by a genie out of a bottle, but by the imagination, determination and hard work of literally thousands of dedicated people. Now we must look to the future. Just what is in store for the Oregon Shakespearean Festival in the uncertain future in this most uncertain world?

"O brave new world."

How else begin a new decade at a
Shakespeare Festival? The 1960
Tempest *had Bob Loper as
Prospero, Shirley Patton,
Miranda and Graham
Woodruff, Ariel.*

*I had a glorious time as Falstuff in the
1961* Henry IV, Part One *especially
with Ed Brubaker as Bardolph and
Eugene Peyroux as Hal. Also in the cast
were Monte Markham as Hotspur, Rod
Alexander as the King, Nagle Jackson as
Westmoreland.*

Then in Part Two *the next year,
I played Justice Silence; Hugh Evans
was Shallow and Chuck Taylor
played Wart.*

In 1963 a Festival newcomer named Stacy Keach played King Henry V.

Richard Hay celebrated Shakespeare's 400th birthday in 1964 by making a rare stage appearance in The Knight of the Burning Pestle. He also designed the Elizabethan Stagehouse used at the 400th year Festival at Stanford.

King Lear in 1964, my last directorial assignment on the Elizabethan stage. Dick Graham was Lear; Laird Williamson, Edmund; Liz Huddle, Regan; Shirley Patton, Cordelia.

In 1964 I played my last Shylock.

It was my

turquoise

In 1970 with a degree of desperation, I put this concept of Shylock on canvas while recuperating from the illness that kept me from playing it.

Mechanicals in the 1966 Midsummer Night's Dream included Pat Patton as Starveling; Jim Baker as Bottom; Bill Oyler as Snout. I'm Quince up a tree.

Construction of the Bowmer Theatre occupied 1969.

Hazel and Andrew Love are shown with Alfred S. V. Carpenter and Earl Collins at the Feast of the Tribe of Will, traditional gathering in Lithia Park to open the summer season. Photo from middle 1960's.

*I was engulfed by
Claudia Wilkens as
Mrs. Peachum in* The
Beggar's Opera,
*performed as a
matinee in the Varsity
Theatre during August
and September 1966.
This was a prelude to
the Bowmer Theatre
matinee series now in
effect during the
summer season.*

*We opened the new
theatre in 1970 with
Rosencrantz and
Guildenstern are
Dead. I directed the
production which
featured Larry
Carpenter as
Rosencrantz, Roger
Kozol as Guildenstern
and Kit Carson as The
Player.*

Richard Hay, in designing the auditorium and stage of the Bowmer, happily made possible his exciting theatre designs with the plasticity so essential in the open space he has provided for both actor and audience.

The 1970 Merchant of Venice.

The set for Beckett's Waiting for Godot.

The 1973 Othello.

Strindberg's Dance of Death.

Ben Jonson's Alchemist *set in California Gold Rush.*

The Time of Your Life.

Gertrude and I,
opening night, 1975.

A standing ovation for
a special student
matinee performance
of Winter's Tale,
spring 1975.

Coda

I STILL REMEMBER an anecdote which I found many years ago while doing research for "Andy Jackson." In spite of his cantankerous, stubborn and frequently violent nature, Jackson won the deep affection and respect of his servants. One of them was asked one day if he thought his master would go to Heaven when he died. According to the story the servant replied,

"I can't rightly say about that. But if he wants to go, who's going to keep him out?"

Barring atomic war, planetary collision or other worldwide or national calamity, what is to keep the Oregon Shakespearean Festival from continuing to prosper and to expand its sphere of influence? I believe we have two sources of potential danger to our wellbeing. One lies in the realm of aesthetics and is a result of the times in which we live.

Because we have no great playwrights currently turning out theatre pieces, directors over the world have felt that an additional creative burden has fallen on their shoulders. As a result, the modern theatre, by and large, has become a director's theatre rather than a playwright's theatre. Therefore, young directors tend to lose confidence in the script as written—even Shakespeare's scripts.

If this trend becomes so prevalent that the only directors available to the Festival Producing Director are those who must introduce their own particular brand of gimmickry, we will be in serious trouble. The changing of words, the re-arranging of scenes, the interruption of the storytelling tempo by the insertion of mood music, extraneous stage business, the modification of Shakespeare's meaning, larding the play with heavy symbolism, shaping his dramatic structure, in other words, substituting the director's craftmanship for Shakespeare's art, all these things and more are done in the name of making the plays understandable to a twentieth century audience.

When Ashland is no longer the place where people can come to see, hear and understand Shakespeare without the aid of these spurious crutches to an alleged mental incapacity, we will be in serious trouble.

When scenic investiture and costume become substitutes for the actors' interpretations of a great author's lines, we will be in serious trouble.

Hopefully none of these regretful practices will become an Ashland trademark instead of an occasional incident. If so, there is no reason why the Festival cannot continue to grow in aesthetic stature and dramatic excitement.

The other source of danger is a practical one which poses frightening possibilities. You will remember that the Festival built the Angus Bowmer Theatre in 1970 to provide room for the expanded audience which had developed during the previous decade. When you have no more seats to sell there is an automatic cap put on your income. This does not, however, put a cap on your expenditures. The natural struggle for excellence encourages further expansion of budget, no matter how judiciously you try to economize. The great spectre, however, is the steady inflation which allows no kind of cap on the outgoing funds.

In England, Germany and other European countries, as much as 60 percent of the operating costs are covered by govermental subsidies. In this country, theatres in large population centers pass the hat every year to provide over half of their expenditures. We have conducted large scale fund drives, but only for major capital expenditures. We have been reluctant to conduct drives for operating costs.

It is quite obvious that we cannot continue to build new theatres to provide more seats (and therefore more income) when we again find ourselves painted into a corner. The building of the Bowmer Theatre, we thought, would give us the much needed expansion room for the present time, and that it would be 10 years before we were again in the position of not having enough seats. In the summer of 1974, however, when only five seasons had passed, we played to a summer audience of over 98% of capacity in both theatres. In 1975 we squeezed two more weeks into the Stage II season and one more week into the summer season. This gives us a little more elbow room, but you see the problem. Eventually we are going to need sources of income other than ticket sales.

One such source of income was opened up by the formation of the Festival's new Southampton Society. This Society, named for the Earl of Southampton (a sixteenth century patron of William Shakespeare) makes it possible for the Festival devotees to become members by individually sponsoring a specific element of our season. This kind of sponsorship has a specific appeal to certain people. It is satisfying to sit watching a production which your ticket purchase helped to make possible. But some people get a much bigger thrill by thinking, as they watch a production, "By my sponsorship, I personally made possible that beautiful scenery, or all those gorgeous costumes, or this specific performance for school children." It is hoped that the Southampton Society will prosper.

Bill Patton believes that one of the long range solutions of this problem is for us to expand our Endowment Fund to the point where the income will substantially supplement our other sources of revenue. All membership fees and many gifts go into this fund and Friends of the Festival have helped to swell this source of income.

We need to continue to enlarge this fund with increased membership fees, and gifts, as we have done in the past. But we also need some large gifts. The endowment of perpetual memorial scholarships has already been started by the Tudor Guild. My new association with the National Council on the Arts has taught me that corporate grants to the arts have been found worthwhile to the corporation as well as to the grantee. Some people have remembered us in their wills. All these methods of enlarging our endowment fund must be put into practice if we are to survive in the manner to which you, our audience have become accustomed.

A fund large enough to provide the income to support our increasingly expanded budget is a dream. But is it nearly as absurd or impossible as that original one back in the thirties?

You can imagine that I look back a bit nostalgically to those early days. I think sometimes of the roles I played, and wonder if I could do some of them again. But this is not a sad time for me. I derive great pleasure from my association with my enthusiastic, dedicated friends in the company and in the audiences, and as I wander through the crowds at the Theatre, I look around me and toast my spiritual toes at the fireside of the many friendships which have been fueled by once or twice a year meetings, some of them for over a quarter of a century.

From my association with the young, creative minds of our ever more challenging company members, I am able to absorb some of their vigor and enthusiasm; and once again, if only vicariously, through them the world is my oyster.

From my office window I look at the clear blue sky, the clean clear green of the trees in the hills above Lithia Park, then feast my eyes on two beautiful theatres—one named for a Queen, and one for me. Then, on the contrasting hue of our red brick courtyard, I see the long lines of patient people waiting for a turned-back ticket or for a place at the "Standing Room Only" gate—then I repeat to myself that unforgettable line of my beautifully inarticulate Italian guide on Capri:

"Da panoram' she is so *very*!"